AVENUE OF SPIES

The Envoy

Escape from the Deep

The Few

The Longest Winter

The Bedford Boys

Blood and Champagne

Jack London

The Liberator

AVENUE OF SPIES

A TRUE STORY OF
TERROR, ESPIONAGE, AND
ONE AMERICAN FAMILY'S
HEROIC RESISTANCE IN
NAZI-OCCUPIED FRANCE

ALEX KERSHAW

 CROWN PUBLISHERS
NEW YORK

Copyright © 2015 by Alex Kershaw

Published in the United States by Crown Publishers, an imprint of the Crown
Publishing Group, a division of Penguin Random House LLC, New York.
www.crownpublishing.com

CROWN is a trademark and the Crown colophon is a registered trademark of Penguin
Random House LLC.

Library of Congress Cataloging-in-Publication Data
Kershaw, Alex.
Avenue of spies: a true story of terror, espionage, and one American family's heroic
resistance in Nazi-occupied Paris / Alex Kershaw.—First edition.
1. Jackson, Sumner Waldron. 2. Jackson, Sumner Waldron—Family. 3. World War,
1939–1945—Underground movements—France—Paris. 4. Spies—France—Paris—
Biography. 5. Americans—France—Paris—Biography. 6. Physicians—France—Paris—
Biography. 7. World War, 1939–1945—France—Paris. 8. Paris (France)—History,
Military—20th century. 9. France—History—German occupation, 1940–1945. I. Title.
D802.F82P37476 2015
940.53'44361092313—dc23   2015016861

ISBN 978-0-8041-4003-4
eBook ISBN 978-0-8041-4004-1

Printed in the United States of America

Maps by David Lindroth Inc.
Jacket design by Elena Giavaldi
Jacket photographs by DPA/ZUMA (top left); Mondadori/Getty (top right); Roger-Viollet/
The Image Works (bottom left); courtesy the author (bottom right)

10 9 8 7 6 5 4 3 2 1

First Edition

For Pete and Loraine

CONTENTS

We lived in the shadows as soldiers of the night, but our lives were not dark and martial. . . . There were arrests, torture, and death for so many of our friends and comrades, and tragedy awaited all of us just around the corner. But we did not live in or with tragedy. We were exhilarated by the challenge and rightness of our cause. It was in many ways the worst of times and in just as many ways the best of times, and the best is what we remember today.

—JEAN-PIERRE LÉVY

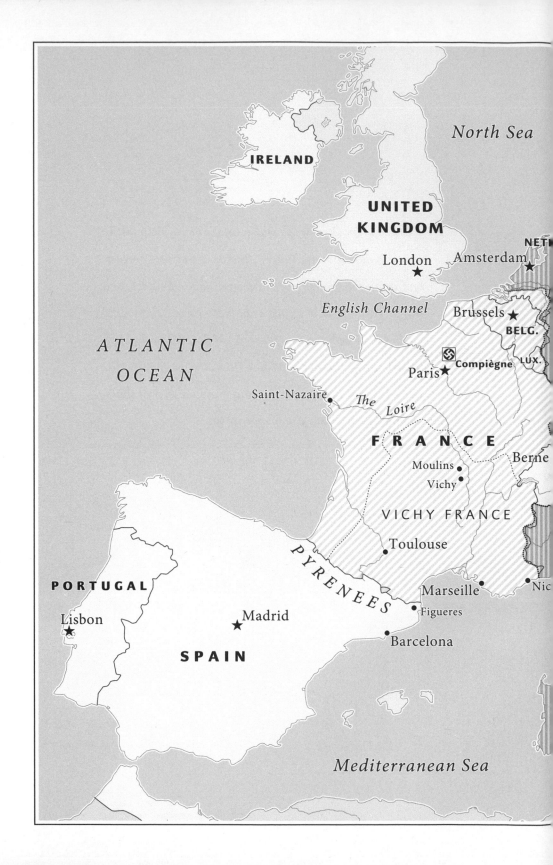

NORWAY

Stockholm

SWEDEN

ESTONIA

LATVIA

DENMARK

Copenhagen

Malmö

LITHUANIA

Baltic Sea

SOVIET
UNION

Neustadt

Hamburg Lübeck

EAST
PRUSSIA

Neuengamme

Ravensbruck

Berlin

Warsaw

GERMANY

POLAND

Frankfurt

CZECHOSLOVAKIA

Munich

Vienna

Zurich

WITZ

AUSTRIA

HUNGARY

ROMANIA

Milan

YUGOSLAVIA

BULGARIA

Rome

ALBANIA

ITALY

Wartime Europe
1944–45

Occupied by Nazis, January 1944

Occupied by Nazis, January 1945

Camps

0   MILES   200

0   KILOMETERS 200

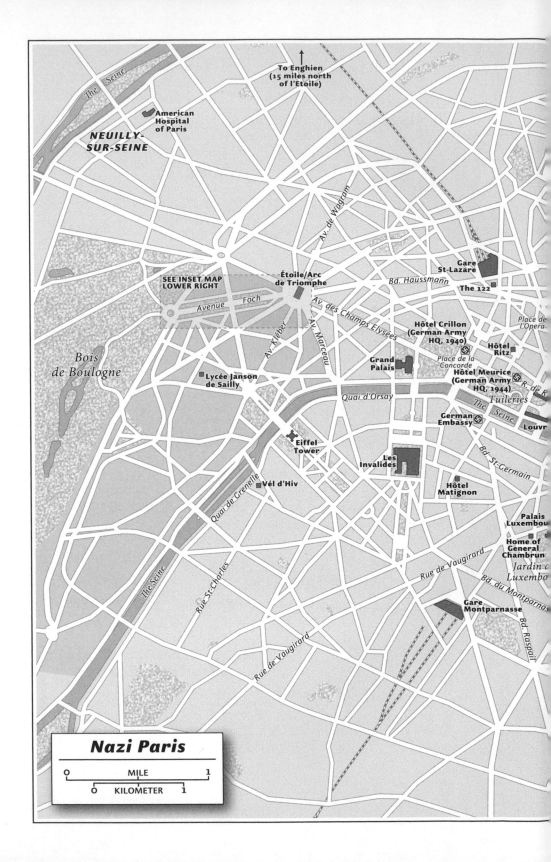

The Seine

To Enghien
(15 miles north
of l'Etoile)

American
Hospital
of Paris

NEUILLY-
SUR-SEINE

Av. de Wagram

Gare
St-Lazare

Bd. Haussmann

The 122

SEE INSET MAP
LOWER RIGHT

Étoile/Arc
de Triomphe

Place de
l'Opera

Avenue Foch

Av. des Champs Elysées

Hôtel Crillon
(German Army
HQ, 1940)

Hôtel
Ritz

Av. Kléber

Av. Marceau

Bois
de Boulogne

Grand
Palais

Place de la
Concorde

Hôtel Meurice
(German Army
HQ, 1944)

R. de R

Lycée Janson
de Sailly

Quai d'Orsay

The Seine

Tuileries

German
Embassy

Louvr

Eiffel
Tower

Les
Invalides

Bd. St-Germain

Quai de Grenelle

Vél d'Hiv

Hôtel
Matignon

Palais
Luxembou

Home of
General
Chambrun

Jardin d
Luxembo

Rue de Vaugirard

The Seine

Rue St-Charles

Bd. du Montparnas

Gare
Montparnasse

Bd. Raspail

Rue de Vaugirard

Nazi Paris

0   MILE   1

0   KILOMETER   1

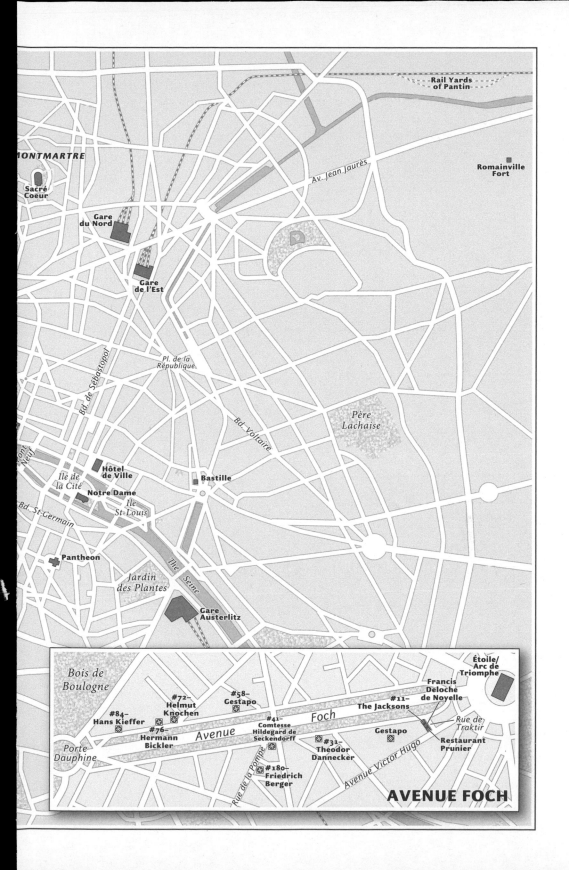

MONTMARTRE

Sacré
Coeur

Gare
du Nord

Gare
de l'Est

**Rail Yards
of Pantin**

Av. Jean Jaurès

Romainville
Fort

Pl. de la
République

Bd. de Sébastopol

Père
Lachaise

Bd. Voltaire

Pont
Neuf

Hôtel
de Ville

Île de
la Cité

Notre Dame

Bastille

Île
St-Louis

Bd. St-Germain

Pantheon

The Seine

Jardin
des Plantes

Gare
Austerlitz

Bois de
Boulogne

Étoile/
Arc de
Triomphe

#72–
Helmut
Knochen

#58–
Gestapo

Francis
Deloche
de Noyelle

#84–
Hans Kieffer

#11–
The Jacksons

#41–
Comtesse
Hildegard de
Seckendorff

Foch

Rue de
Traktir

#76–
Hermann
Bickler

Avenue

Gestapo

Porte
Dauphine

Restaurant
Prunier

#31–
Theodor
Dannecker

Rue de la Pompe

Avenue Victor Hugo

#180–
Friedrich
Berger

AVENUE FOCH

Part One

CITY OF DARKNESS

What Nazism, epitomized by the Gestapo, tried to realize (and almost succeeded in realizing) was the destruction of man as we know him and as thousands of years have fashioned him. The Nazi world was an empire of total force, with no restraints.

—JACQUES DELARUE, *The Gestapo: A History of Horror*

THE FALL

A SHELL EXPLODED. Fragments of shrapnel hit a young soldier. He fell to the ground. Before long, nurses with East Coast prep school accents, volunteers at the American Hospital of Paris, helped the young man into a makeshift operating theater. The emergency surgery was in the elegant ballroom of a casino in Fontainebleau, forty miles south of Paris. A tall man with thick dark hair, blue eyes, bushy brows, large but nimble hands, and a boxer's face was soon at the shattered young man's side. His name was Dr. Sumner Jackson, a fifty-six-year-old American and the chief surgeon of the American Hospital of Paris.

Sumner began to examine the young man's leg and decided there was only one thing for it. It would have to go. He needed a saw. It would be no easy operation given the poor light in the casino. A few minutes later, the boy lay in agony on a roulette table as Sumner prepared to remove his leg, carefully cutting off the flow of blood through his arteries. If Sumner made a mistake, the boy could bleed to death.

Sumner took a scalpel and sliced across the boy's muscles, revealing the underlying bone. With an oscillating saw he cut through the bone and filed down the rough edges before delicately laying muscle and skin flaps over the stump. It was painstaking work that took great care and concentration in the dim light, and Sumner took intense pride in his expertise. A superb combat surgeon, arguably the finest of his generation, he had vast experience, having spent much of the last war trying to repair shattered young bodies. In 1916 he had volunteered for Britain's Royal Army Medical Corps and had arrived in Flanders with other Americans who had defied U.S. president Woodrow Wilson's call for neutrality. He was assigned to a surgery near the Somme battlefield, where over ninety percent of those who "went over the top" and attacked German positions ended up being killed or wounded.

Sumner had operated on hundreds of young men whose limbs had been torn asunder by shellfire. Twenty-five years later, he was once again doing his best to save lives, but there was something particularly unnerving about the nature of men's wounds in this new war. It only took one German 88mm shell to kills dozens of troops if caught out in the open. Hitler's modern weapons were designed to rip humans to small pieces of flying flesh, to turn them to hamburger.

Sumner completed the amputation, ensuring that the boy's leg was carefully bandaged. There was no time to rest. Dozens of other gravely wounded men lay waiting their turn. Sumner was working sometimes deep into the night—often beside a fellow American doctor named Dr. Charles Bove—sawing, cutting, stitching, trying to save as many soldiers and civilians as they could. The casino's corridors were filled with emergency surgical cases, patients begging for water or lying in grim silence, resigned to death. Whenever Sumner straightened his back and took a drink of coffee or water, he could see yet more who had been laid out on the baccarat tables, waiting to suffer the saw. There were as many urgent cases awaiting Sumner when he returned to his base, the American Hospital of Paris, reputedly the best equipped in Europe, where he had worked since 1925. He made the journey back and forth in a white ambulance, sometimes driven by an upper-class young American volunteer, through the working-class outskirts of Paris and then to the leafy streets of upscale Neuilly-sur-Seine.

Many Parisians could not remember such a glorious spring. The chestnuts along the Avenue Foch, where Sumner and his wife and twelve-year-old son lived in a ground-floor apartment at number 11, were a wonderful green. Breezes carried the sweet scent of purple lilacs and lilies of the valley. From a wide terrace adjoining his office on the fourth floor of the hospital, when Sumner was able to take a break from surgery, he could see the city's immense elegance as he stood for a few minutes relaxing, usually smoking a cigar or more often a cigarette.

Sumner's view of Paris, spread out before him, was fabulous, with the Eiffel Tower clear in the distance a few miles to the southeast. In the courtyard below, ambulances pulled up all that May, their bells ringing, returning from the front lines. The impossible was happening. France was falling. Anyone who could get out of Paris was doing so. Many of his American colleagues at the hospital, a cornerstone of the expatriate community since 1910, and his wealthy neighbors on Avenue Foch, several of them Jews, had already fled.

Sumner had seen the rise of fascism in Europe, the weakness of European democracies, and the appeasement of Hitler, whom he despised. He had been convinced the previous fall, after war had broken out, that the United States would join her allies from the last war to once again put Germany in her place. Hitler would be stopped. Sumner could not believe that America would stay neutral and let Europe fall into the abyss once again. But now his worst fears were being confirmed.

A fortnight earlier Europe had exploded as the Nazis launched a massive spring offensive in the West. Since May 10, Sumner had read headlines that grew more ominous by the day. The Wehrmacht had stormed with seemingly unstoppable force through Belgium, Holland, and northern France. Hitler's armies were less than a hundred miles from Paris. The French were in retreat, the nation losing heart, it seemed, and the unimaginable happening. Indeed, Sumner knew, it was no longer a question of whether France would be defeated but when.

Operating on severely wounded young men consumed all of Sumner's waking hours. When he did have time to wipe his brow, take a long gulp of coffee, and drag on a cigarette as he gazed to the south from his terrace, he could not help but think about his fifty-two-year-old wife and their son, Phillip, at home on Avenue Foch, a couple of miles from the Eiffel Tower.

After twenty-one years of marriage, Sumner was still utterly devoted to Swiss-born Charlotte Sylvie Barrelet de Ricou, whom Sumner had always called Toquette. She was petite with sandy brown hair and the lean physique of a keen tennis player. In her youth, she sometimes boasted, she had beaten the best French tennis player of the time, Suzanne Lenglen, who had won thirty-one championship titles. After the last war, Sumner had taken her back to New England, but she was so dreadfully unhappy, missing Paris and her family so much that she fell ill. "It's me or America," she finally demanded. Sumner chose her, abandoning a good job in a Philadelphia hospital and returning to Paris, where he was forced to spend years studying French and taking endless exams in order to practice medicine in France, much to his bitter frustration. He was in fact compelled to repeat six of his seven years of medical school. Finally, at age thirty-five, he had been able to earn a living as a doctor once more.

Toquette had been more than worth the sacrifice. The youngest of six children whose father was a successful Swiss lawyer, she had a remarkably powerful spirit. Sumner also greatly admired her courage and stamina. She had won a Red Cross award for four years of service in bloody surgeries in World War I and shared his belief that one should give back, not just take, in a civilized society. He had first met her when she was a feisty twenty-eight-year-old nurse working at his side in a hospital on the Rue Piccini in Paris in 1916. "The first time I kissed your mother," Sumner jokingly told his son, "was in a linen closet at the Rue Piccini. . . . It was a very long kiss."

Toquette was witty, spoke flawless English, and quickly discovered that the equally pithy Sumner also loved to swim, sail, and play tennis. Soon, thirty-one-year-old Sumner, whom she called Jack, was seriously wooing her, often visiting her family home in Enghien-les-Bains, an upscale suburb of Paris. Neither Toquette nor her family needed any persuading, and the couple was married at the family home in Enghien in November 1917. Over a decade later, their son, Phillip, known to all as Pete, was born on January 10, 1928, in the American Hospital. Phillip's birth when Toquette was thirty-nine, after she had all but given up hope of conceiving, prompted a raucous party with several bottles of Bollinger 1921 champagne being drunk to celebrate the new arrival.

Sumner and Toquette had since doted on their only child, and he had grown up very much aware that his parents had a great love for each other. Toquette did all she could to make Sumner happy, determined he would never regret his decision to forsake his family (he was close to his brother, Daniel, and sister, Freda) and a life in America for one in France. Yet on the outbreak of the Second World War, the previous September, Sumner and Toquette had once again been forced to decide whether they should stay in Europe or leave. Sumner had thought it best they go to America for Phillip's safety. But Toquette had insisted on staying. The idea of living in the United States again filled her with almost as much dread as the approaching Germans.

Eight months later, Toquette was just as determined to stay in Paris, close to her family. And Sumner still faced an agonizing choice. Should he continue to do as his wife wanted? Or should he ignore her wishes and take his family back to America while there was still time to escape?

FLAMES JUMPED into the sky. Near Amiens in northern France, an ambulance driver tried to make his way past burning buildings, avoiding downed telephone wires, rotting horse carcasses, and bomb craters, pitiful evidence of the immense ferocity of Hitler's Blitzkrieg.

It was early on May 18, 1940, when a well-spoken Princeton gradu-ate, thirty-two-year-old Donald Coster, looked up from the ambu-lance and saw German planes, wave after wave of them. There were the whistles and screams of bombs falling. Stuka dive-bombers with inverted gull wings attacked, dropping five-hundred-pound bombs, leaving behind a blanket of acrid, sickening fumes. Coster made it to a hospital in Châteaudun just as the bombing became most intense. Terribly afraid, the volunteer ambulance driver took shelter in the hospital's basement.

After about an hour, the sound of bombing ended. There was a tense silence. Coster knew the Germans were close by, approaching Amiens itself, one hundred and fifty miles north of Paris. Like mil-lions of French, Coster had tried to escape their lightning advance. That was why he was now cowering in a cellar beside several dozen doctors, nurses, and wounded soldiers. The bombing began again. This time the explosions were much closer. Coster felt them like "punches" against his chest. It was quiet once more. He could hear his heart beating fast and then came the sound of heavy jackboots on cobblestones. For several minutes Coster waited, expecting grenades to be thrown down into their shelter. He stood up and climbed the steps leading out of the cellar.

Daylight blinded Coster as he left the shelter and walked into a courtyard. For the first time he caught sight of a German soldier. The storm trooper was aiming at a line of French prisoners backed against a wall. They were civilians. The German looked as if he was going to finish them off. Coster waved his identification card at the German, who instantly turned his gun on him and was about to pull the trigger when someone called out in German, begging the soldier to spare Coster and take him to his commander instead.

Coster and some of his fellow ambulance men, under guard, walked fifty yards or so until they reached a main junction on the road to Amiens. There was a roaring of engines, a clanking of tank tracks. A Panzer column was moving into the city—the tip of the

Nazi spear thrusting toward Paris. There had been no more mobile and powerful force in the history of war, and Coster looked on in awe. The column seemed to stretch forever and moved so fast, the tanks thundering by at forty miles an hour, bristling with heavy weapons, the eight-foot-high steel behemoths surely unstoppable. Armored cars followed, pulling camouflaged antiaircraft guns, their 20mm barrels pointing skyward. One tank rolled toward a barricade farther down the road and smashed through, making light work of heavy logs. "Nothing invented by man, you felt with a shock of despair," recalled Coster, "could possibly withstand this inhuman monster which had already flattened half of Europe."

A German officer ordered Coster to help at a nearby hospital and bring in wounded from the battlefield. In a field of high grass were many English dead rotting in the sun, their faces purple and black. There were a few men whose wounds were already gangrenous, and they gritted their teeth as they called for help from where they lay amid dozens of dead cows with huge bloated stomachs. The stench was nauseating. Three hundred British soldiers had been riddled with bullets from the Panzers' machine guns. Fewer than thirty had survived.

A German approached as Coster helped the wounded. He thought Coster was a British soldier, mistaking his uniform, and snatched his gloves away. Coster stupidly tried to grab them back and the German whipped out his pistol and aimed it at his stomach. Coster pointed to the band on his arm, showing the symbol for the American Field Service, a volunteer ambulance unit.

"*Amerikanisch,*" said Coster.

To Coster's surprise, the German officer stood to attention, saluted Coster, shook his hand, and then left without another word. Other German soldiers nearby talked with Coster. They regarded Americans with bemused contempt, especially President Roosevelt, a vacillating windbag compared to their glorious, decisive Führer. One of them said: "We never see any of you on our side."

There was more good news from the front—for the Germans. After advancing through southern Belgium, the Germans had crossed the Meuse River and pierced the French line at Sedan. The Allies had been forced to retreat toward the port of Dunkirk. Disaster loomed. Nothing, it seemed, could stop the Nazi juggernaut as it barreled toward Paris.

TWO

TO SAVE FRANCE

AT THE AMERICAN Hospital in Neuilly, the chaos and crisis worsened. One of the patients was RAF fighter pilot Paul Richey, who had been hit in the neck by a German bullet. He would later recall Sumner and the other colleagues, in particular Jackson's close friend, sixty-five-year-old Dr. Thierry de Martel, France's leading neurosurgeon, who had operated on Richey with great success. De Martel had a noble face, short gray hair, and had an aristocratic, intellectual air. With Sumner and others all through that late May of 1940, he had removed German shrapnel from Allied soldiers' skulls. Never before, not even during the darkest days of World War I, had de Martel and his close friend Sumner worked such long hours; all of Paris's hospitals were now flooded with the badly wounded.

The news was ever more unsettling: Sumner and his colleagues learned that some of the hospital's female ambulance drivers had been reported missing. Hopes of stalling the German advance began to fade. Patients like Richey were advised not to wear insignia on their uniforms in case the Germans captured the hospital. Then, on June 1, 1940, the hospital's board of governors agreed that new leadership was required if the hospital was to be safeguarded in such trying times, and so they appointed Sumner "resident physician in charge." He was proud to accept the role, but it came with a high price. Even if he wanted to, Sumner felt that he could not now leave Paris, however much he still toyed with the idea of taking Toquette and Phillip back to Maine, or the hospital might collapse without him. It was his duty to stay on in Paris, but he was also more and more convinced that his wife and child must leave even if he no longer could.

Two days later, on June 3, came the first great intimation of what lay in store for the city. It was a hot and humid day, unusually so for early June in Paris. Shortly before lunch, Sumner heard air raid sirens begin to wail. He went to the terrace adjoining his office with several colleagues to watch the raid. There was the repeated crump of exploding shells, piercing whistles, and the clatter of shrapnel as it fell on the hospital roof. Huge clouds of black smoke billowed across the city, obscuring the famous landmarks. "I'm glad we painted out our red crosses!" said one of Jackson's colleagues. The Germans were targeting hospitals and ambulances. Would they destroy Paris just as they had leveled central Warsaw the previous September and, more recently, the heart of Rotterdam on May 14, when hundreds of innocent civilians had been killed and 30,000 people left homeless?

After dark, the bombers returned. On Avenue Foch, it was fifty-two-year-old Toquette Jackson's turn to hear the sirens and try to stay calm. As with so many mothers in Paris, she worried about what would happen to her family. Twelve-year-old Phillip, her only child, slept each night in a room on the ground floor. She was prepared to do anything to keep him safe. All along the avenue, the streetlights were out. In some of the neighborhood's newer buildings with large windows, there were odd flashes of light as servants on the top floors descended by torchlight to the basement shelters. Parisians were supposed to observe a strict blackout, but no one wanted to trip and fall six flights. People spoke in whispers as if the Germans had already set up camp on the Champs-Élysées. There was no unseemly rush for the metro. Avenue Foch residents preferred to sit huddling close to their concierges in the basements of their mansions.

That day, 257 Parisians were killed and aerodromes around the city destroyed. At the American Hospital, patient Paul Richey believed the targeting of civilians for the first time was "a well-calculated psychological stroke." The hospital's windows were all taped, sandbags piled high. "More and more French wounded were flooding in," recalled Richey. "Several women ambulance drivers were shot up by Hun aircraft, and one drove back pluckily with a bullet in her buttock. Ambulances disappeared without a trace and were presumed casualties. The Huns seemed to be deliberately strafing vehicles marked with red crosses, and the hospital authorities ordered them to be erased."

A couple of days later, a young soldier—a badly wounded twenty-year-old Algerian—was brought to the hospital in an ambulance. He had been hit by shrapnel from a German artillery shell and thrown from his motorbike. The young man's father, a much-respected French general, soon arrived at the hospital to check on his son. Sumner watched as the father pinned the Croix de Guerre and the Médaille Militaire onto his son's chest.

Among those gathered in the hospital to witness the medal ceremony was Toquette Jackson. She had spent all of the last war working in nursing whites and was helping out at the American Hospital, so acute was the medical crisis.

Sumner and Toquette watched as the French general, who had lost an eye at Verdun in 1916, comforted his wounded son.

"*Tel père, tel fils* [Like father, like son]," Sumner told Toquette and others after the award ceremony.

Throughout that frantic May of 1940, the Jacksons managed to take the odd break, retiring together to the veranda adjoining Sumner's office on the fourth floor of the hospital. Sumner was so busy that he often slept in his office rather than return to 11, Avenue Foch, where, before the war, he had run a highly lucrative private practice specializing in urology, which often meant curing rich Americans with venereal disease. According to a middle-aged Frenchwoman, Clemence Bock, who had tutored Sumner in French and become a good friend: "Some of the most beautiful women in Paris came to his

office at avenue Foch or to the hospital. . . . Mademoiselle Diplara-
kos, the beauty queen of Greece, was in love with him."

As the Jacksons looked out over Paris, smoking cigarettes, they
would undoubtedly have discussed what they should do next. Toquette wanted to stay at her husband's side, come what may, but
Sumner was increasingly insistent that she should leave before the
Germans arrived.

One day, Dr. Charles Bove, one of the hospital's finest doctors,
joined the Jacksons on the terrace. To their surprise, he announced
that he was going back to the United States while there was still a
chance of escaping the Germans. "It's only a matter of a few weeks
before Roosevelt brings America in and declares war on Germany,"
added Bove. "But this time the Boche will have Paris, and if we stay
they'll lock us up."

Others also gave up hope in the next few days. A depressed
Thierry de Martel told Sumner that he could not bear the idea of
German troops in his beloved Paris. His sadness cast a further
shadow over the hospital and staff, who had only ever known him to
be upbeat. "He was a debonair dresser with perpetually smiling eyes
and a tongue that was always ready to burst into humorous sally,"
recalled a colleague. "He was the eternal playboy who had refused to
surrender to his years. But he had become a man transformed. For
days he had scarcely spoken a word to us, and then only on business.
It was terrible to see his laughter strangled."

At some point early that June, Toquette agreed to leave Paris
with Phillip until the battle for France had been decided. Sumner
had learned from sources within the hospital that the Germans were
indeed unstoppable and in a few days would be in the outskirts of
Paris. There was no telling what would happen to the city and those
who chose to stay if the French decided to defend it.

It was hard for Toquette to have to say good-bye to Sumner. She
had never left his side during a crisis. Although he would have joined
her if she had wanted him to, she had insisted that he stay on without

her. There was no question of him abandoning his duties as other colleagues had. Given how many doctors were deserting the hospital, his departure would send the worst signal; others would follow his example and the superbly equipped hospital would end up in Nazi hands—exactly what the enemy would want.

Toquette told Sumner she was confident that the Allies could stop the German advance and hold them off north of Paris. The city could still be saved. They would be reunited soon. She was convinced of it. Any other outcome was too terrible to contemplate.

One morning early that June, twelve-year-old Phillip Jackson awoke in his family's L-shaped *"rez de chausée"*—ground floor apartment—on the Avenue Foch. His spacious bedroom opened onto a wide hallway where there was a telephone. Across the hallway was Sumner's office, part of which was a laboratory, which connected to an elegant living room that led to his parents' bedroom and then a kitchen that looked out onto the Rue Traktir. The elegantly decorated apartment had two entrances and access to an inner courtyard where Sumner kept the family's car.

A dark-haired and rather sensitive boy, Phillip could see through his window into a small garden and then through black iron railings to the broad avenue beyond. In recent days several of his neighbors had left for the country, and he was about to do the same. He got dressed and later that morning—along with his mother and his fifty-nine-year-old aunt Alice, nicknamed "Tat," and Rosalee, the Swiss maid from the family's country home in Enghien—climbed into the family's jet-black Citroën 11, the first front-wheel-drive car to be built in France. There was little room for luggage, so he took only what he absolutely needed. He was happy that his summer vacation had started two months earlier than planned, and excited that he was headed to the country.

When the war had broken out the previous fall, life had been imbued with a brilliant intensity, as if Phillip were living in one of the adventure stories Toquette read him every night, never neglecting to close the book at a well-marked cliffhanger. The previous winter at the family country home in Enghien, just outside Paris, he had stood in his thick winter coat, all smiles, at the opposite end of a draw saw, helping his father prepare firewood for what were bound to be hard times ahead. To Phillip it seemed that his father, usually so busy at the American Hospital, was always at his happiest when he was working outside with his hands, be it cutting firewood or carving small boats from pieces of flotsam that father and son collected from the beaches in Normandy on summer vacations.

For Phillip, a great adventure was beginning as Toquette drove along the Avenue Foch with her sister, Tat, who had the same thin face, bright eyes, and prominent brow as his mother, seated beside her on the bench seat. The Citroën carried them across the gray Seine and headed south, along the straight and flat roads that crossed the broad plain below Paris, through the endless wheat fields, toward the Massif Central, the region in central France famous for its volcanic ranges and wild river gorges. There was plenty of time for Toquette to worry about her husband as she followed the route of the Loire River toward the mountains. What would happen to Paris? There was no knowing what the Germans might do. Would they sack the city? Would it become a beautiful battleground before being reduced to ruins?

The roads were clogged but Toquette made steady progress, passing through the towns of Nemours, Nevers, and Moulins, with its four-spired cathedral. Phillip stared out of the car window at the neat vineyards of the upper Loire Valley near the town of Sancerre, famous for its fruity wine, and Pouilly, equally celebrated for its fine whites. Finally, Toquette pulled up outside a small hotel on the banks of the Allier River in the village of Villeneuve d'Allier, a few miles from the spa town of Vichy. Her eldest brother, sixty-one-year-old Hermann, a keen fisherman, had recommended the hotel. The owner's daughter, Paulette, around Phillip's age, would be only too happy to teach Phillip how best to hook brook eel and whitefish.

Toquette and Phillip had left Paris just in time. By June 9, it seemed, the whole city was on the move. All roads south were jammed with a pitiful exodus. More than a quarter of those fleeing were children. No one wanted to be caught "like a rat in occupied Paris," in the words of the writer Simone de Beauvoir. A quarter of France's population was fleeing the German advance, headed anywhere so long as it was south. The French writer and aviator Antoine de Saint-Exupéry flew above the exodus and recalled: "Roads completely blocked, fires everywhere, supplies scattered helter-skelter, villages devastated, everything a shambles—a total shambles." France looked "as though a gigantic ant hill in the north had been kicked open and all the ants were running away." Most had believed the Germans would be repulsed. As recently as May 24, French prime minister Paul Reynaud had broadcast: "France has been invaded a hundred times and never beaten . . . our belief in victory is intact."

Meanwhile, back in Paris, Sumner prepared for the worst, sleeping in his office on the hospital's fourth floor and continuing to work all hours, even donating his own blood. On June 10 the French government left Paris for Tours, prompting a wholesale desertion. The next day Sumner awoke to find the city he loved more than any other desolate, as if in early mourning. From his terrace he could see the broad streets around Neuilly. They were unusually dark. Rolling clouds of soot were blocking the sun. There had been no dawn chorus. The birds had fled.

Street sellers' wagons lay abandoned, fresh flowers strewn across the pavements. Dead dogs littered the city; their owners had killed them before leaving. Abandoned farm animals grazed in the Tuileries Garden. Along the Avenue Foch, as in so many upscale areas of the city, most homes were empty, their windows shuttered. Since moving to the avenue in 1925, Sumner had come to know many of his neighbors, several of whom had wisely fled Paris well ahead of the Nazis. They included Pierre Wertheimer, a partner in the House of Chanel perfume business, who had left number 55 and decamped to New York. So, too, had Mr. Alfred Lindon at number 75, leaving sixty-three precious paintings under lock and key at the Chase Bank. At number 58, there was also no sign of banker Nelson Dean Jay, president of the American Hospital's board of governors.

Others in the city's wealthy 16th Arrondissement had packed up and left in a hurry too: The Duke of Windsor, although a keen admirer of Hitler, had not stayed to welcome his storm troopers, absconding at dawn without even telling his aide-de-camp. Also absent were the Astors, the Guggenheims, the Vanderbilts, and the Rubinsteins—the international set who had before the war been patients of Sumner Jackson. The few families left on Avenue Foch wondered what might happen when the Germans arrived, given that their homes would be much prized. They became even more anxious when they heard shellfire so close to Paris that with every sudden explosion small clouds of birds rose from the top of the Arc de Triomphe, at the far eastern end of the avenue.

Sumner had read about the Germans' actions in Poland the previous fall, the indiscriminate targeting of civilians—indeed, the thousands of innocents killed in terror bombings—and the destruction of Warsaw and Rotterdam that May. Hitler's armies and his Luftwaffe clearly had little regard for human life and scant mercy wherever they chose to attack. The American embassy had assured Sumner and his fellow American citizens, around five thousand of them still in Paris, that the Nazis would respect their neutral status and their property. Over a thousand so-called red certificates had been issued, meaning properties could not be commandeered by the Germans when they arrived. But would the Germans really honor such paperwork? Sumner knew that his home at 11, Avenue Foch would make some senior Nazi official a superb pied-à-terre. There was no telling what might happen. Certainly, after his time treating the victims of German aggression in the First World War, Sumner was far from inclined to trust the "damned Boche," as he often called the Germans, when it came to any assurance that they would respect the law.

By June 13, 1940, preparations throughout the city were being made for what seemed to be inevitable conquest. In Neuilly, Sumner and his colleagues decided to evacuate French soldiers from the American Hospital in case the Germans decided to send them to POW camps. The Germans were fast closing on the capital, skirting the Seine as they stormed south from the ancient city of Rouen. The Gare d'Austerlitz had been closed after the last train headed south had pulled out of the station. Four million people from the city and its neighboring towns had also departed, leaving just a fifth of the original population. Those staying mostly could not afford to leave, or were infirm, or, like Sumner, were needed in essential jobs. Most of the city that evening was deathly quiet. In a few quarters the only people on the streets were deserters from the French army, still in their khaki uniforms, staggering around drunk outside looted bars and cafés. From the terrace of Sumner's office in Neuilly, it was possible to see flashes of light from bursting artillery shells splashing across the horizon. Hitler's storm troopers were less than twenty miles away.

THREE

THE FOURTEENTH

A LONE GERMAN on a motorbike crossed the deserted Place Voltaire in eastern Paris, his headlight stabbing a cruel shaft of light into the pitch darkness. It was 3:40 a.m. on Friday, June 14, as the first of Hitler's men arrived in the City of Light, headed toward the Bastille, passing boarded-up homes and walls where propaganda posters had been hastily pasted earlier that spring: *Nous vaincrons parce que nous sommes les plus forts.* (We will win because we are strongest.)

Other men with weather-beaten faces from the Eighteenth Army followed, marching through the Porte de la Villette unopposed. Paris had been declared an open city, abandoned to the Boche without a fight. As dawn broke above Haussmann's hushed boulevards, two German units headed for the most symbolic landmarks: the Arc de Triomphe and the Eiffel Tower. By 8:00 a.m. the Germans had set up a headquarters at the Hôtel de Crillon, a stone palace dating from 1758 that overlooked the Place de la Concorde at the foot of the Champs-Élysées, in the very heart of the city.

A hundred yards from the Jacksons' home, the Arc de Triomphe was crowded with smiling German soldiers. At 9:45 a massive swastika was raised and was soon fluttering above the Tomb of the Unknown Soldier. A military band began to play. Nearby, German soldiers set up their MG42 machine guns, aiming them along each of the twelve avenues that converged at the Place de l'Étoile. Then they set up four cannons and pointed them down the four main arteries leading from the Place de l'Étoile: the Champs-Élysées and the Avenues Foch, Victor Hugo, and Marceau. General Kurt von Briesen, commanding the 30th Infantry Division, took his men's salute around midday as they marched down the Champs-Élysées. He was on horseback but stood up in his stirrups every few minutes out of sheer delight.

That lunchtime, the new Nazi ambassador to Paris, thirty-seven-year-old Otto Abetz, who had arrived that very morning, sat down to eat at the Ritz. An ardent Francophile married to a Frenchwoman, the handsome former art teacher at a girls' school in Karlsruhe was in his pomp, talking with General Otto von Stülpnagel, the new military commandant of Paris. The Ritz's head chef had noted the likely nationality of that day's guests and had obsequiously included an entrée choice of *filet de sole au vin du Rhin* (sole cooked in a dry German wine from the Rhine), or *poularde rôtie* with sumptuous rissole potatoes and asparagus with hollandaise sauce.

On other major buildings throughout central Paris, bloodred flags with crooked crosses were soon flapping lazily in the summer breezes. In Neuilly, at the American Hospital, from Sumner's terrace, German troops in field gray were visible in the tree-lined streets. The men's faces were dirty with dust and sweat. Elsewhere a few Parisians stood, nervous but with no hatred in their eyes as they watched large chestnut horses with bleached tails pull well-used artillery pieces toward the city's center.

Along the Avenue Foch, as in most of Paris, there was still a heavy silence. Most homes were shuttered. It seemed no one had stayed to see the Germans arrive. That afternoon a depressing drizzle fell on the iron fences and lamps that were a feature of the widest avenue in Paris, 120 meters wide and 1,300 long, flanked by sidewalks and riding paths that led to the Bois de Boulogne at the western end, shaded by rows of towering chestnut trees.

At the Ritz, senior German officers, in spotless gray uniforms covered in gold braid, were finishing their dessert of fresh fruit.

Meanwhile, less than a mile away, in the study of his home at 18, Rue Weber, sixty-five-year-old Dr. Thierry de Martel, Sumner Jackson's close friend, sat on a couch. The previous day de Martel had written to William Bullitt, the American ambassador: "I made you the promise that I wouldn't leave Paris. I didn't say whether I would stay in Paris alive or dead." He had lost his only son in the First World War in the great bloodletting that had prevented the Germans from destroying France. Now the Nazis, the Jew-haters, the philistines, the heralds of a new dark age, were almost at his door, their tanks' tracks clanking on the cobbles of the Champs-Élysées. So de Martel pulled out a syringe, placed a needle in his arm, and pushed the plunger, injecting strychnine. Even a small dose would have acted almost immediately. The strychnine sent his body into seizures, then violent convulsions, before he became unconscious.

At the American Hospital in Neuilly, Sumner learned that an important colleague, Dr. Edmund Gros, had suffered a stroke. If he kept losing staff at this rate, the hospital would not be able to function. Around this time, one of Sumner's fellow doctors found that "a stillness like the quiet of a human being who has stopped breathing permeated the grounds" of the American Hospital. The doctor went into the reception room. "The cork-tiled floor deadened [my] footsteps as always; but for once the silence was disquieting."

The doctor came across a colleague. "What's wrong here?" he asked. "Everything looks dead."

"Everything *is* dead," replied his colleague. "I'm going home to America. I advise you to get out too."

THE SOLDIERS that Helmut Knochen passed early that morning, the vanguard of the mighty Wehrmacht, had been hunched down in their heavy gray field coats, weary and wet from the rain. By contrast, his face was not deeply bronzed. He had not been fighting for over a month to take Paris. Nor were he or his entourage in combat uniform. They were in fact in disguise, wearing the uniforms of military police, the Feldgendarmerie, their epaulettes trimmed with orange, small bull's-eyes on their caps, as they entered the outskirts of Paris.

Thirty-year-old SS-Standartenführer Helmut Knochen, the man with the pale face, recognized many of the landmarks as his car headed to the heart of the city, sites he had grown to adore on his last visit in 1937 to attend the World's Fair: the golden dome of Les Invalides; the Place de la Concorde, where that morning two Storch light planes had deposited senior German officers; the Tuileries Garden; the Palais du Louvre. This highly effective agent had auburn hair and a rather weak chin, and stood around five feet ten inches tall. A source for British intelligence had described him more generously as having a wide, somewhat feminine mouth that had a slight twist to the left that made him always look sardonic.

Knochen was certainly no foot soldier. He had been in an office, working heroic hours, planning the greatest moment of his already distinguished career: the occupation of Paris, his beloved Paris. He must have been utterly elated, energized, for he and his men had long prepared for this day. He himself had studied the French political situation and closely followed events in Paris, known within his department by the code word "Region V," since 1935. It was a glorious moment for any Francophile German—to enter the fabled city as its conqueror, as part of its new master race, as momentous a day as when he had been decorated with the Iron Cross by Hitler himself at a special ceremony the previous November in the vast Reich Chancellery in Berlin. The Führer's extraordinary magnetism had of course totally seduced him, just as it had captivated so many millions of Germans. Paris was Knochen's reward for excellent work: he had played a critical key role in the greatest German intelligence coup of the war so far, the kidnapping of two British spies in November 1939 in Holland, which would be known in espionage folklore as the Venlo Incident.

Knochen's fleet of fast cars sped through the empty streets, dull and gray beneath heavy clouds, seemingly in grief. The unmarked cars pulled up on the corner of the Rue Saint-Honoré before the Hôtel du Louvre, one of the grand dames of Paris hotels. Two dozen or so Germans stepped out of the cars and made their way into the lobby, among the finest in the city. The front desk was a few yards from two huge Doric columns of black marble.

The Germans' watches were set to Berlin time; all of France would now live by it. Their mission was to make sure of that and much more, for they were not soldiers but men of the Geheime Sta-atspolizei, the Secret State Police, otherwise known as the Gestapo. They were, notably, under the administrative control of the SS, the so-called Schutzstaffel, which would ultimately be responsible for most of Nazi Germany's crimes against humanity. Ardent anti-Semites, among the more intelligent and cultured of the Nazis' se-cret policemen, their remit was wide indeed. They were to investigate cases of espionage, sabotage, and treason, and all criminal attacks on the Nazi Party and Germany. In 1936 they had been given carte blanche to operate without legal oversight, meaning they were effec-tively above the law, unlike the military. As SS-Obergruppenführer Werner Best, one of Knochen's colleagues and a former head of legal affairs in the Gestapo, had explained: "As long as the [Gestapo] car-ries out the will of the leadership, it is acting legally."

Knochen stepped forward and then entered the hotel. Mr. Bones—that was what his name meant in German. He was from bourgeois origins, not the gutter, a polished performer with a first-rate intel-lect. His father, Karl, had been a strict schoolmaster and just as tough a disciplinarian when it came to his own son. As soon as possible he had enrolled Helmut, at age sixteen, in the Stahlhelm, a violent paramilitary organization. Helmut had excelled academically and attended the universities of Leipzig, Göttingen and Halle, where he had gained a doctorate in medieval English literature. But instead of becoming an academic he had joined the Nazi party's official press agency in 1936, working as an editor, and while covering the Berlin Olympics he had met a former professor who soon recognized his fine analytical mind and recruited him to the Gestapo. His first job had been to monitor the German press, on the lookout for articles written by possible subversives.

It was a heady evening in the City of Light. In some restaurants the Germans, sick of army rations, sat down at tables and, grinning from ear to ear, ordered two-pound steaks and dozen-egg omelettes. At the headquarters for General Gerd von Rundstedt's forces in the Parisian suburb of Saint-Germain-en-Laye, about twelve miles from the city, brisk orderlies placed a large map of Paris on a wall and then studded it with pins. Blue pins indicated the best restaurants. The red ones were for the best brothels. There would be nothing but the finest for the victorious *Übermenschen*.

Like his idol, Adolf Hitler, Knochen had a great deal to celebrate. But he and his men did not venture into the grand hotels nearby, the Meurice, the Crillon, the Majestic, and the Ritz, already occupied by the German army's top generals. The head of the Reich Main Security Office, Reinhard Heydrich, Knochen's mentor and boss, had ordered him to keep a low profile. Many of the Prussian aristocrats in the top ranks of the Wehrmacht despised the "black men" of the SS, who personified everything they loathed and feared about Nazism. They had fought hard to make sure the Gestapo would have no supremacy in Paris, unlike in other conquered cities in Nazi Europe where mass arrests and executions had rapidly turned civilian populations against their new rulers.

The best brothels were already open for business. A few minutes' walk from the Hôtel du Louvre was the legendary Chabanais, a whorehouse much frequented by European nobility. And a few more minutes farther west on foot was number 122 Rue de Provence, the address of what would become the most celebrated of Paris's many wartime brothels, the One Two Two. It was unlikely that Knochen visited either, unlike so many of his compatriots, that first night in

Paris. He had to be up early the next morning, ready to raid the pre-fectural offices for records containing the names of German émigrés and other potential enemies of the Reich. Indeed, there were urgent tasks, work that would within just a few days earn him, according to an Allied intelligence report, the goodwill of General Alfred Strec-cius, chief of the German military administration in France. He could truly indulge later. In any case, he was interested in a more refined breed of mademoiselle: the aristocratic and sensual elite, the women of Parisian high society, Le Tout-Paris, who were drawn to men of power like moths to a flame, whether or not they were dressed in an SS uniform.

Knochen had a burning ambition. One day France would be an SS state, totally controlled by the "black bastards" of Hitler's elite security force, and Knochen would be running affairs. While his powers were limited for now—he could not yet even make arrests—Knochen was confident that eventually, if he was as cunning as he was patient, he would be able to do what he wanted: ruthlessly de-stroy all opposition to German rule in France.

THAT EVENING, as the light began to fade, German vehicles fitted with loudspeakers trundled along the Avenue Foch and the other grand avenues leading from the Place de l'Étoile, then fanned out across Paris, passing through suburbs like Neuilly.

"Parisians!" they announced. "German troops will be passing through Paris for the next forty-eight hours. Stock what provisions you need, then go home and stay there. No demonstrations will be allowed."

It had been perhaps the saddest day of Sumner's life. That night he was bereft and full of grief: his close friend and colleague was dead. At some point that day, Dr. Thierry Martel had been admitted to the American Hospital. He had been found in his apartment lying next to an open book, Victor Hugo's play *Hernani*. Among the last words he had read were: "Since one must be tall to die, I arise." According to one of his colleagues, Martel died after three hours without even opening his eyes. He had made certain he would be "dead on the day the Germans entered Paris." Sumner and his colleagues had done everything they could to save him.

That night the lights did not go on in Paris. The unthinkable had happened. The Nazis had taken over without a shot being fired. No one had imagined they would so quickly and easily become the new masters of the most beautiful capital in Europe. There was a strict curfew at 11:00 p.m. Seen in the distance from Sumner's terrace, the Eiffel Tower no longer glittered. From its peak flew a huge swastika. The stunned city spread out below lay hushed in a darkness it had never known.

FOUR

DAY TRIPPERS

ALL OVER CONQUERED Europe that dark summer of 1940, countless people tuned in to the BBC. Sumner Jackson listened to the British broadcaster regularly now that it was the only news source that he could trust. He would have heard the news reports with the volume turned low, the radio set placed far from a door or window so a potential informer did not hear. One could never be too cautious, and in the first days of the occupation those, like Sumner, who despised the Nazis were understandably somewhat paranoid. Indeed, he had good reason to be careful. The Germans had set up their headquarters in Neuilly, their *Kommandantur*, right opposite the American Hospital's main entrance gate. Sumner was no doubt relieved that, thankfully, at least for the time being, they had not demanded to take over the hospital.

In several BBC broadcasts that June, fifty-year-old general Charles de Gaulle implored patriotic Frenchmen to join him in London and continue to fight the Germans.

"Is the last word said?" asked de Gaulle. "Has all hope gone?"

The war was yet to be won even if France had been occupied.

"The cause of France is not lost," declared de Gaulle. "The very factors that brought about our defeat may one day lead us to victory. For, remember this, France does not stand alone. She is not isolated. Behind her is a vast empire, and she can make common cause with the British empire, which commands the seas and is continuing the struggle. Like England, she can draw unreservedly on the immense industrial resources of the United States."

Finally, de Gaulle exhorted his fellow citizens to never give up, assuring them: "Whatever happens, the flame of French resistance must not and shall not die."

The first call to the French to resist Nazism had been made.

Like de Gaulle, Sumner was determined to fight back in some way.

ON JUNE 22, 1940, Knochen and his fellow Gestapo members were issued telephone directories of the military administration. The numbers were mostly for the city's swankiest hotels: the Lutetia, the Majestic, the Meurice. Knochen had spent a week in the capital making sure he and his men stayed away from the places where the Prussian generals of the high command and their effete aides could be found quaffing the best vintages. The non-Nazi elites had no idea as of yet that the "black men" of the SS, the Gestapo, were even in the city.

Armed with his new telephone directory, Knochen could quickly contact anyone who mattered in Paris. That night of June 22, he faced his first major task of the occupation: helping arrange security for Hitler. The Führer would arrive the very next morning.

It was just after dawn when Hitler's Storch rumbled along the runway at Le Bourget airfield. A giant cloud of oil fumes that had hovered over Paris since June 1 had miraculously disappeared, just in time for the Führer's visit. Five large Mercedes sedans with their leather roofs rolled back were soon cruising along empty boulevards, their occupants dressed in smart uniforms, heads bobbing in unison whenever they went over cobblestones.

At 6:35 a.m., Hitler's convoy circled the Arc de Triomphe twice and then set off down Avenue Foch, the wealthiest street in all of vanquished Europe. The fifty-one-year-old Führer was soon passing the street lamps and elegant black iron railings designed by Gabriel

Davioud that fronted the Jacksons' ground floor home at number 11 and other buildings along the avenue. To Hitler's right, on the north side of the avenue, which was totally deserted, stood a white memorial to Jean-Charles Alphand, the chief engineer responsible for the avenue's construction during the reign of Napoleon III. Alphand purposely made the promenade extra-wide so that wealthy Parisians in their open-top coaches could pass directly from the center of the city to the Bois de Boulogne. Named Avenue Foch in 1929, many of the elder residents still called it by its popular name during La Belle Époque: Avenue Bois.

Hitler was not impressed by the neat gardens with exotic flowers, the riding paths, the crisscrossing alleys, and the honey-colored mansions. Perhaps it was simply the avenue's name that displeased him. It was Marshal Foch, no less, who had taken the German surrender in 1918. In the eyes of rabid German nationalists, Foch was the anti-Christ. It was also Foch who had urged that extremely severe peace terms be imposed so Germany could never threaten France again. When Germany was not dismembered, Foch had been furious. "This is not a peace," he had warned. "It is an armistice for twenty years." He had been wrong by just 68 days.

Whether it was the buildings or the name, Avenue Foch held no appeal for Hitler. He was blind to its magnificence. For the first time, he seemed to lose interest in his surroundings. The motorcade made a sharp left midway along the avenue and headed south, toward the Seine. By 9:00 a.m. the tour was over. Hitler would never return. "It was the dream of my life to be permitted to see Paris," he told his favorite architect, Albert Speer, who had accompanied him around the city. "I cannot say how happy I am to have that dream fulfilled today."

That evening Speer met with Hitler in a room in a village in northern France. Hitler was seated alone at a small table.

"Wasn't Paris beautiful?" he mused. "But Berlin must be made far more beautiful. In the past I often considered whether we would not have to destroy Paris. But when we are finished in Berlin, Paris will only be a shadow. So why should we destroy it?"

Hitler was lying. When the time came, he would destroy anything that suited his sadism. But Paris would be looted first—carefully—and the best of its portable wonders brought to him. In *Mein Kampf,* his autobiographical manifesto published in 1925, Hitler had clearly stated his true views about France. It was a great rival, its capital full of Bolshevik Jews, its people the "mortal enemy" of Germany. In his masterpiece of fascist and racist cant, one theme dominated: his hatred for the Jews. Once Helmut Knochen and his colleagues—Hitler's most loyal servants—had purged the city of these and other degenerates, Paris would enjoy a true golden age—a National Socialist "Belle Époque."

FIVE

SPIES OF SUMMER

THE GIRL'S DRESS was torn and soiled. She had not washed for several days. She looked haunted. Her face was etched with permanent disillusion. A tall American in a small car would never forget her expression as he passed her on a road leading to Paris. In his eyes she symbolized defeated France. She had seen the complete "moral breakdown and degradation of her own people," recalled the American diplomat George F. Kennan. "She saw them fight with each other and stumble over each other in their blind stampede to get away and to save their possessions. . . . She saw her own people pillaging and looting in a veritable orgy of dissolution as they fled before the enemy . . ."

Kennan had left Brussels that morning of July 2, 1940. A slim, balding thirty-six-year-old destined to become one of the great statesmen of the twentieth century, he was at the wheel of a rickety Chevrolet. Beside him sat Donald Coster, the volunteer ambulance driver who had witnessed the Blitzkrieg late that spring. Coster had told Kennan he was trying to get back to Paris to recover his clothes. It was a rather odd motive for leaving Brussels in a hurry, a poor rationale for making the hazardous and distressing journey through the ruins of northern France. The two Americans had water and some chocolate to fortify them, and had been warned that the country between Brussels and Paris was, in Kennan's words, as "uncharitable to travelers as a desert." The devastation was enormous. Some towns were totally gutted.

On June 14, Coster had persuaded a Belgian Red Cross official to drive him to Brussels, where he and other Americans were granted safety at the American embassy. Before long, Coster encountered Kennan, who agreed to give him a lift to Paris. Coster had not told Kennan that he was trying to stay a step ahead of the German military intelligence service, the Abwehr, or the Gestapo, or perhaps both. But he had told him he could not sit around and wait for the Germans to reach Brussels. He had to keep moving.

German troops were up ahead. The Chevrolet slowed. Kennan pulled out his diplomatic pass. Anxious seconds followed as the Germans examined it. The Americans were allowed through but it was slow going. Traumatized refugees returning to their homes clogged the roads. Finally, Paris was in sight. It was July 3 when Kennan dropped Coster off at the Hôtel Bristol, on the Rue du Faubourg Saint-Honoré, not far from the Élysée Palace. The grand hotel with a spacious courtyard was one of Paris's finest and home to a disparate band of American refugees.

Soon, though, Coster was starting to feel positively paranoid, like a "sitting duck." Germans were everywhere, "all over the place," he remembered, "filling the best hotels, shopping with their Credit Marks in the luxury shops: snapping cameras and jotting down notes in their pocket diaries. Busloads of soldiers made conducted tours of the principal monuments." The hotel's telephone was working. But when he picked it up, he heard clicks as the line opened to listeners at German headquarters. He had to keep moving.

One day that July, Coster left the hotel. He headed northwest, crossing the Seine, and made his way to the American Hospital in Neuilly. Somehow he knew of an American doctor called Sumner Jackson. Once he had found him, he asked the harried surgeon—a decorated veteran of the First World War, and well-known figure in expatriate circles—for help. Could he hide in the hospital until it could somehow be arranged for him to get out of France undetected by the Gestapo or the Abwehr, German military intelligence?

It was a momentous decision for Sumner. He knew the risks were enormous. Coster was clearly on the run. Why else would he need to hide in the American Hospital? But how did he know about Sumner? If the Germans made a surprise visit, or their intelligence services tracked Coster to the hospital, what would happen? Sumner had a family to worry about, unlike in the last war. Now, suddenly, he was being faced with a defining choice, far more significant than whether or not to listen secretly to de Gaulle on the BBC. If he helped Coster, hiding him from his pursuers, he would be gambling not just with his own life but with the lives of those he cared most about: his family and the people at the American Hospital.

THE ALLIER River flowed fast past Phillip Jackson, standing on a riverbank with a fishing rod. Nearby was the free-spirited French girl, Paulette, around his age, the daughter of the man who owned the inn where Phillip, Toquette, and his aunt Tat were staying. The girl was a little cross-eyed, not at all attractive, and a true tomboy, but Phillip thoroughly enjoyed her company. She had a talent for fishing and had taught him several tricks, including how to set poaching lines in the gushing rock-strewn river at night to catch eel and trout. Phillip enjoyed the risk, the adventure, and spent most days with her, getting up early so the pair of them could sneak out of the inn, dew soaking their shoes, and check their lines, baited with gudgeon, before anyone came along and they were caught.

For Phillip, that summer of 1940 was a wonderful interlude, never to be forgotten. He loved being in nature, fishing, hunting, and studying wildlife. One of his favorite books, which he had read from cover to cover, was *La Pêche et les Poissons,* an illustrated dictionary of fish and fishing. He knew all about the migration of the silver-backed salmon, how they swam across the mighty Atlantic to waters around Greenland and returned every couple of years to spawn in the Allier. He had learned to hunt and shoot with his father, bagging his first prey—a barn owl—with a 9mm child's rifle two years before. During summers in Normandy before the war, a local fisherman, René Ligard, had shown Phillip how to gather gray shrimp with a large net when he wasn't teaching the boy, at Sumner's insistence, how to swim, which entailed coping with the cold and choppy waters of the English Channel.

Phillip adored animals. But it was Toquette who had a true obsession with them. Along the Avenue Foch, she was known as "*la mère des animaux*"—the mother of animals. She had even been seen on several occasions leading a lamb along the avenue so it could graze on the lush lawns that flanked the riding paths. She took in every stray that came her way, even caring for a fox. At one point Phillip had counted no less than twenty-seven animals in the house and garden at Avenue Foch. Before the war, with his mother's blessing, he had bred white mice to feed two snakes in an aquarium he kept in his bedroom. He sold the spares down on the quays along the Seine for pocket money.

Toquette's sister, Tat, kept a diary that summer. The twelfth of August was a particularly pleasant day, she noted, as she watched Toquette chase butterflies with Phillip in a meadow beside the Allier River. It was clear that her sister and nephew were as close as a mother and only child could be. The idyll was only briefly disturbed by the sight of a German fighter plane passing over, black crosses on its wings.

BACK IN Paris, Sumner was just as busy after the occupation as before. He expanded the American Hospital's activities, determined to help at least some of the two million Frenchmen who had been taken prisoner by the Germans. Each morning Sumner watched from his terrace as a line of ambulances, manned by American and French volunteers and packed with bread and other essential products, left the hospital bound for camps around Paris where some 250,000 of the POWs languished. It enraged Sumner, who was at the best of times feared by patients and colleagues alike for his fierce temper, that more was not done to provide food and medicine to the camps. He blamed the situation on what he called the "bullshit bureaucracy of old men."

Sumner fought to get as much help to the camps as possible. Many of the ambulances sent out with food and other aid returned with seriously ill patients, who were struck by the cold air of neutrality in the hospital but soon warmed to Sumner despite his stern demeanor. According to one observer, these patients "feared and loved him. He was often intimidating, but he was mostly gentle, well read and forever telling interesting stories about America and the Great War." He attended to as many of the POWs as he could, in the process learning a great deal about the camps and their locations and the security measures the Germans had or had not taken.

Sumner saw an opportunity to do more than just treat the sick. He went a dangerous step further by falsifying records so that when some prisoners had recovered they were listed as deceased and did not have to return to captivity. Because the Germans had no presence in the hospital—not even sentries posted at the entrances—Sumner was able to hide some of these patients until they could safely disappear. A detailed report from the hospital to the United States, where its governors were based, of course made no mention of Sumner's covert actions. Instead, it stressed that "too much praise cannot be given to Dr. Sumner W. Jackson, who had been a member of the attending Staff since 1925 and who accepted the professional supervision of the wounded for the period of the war."

Among Sumner's patients was a French-Jewish officer, known to others on his ward only as "Captain M," who told a fellow patient that he had to escape France because the Germans had already warned him he would not be treated as a French officer but as a Jew, who would not be afforded any rights. Sumner made sure that when Captain M did leave his ward for good, there was no record of his stay in the hospital. The same was true of Donald Coster, the American ambulance driver, whom he had in fact kept hidden in the hospital's basement until false papers could be found for him a week after his arrival.

Two years later, in the fall of 1942, Coster would be one of twelve American spies operating in Morocco, known as "FDR's Apostles," who would help pave the way for Operation Torch, the Allies' successful invasion of North Africa. Coster told a researcher in an interview in 1981 that it was Sumner, and no other, who had concealed him in the basement. Perhaps Kennan had provided Coster with Sumner's name. The United States had no formal foreign intelligence service at this time: America's spies worked for the State Department, most often under the guise of diplomats like Kennan.

During his time as an ambulance driver, Coster had in all likelihood also been collecting intelligence for the United States: firsthand reports on the might of the Wehrmacht and the terrors of Blitzkrieg. It remains unclear if he believed Sumner was also an intelligence asset. But somehow, after meeting with the tall doctor from Maine, he managed to acquire the right papers and perhaps a new identity to allow him later that July to make his way through France and Spain to Lisbon. "And there," he recalled, "was a sight I had often despaired of ever seeing again—an American ship, ready to sail for New York."

SADLY FOR PHILLIP, his summer vacation of 1940 ended all too soon. Sumner learned that the Germans were requisitioning buildings throughout Paris. Even though he had been assured by the American embassy that the Germans would leave American properties well alone, he wanted to make doubly sure the Nazis did not seize the family's homes at 11, Avenue Foch, and in Enghien. They had to be occupied if they were to stay out of the hands of the Nazis, just as the hospital needed to be full of patients to prevent the Germans from moving their own troops in. It was decided that Tat would stay in Enghien, while Phillip and Toquette returned to their first-floor home on Paris's most prestigious avenue.

Phillip and Toquette arrived back in Paris on August 19, 1940. The city looked very different to Phillip. He had never seen so many bicycles and so few cars. The Place de l'Étoile resembled a scene from a schoolbook about Shanghai or Peking with velotaxis and pushcarts everywhere. Swastikas, bloodred and garish, flew from buildings along the Avenue Foch. There were new signs outside restaurants around the Place de l'Étoile: *"Mann Spricht Deutsch"* ("German Spoken Here"). The smug Germans in gray uniforms gathering at the upscale boîtes and bars near Phillip's home were not lean and mean, terrifying Supermen—the Aryan storm troopers of June. They were not shock troops. Those men had moved on. The legions of Fritzes in field-gray uniforms with cameras were mostly wide-eyed tourists eager to see the greatest prize of the Third Reich.

Barely ten weeks into the occupation, Parisians were starting to chafe against rationing and other restrictions despite their occupiers going to extraordinary lengths to foster good relations. German soldiers were not allowed to smoke or loosen their ties in public, buy cocaine in bars, go swimming in the Seine, sing or dance in the street, ride horses in the Bois de Boulogne, be seen with black or Jewish women, or buy pornography. They could visit certain designated brothels only. However, the last rule was universally disobeyed: within the first month of the occupation, more than 750 hotels and 300 restaurants were placed on a German soldiers' no-go list due to rampant prostitution.

The Eiffel Tower, which Phillip could clearly see in all its majesty from the Trocadéro, was hung with a giant sign: *"Deutschland Siegt an Allen Fronten"* ("Germany Is Victorious Everywhere").

SIX

WINGED VICTORY

THE BLACK GESTAPO car pulled up in front of armed guards by a sentry box at 72, Avenue Foch. The guards had the silver runes of the SS on the lapels of their uniforms and a silver skull, the famous death's-head symbol, on their caps. SS-Standartenführer Helmut Knochen had only to step out of the car and take a few brisk paces to reach the imposing entrance to the five-story villa from the Second Empire period, two hundred yards to the east of the Jacksons' home. On the northern side of the avenue, it boasted wide staircases and a well-tended private garden, and had the notable distinction of being the first of many buildings on Avenue Foch to be requisitioned by the Germans.

Knochen's office was a large, well-lit room with high ceilings. The furniture was as elegant as the building, which before the war had been called the Hôtel Lyon-Broussac. After several weeks at the Hôtel du Louvre, he had set up Gestapo headquarters at number 72. So opposed to the SS "black men" were the German general staff that it had taken quite some time before Knochen and his men were even allowed to don their uniforms. In any case, Knochen preferred most days to wear well-cut gray tweed suits. Though formally allowed to stay in Paris, he and his two dozen colleagues did not yet have the power to make arrests. They were still a puny bridgehead, busy creating connections and gathering intelligence, waiting patiently for the day when they would gain real power.

It was no accident that Knochen and his fellow Gestapo had chosen the Avenue Foch as their stomping ground. It was, after all, arguably the most exclusive address in all of Europe, boasting mansions of the Rothschilds, the Aga Khan and other royalty, and the American socialite Florence Jay Gould. And, of course, it bore the name of Marshal Foch, the colossus to whom the Germans had surrendered in World War I. The symbolism of setting up their base on the street named after Hitler's most despised Frenchman was quite deliberate. Even the SS were capable of irony.

Early that fall of 1940, Knochen started to lay down the foundations for the SS state that he hoped to help establish eventually in France. He began to recruit a private army of informers and enforcers who would carry out some of the more unpleasant tasks required, jobs he didn't want to be officially associated with, errands essential to exerting his will—spying, bribery, informing, torture, and assassination. Once the French had recovered from the shock and trauma of defeat, such practices would be essential to maintaining order and security.

Knochen's most able recruits were easy to locate—all the Gestapo had to do was trawl local prisons for the toughest career criminals, men like thirty-eight-year-old Henri Lafont, a charismatic and seasoned bank robber, who would soon set up a torture chamber at 93, Rue Lauriston, less than a mile from Avenue Foch. Perhaps no other sociopath, not even Knochen's closest SS colleagues, would see how low "Dr. Bones" was prepared to stoop in his quest to pull the levers of true power.

Knochen's official functions also continued and he prepared detailed reports on the political situation in France for his SS superiors in Berlin. German rule had been established with remarkable ease. The French had proven surprisingly accommodating. Following the armistice on June 22, the French Third Republic had been dissolved and France partitioned. An unelected regime headed by the deeply reactionary Marshal Pétain had been established in Vichy, capital of the so-called Unoccupied Zone, which encompassed most of central and southern France. Soon after, on July 11, the notorious appeaser, fifty-eight-year-old Pierre Laval, became France's 120th prime minister, serving under Pétain, and rapidly fostered excellent relations with Occupied France's new masters, the Germans. The eighty-four-year-old Pétain had commanded French forces in World War I and to many traumatized and frightened French the "Lion of Verdun" with the distinctive white handlebar mustache was more than ever the nation's savior. They agreed with him when he blamed an unholy trinity of socialists, agnostics, and urban intellectuals for France's defeat. Liberal decadence had seen France humiliated as never before in her long martial history. The republican motto of *"Liberté, égalité, fraternité"* ("Freedom, equality, brotherhood") was soon abandoned under Pétain's "National Revolution," which illegally replaced the French Third Republic, in favor of a slogan that better fitted his authoritarian and increasingly fascist regime: *"Travail, famille, patrie"* ("Work, family, fatherland").

On September 4, from his spacious new office at number 72, Knochen noted in one missive to Berlin that an "anti-German attitude is beginning to take ground." He could not yet detect any signs of armed resistance. But he knew it was only a matter of time before some of the youths, who made "loud whistles" in cinemas when newsreels showed Hitler or Goering, would do more than clap loudly at bomb damage caused by the British, and strike back with bullets and bombs.

It did not take Knochen long to familiarize himself with his new neighborhood and its many attractions. Paris was a different city from the one he had come to know in 1937 on an extended stay. Then cars had scarred the grand boulevards, coughing exhaust fumes. Now the city was more beguiling than ever. Knochen could appreciate its elegant lines, the uncluttered avenues and boulevards given a new perspective. With the city stripped by German decree of civilian cars and trucks, trees could breathe deep again, and that fall of 1940 the foliage, russet and golden, would stay longer than before. Sounds from previous centuries returned: the hammering of a cobbler or a blacksmith. Some evenings Knochen would have heard nightingales sing as he strolled up the avenue toward the Place de l'Étoile, breathing air that was almost as pure as that in Berchtesgaden, Hitler's mountain retreat.

Each day brought better news for the occupiers. On October 3, 1940, the Vichy regime passed a law, unprompted by Knochen and his Gestapo colleagues, that excluded Jews from any kind of public service. The next day Field Marshal Walther von Brauchitsch, the head of army high command, gave formal permission for Knochen to "investigate anti-German activities carried out by Jews, immigrants, communists, and church groups in the occupied zone." Knochen and his colleagues could also seize these enemies' assets: artwork, furniture, and countless cars. Before long, Knochen's and other Gestapo offices on Avenue Foch were among the best decorated in all Europe.

On October 18, Jews were banned from owning or directing any business, much to the delight of many envious French. So began the process of Aryanization, in other words state-sanctioned theft, by which Jewish concerns were taken over by gentiles. The owner of number 55, Jewish businessman Pierre Wertheimer, had long since fled, moving to the United States, but he had arranged for an associate to take over his stake in Chanel Perfumes to keep it out of Nazi hands. The designer Coco Chanel wrote to the German authorities demanding that she, not the associate, receive Wertheimer's share. "Parfums Chanel is still the property of Jews," she complained. "Your mission is to make these Jews cede their property to Aryans."

As the last leaves fell throughout France, on October 24, 1940, Marshal Pétain and Hitler met at Montoire-sur-le-Loir (Montoire on the Loire). As London suffered the worst of the Blitz, the eighty-four-year-old Pétain was photographed shaking Hitler's hand. "It is with honor," Pétain declared, "and in order to maintain French unity, a unity which has lasted ten centuries, and in the framework of the constructive activity of the new European order, that today I am embarking on the path of collaboration."

By the time Pétain had met Hitler, there was another new occupant on Avenue Foch, perhaps the most sinister, certainly among the most deranged. It was in late September that twenty-seven-year-old SS Hauptsturmführer Theo Dannecker, a former textile salesman, took up residence at Number 31 as head of the Gestapo's Jewish Affairs Office in Paris. He already knew one of his neighbors. "Dr. Bones," or rather Knochen, had been his boss for two years, from 1937 to 1939, at Gestapo section II-11, specializing in "Churches, Jews, and Freemasons." How times had changed. Dannecker and Knochen were no longer ambitious outsiders, bonded by their shared fascination with the secrets of European freemasonry and hatred of the Jews. Each now had his own mansion on the most exclusive avenue in Nazi-occupied Europe. Dannecker's new base was in fact less than fifty yards from Knochen's offices at 72.

Dannecker was determined to solve the "Jewish problem" in France as swiftly as possible. That fall, with Knochen's help, he quickly set about doing so. He did not of course see himself as a psychopathic racist. He was an irrepressible warrior, just like Knochen, in Hitler's war against the Bolshevik Jews. In fact, he was evil incarnate, a nihilistic predator who would soon send thousands of Parisians to the gas chambers in Auschwitz, committing mass murder from his elegant new office just a short stroll from the Jacksons' home.

ONE DAY that October, at the Jacksons' lakeside home in Enghien, Sumner pulled an envelope from a pocket and handed it to Toquette.

Phillip watched as his mother read out a letter from the director general of the American Hospital:

Dear Dr. Jackson,

*Please advise the medical staff that the Republic
has awarded the Croix de Guerre with Palm [a
military honor] to the hospital and staff. . . . I am
pleased to advise you personally that you are among
those decorated and cited for "A magnificent effort,
voluntarily treating the wounded and aiding prisoners
day and night in the face of the enemy . . . saving
a great number of human lives." Please accept my
warmest thanks and appreciation for your exceptional
devotion to duty in this trying period.*

Sumner was silent. He was never one to claim sole credit for any of the hospital's achievements. According to Toquette's sister, who was also present, Sumner had simply stood with his arms folded across his chest, speechless, as Toquette read out the citation.

Phillip was proud of his father but rather less pleased with his decision to send Phillip to a strict Catholic school near Enghien that October. Sumner believed it would be better for Phillip to be away from Avenue Foch, known now as "Avenue Boche" by Parisians because so many of Helmut Knochen's fellow Gestapo had set up base there. Phillip badly missed his old school and classmates at the Lycée Janson de Sailly, a ten-minute walk from 11, Avenue Foch. He kept in touch with several friends, eager for their news, yearning to rejoin them the following year.

Phillip learned that some of the older students from his school were involved in the first noteworthy act of resistance in France. On November 11, Armistice Day, several hundred pupils from Phillip's school and others near the Place de l'Étoile disobeyed their teachers, walked out of their classrooms and marched toward the Arc de Triomphe singing "La Marseillaise." Around three thousand students soon gathered at the Étoile, hemmed in by French police. German

soldiers watched apprehensively. The students had organized a collection to pay for a wreath that they planned to place that afternoon
at the Tomb of the Unknown Soldier, a favorite with visiting German
soldiers. However, the wreath was made in the form of the Cross of
Lorraine—the same symbol that General de Gaulle, condemned to
death by Pétain that August, had adopted for his Free French Forces
in London.

It was just before four o'clock when two brave students laid the
wreath on the Tomb of the Unknown Soldier. Some of Phillip's
schoolmates were dressed from head to toe in black and wore rib-
bons colored red, white, and blue—the French tricolor had been
banned in Occupied France. Loud cries of "Down with Hitler!"
and "Down with Pétain!" could be heard close by on Avenue Foch.
Pandemonium broke out as the French police and heavily armed
German soldiers tried to break up the crowd. Around 150 people
were arrested, most of them students. Some were taken to a military
prison, where they were beaten, dragged by their hair, and forced to
stand in the pouring rain, hour after hour, with their hands on their
heads. Others were ordered to line up against a wall by a group of
soldiers. These students believed they were going to be shot until a
senior German officer appeared and cried out in protest: "But they
are just children!"

Had Phillip not been at the Catholic school in Enghien, where he
had to recite Ave Maria each morning, he, too, could have walked
out of class and marched shoulder to shoulder with his former
schoolmates who, just like him and his parents, hated Hitler and admired de Gaulle. But there was one advantage to being in Enghien,
the upscale spa resort eight miles north of Avenue Foch. As the first
snows fell, promising a bitter first winter under the "Fritzes," Phillip
was able to spend much of his free time with his mother, who was no
longer working at the American Hospital.

The family home in Enghien stood beside a large lake where Sumner and Toquette had boated while they were courting twenty years

before. On sunny days, after the lake had frozen, locals gathered to skate across the gleaming ice, visible from the Jacksons' living room. However, reaching the ivy-covered three-story home from Avenue Foch or the American Hospital in Neuilly was an ordeal for the Jacksons, who were forced to cycle all the way to Enghien, well over an hour's ride from central Paris.

Sumner had reluctantly given up using the family car after quickly burning through the last few gallons of fuel after the Germans imposed severe restrictions on private ownership of vehicles. For a while he roared around on a motorbike but then it, too, ran out of fuel and he, like Phillip and Toquette and indeed millions of other Parisians, was compelled to hop on a bicycle instead. Less than five thousand people were allowed driving permits in a city that officially had 350,000 parking places for cars. At gasoline pumps in central Paris, there was never a queue. Bicycle garages, specializing in repairs and tune-ups, sprang up on corners of some of the busiest boulevards.

While the Jacksons spent most of their weekends together in Enghien, they did still visit their home on Avenue Foch from time to time. Phillip would sit in his old bedroom, which faced a small garden enclosed by tall black iron railings, and look out of the window as Germans passed by, riding horses along a bridle lane on the north side of the avenue. The only vehicles allowed on the broad avenue belonged either to collaborators or the Gestapo, and so Phillip could actually hear the thump of the horses' hooves. Sometimes he was woken by the guttural songs of German soldiers marching in the freezing morning air along the avenue on their way to exercises in the Bois de Boulogne.

Because he spent so much time with Toquette, Phillip was aware of how much energy she devoted early that winter of 1940 to finding food. Toquette, her sister Alice, and the family's maid, a proud Alsatian in her thirties called Louise Heile, had to spend long hours

hunting for rutabaga and potatoes, which had fast become staples at breakfast, lunch, and dinner. Rationing was strict, though undreamed-of delicacies could be found on the blossoming black market. Sadly, many Parisians stopped inviting friends over for dinner. Toquette was in the same bind as so many others: she would have to ask invitees to bring food obtained with their food tickets or she would have to sacrifice the family's ration, which she could not do, as it was barely enough to get by on.

It was galling indeed for Toquette and her French neighbors to live so close to some of Paris's finest restaurants. She had only to step out of a side door and then walk to her right for a few yards to reach the Restaurant Prunier, all the rage with fur-clad collaborators and the more refined SS men like Helmut Knochen. Many evenings, his gluttonous colleagues could be found feasting on superb seafood, washed down with a nice, crisp white like Pouilly-Fuissé or Sancerre, while flirting with some Russian countess or other at the marble oyster bar.

While Toquette lined up in the cold for their ration of root vegetables, Phillip sometimes watched films at the cinemas on the Champs-Élysées, but mostly he spent the long winter evenings with his head in a good book: record numbers of novels would be published during the occupation despite paper rationing. Phillip's favorites were *The Swiss Family Robinson,* with its thrilling shipwreck scenes; *The Marvelous Voyage of Nils Holgersson,* the story of a boy flying to strange lands on the back of a swan; and James Fenimore Cooper's *Last of the Mohicans.* His father reminded him with his rugged frame of one of the book's Yankee heroes.

When Phillip grew tired of reading, he could while away his time by performing chemistry experiments in the laboratory that Sumner no longer used, located just across the hallway from his bedroom. He would create special concoctions with chemicals his father had once mixed to treat his wealthy private patients before the war. He

had no idea what was happening elsewhere on the avenue after dark that first December of Nazi rule as sleek Hotchkiss cars sped by the window, driven by Gestapo officers, headed for one of the grand villas sequestered by Helmut Knochen and his colleagues.

The only time Phillip spent with Sumner, who was busier than ever at the American Hospital, was at weekends when they would wrap up warm and go into the garden at the house in Enghien to cut wood together. It was as if such chores reminded Sumner of all that he missed about America—the woods, his family in Maine, and the gritty values of small New England towns. Even though he had treated royalty and the rich and famous, including Ernest Hemingway, who had come to him with a nasty gash in his head, he was still a practical, forthright man, "a man of Maine" according to a colleague at the American Hospital, "who had never become Frenchified," so much more comfortable in the woods, hunting, and on the ocean, fishing, than in the status-obsessed salons of Avenue Foch.

The sawing, chopping, and stacking was an important task now that there was precious little coal and Paris was soon in the grip of one of the coldest winters on record. Throughout the city, people sat in cafés and restaurants wearing their heaviest overcoats and donned ski jackets indoors. Women could be seen wearing wool trousers, suddenly high fashion. Demand for fur—of any kind—soared. Some wore crazy striped designs using the pelts of cats and dogs and horses. That winter would break every record in the book with its extraordinary number of days below freezing—seventy in all.

The first Christmas under Nazi rule approached. On December 23 red posters appeared, emblazoned on buildings around the city. They announced the execution of a young man, Jacques Bonsergent, the first Parisian to have stood and faced a Nazi firing squad. His crime had been to jostle a German officer in the Gare Saint-Lazare. The posters announced not just an execution but also the Germans' true intentions: to control every aspect of French society and, when

necessary, terrorize. Two days later, the Jacksons, as with all other Parisians, were forbidden from attending Christmas Mass at midnight. France's new masters had decreed that all services be held at 5:00 p.m. because of a specially imposed curfew. Nothing in the French tradition—no date of worship, even—was any longer sacred.

PART TWO

ARMIES OF THE NIGHT

SEVEN

ON DOCTOR'S ORDERS

THE MAN WAS totally blind. Once in a while that January of 1941 he would say something to a nurse or doctor he trusted. He felt protected in the American Hospital. Dr. Sumner Jackson had made sure of that. He was sometimes spotted walking through the hospital's grounds, using a stick, no doubt following Sumner's advice, trying to regain strength in his legs and restore his muscle tone.

The man was an RAF pilot who had lost his sight when he was shot down. He was not the only Allied soldier whom Sumner had decided to help rehabilitate as best he could before he was sent along an escape line, bearing false papers. Others may have been smuggled out of Paris in the hospital's ambulances, which the Germans often neglected to search at the so-called Line of Demarcation at Moulins, the border crossing between Occupied and Vichy France. Then, at great risk, volunteers would accompany such escapees to Toulouse, from where guides would lead them across the Pyrenées to neutral Spain.

Sumner was not acting alone at the hospital. Other doctors and nurses helped him hide Allied airmen and soldiers until they could be sent to safety. Nothing was formally organized and no real names ever used, not a word written down. All those involved were sworn to utter secrecy. Sumner may not even have told Toquette. Only after the war would piecemeal accounts emerge of how evaders had checked into the American Hospital and then several weeks later appeared in London. There was, for example, the case of a wounded soldier who one day confided to André Guillon, a fellow Frenchman at the hospital, that he was suffering from a bad case of gonorrhea. "The American doctor [Sumner] who took care of him with sulfa drugs at a very high dosage . . . accomplished an exploit in healing," recalled Guillon. "We learned that three weeks after he left the hospital, he was in London." One morning there was no sign of the blind RAF officer who had been wandering the grounds and corridors of the American Hospital. He, too, had gone missing. Several weeks later he also turned up in England.

To avoid detection, it was essential to keep the Germans out of the American Hospital. Sumner had to ensure the beds were all full and therefore he arranged for the hospital to take patients from internment camps for the British near Paris, and at Vittel and Saint-Denis. One of those Jackson treated was a young Englishwoman. One day, she pinned a poem on a bulletin board:

PORTRAIT OF AN AMERICAN

We all agree he's a perfect dear
Altho at times he inspires fear
And we quake in our beds as he draws near
Oh! so severe!
But those eyes so stern and steel blue
Can gleam with humour and laughter too
And life takes on a brighter hue
When he smiles at you.

Sumner soon found the poem and, embarrassed, took it down. The following day the poem was back in place. Whether he liked it or not, this patient was determined that everyone should know how much she appreciated him.

Sumner's famously short temper was fully tested that spring of

1941, as keeping the hospital going as an independent organization, not under direct Nazi supervision, became a huge challenge. Thankfully, the hospital's governors appointed a governor-general, seventy-year-old General Aldebert de Chambrun, who quickly proved highly successful when it came to finding food and other essentials. The white-mustached decorated veteran of World War I was, much to Sumner's distaste, a supporter of Pétain, but his gallant past compensated for his politics. He had fought valiantly for France throughout the bloodbaths of the Marne, the Somme, and Verdun, perhaps too much so. The general, a direct descendant of the Marquis de Lafayette, had reportedly written to his wife from the trenches about the "great pleasure" he had in shelling his own château with artillery, seeing "piece after piece come down" because it was occupied by German forces. The general's wife was as well bred as her husband: sixty-seven-year-old Clara Longworth, a snobbish Shakespeare authority with a doctorate from the Sorbonne, was in fact a true American blueblood. Clara's elder brother, Nicholas Longworth, was married to Alice Roosevelt, a rabid right-winger and the only daughter of the great American president Theodore Roosevelt.

Sumner was no admirer of French or American aristocrats. But he was determined to work as best he could with General de Chambrun for the sake of his patients and the hospital, and theirs soon became a formidable partnership. The general was a smart, savvy operator, just as Sumner was, being an experienced diplomat who had served as French ambassador to Rome in the thirties. Few were better connected. The general was able to call on the support of the most powerful collaborator in France after Pétain: no less than Pierre Laval. The general's only child, thirty-seven-year-old René, a wiry figure with an intense, coiled energy, was actually married to Laval's only child. According to *Time* magazine, René's glamorous thirty-six-year-old wife, Josée, was as politically ambitious and swarthy as her father—his "right-hand woman." They had traveled the world together. She had accompanied her father on his first visit to the United States as French premier in October 1931. Ever since, she had been his most loyal confidante.

According to René, who had made a considerable fortune on both sides of the Atlantic as a corporate lawyer, it was none other than his father-in-law who, after conferring with the general, first pressed the Germans to leave the hospital alone, and then "received assurances from [Nazi ambassador] Abetz that the American Hospital in Neuilly, one of the most modern in Europe, would be placed under the protection of the French Red Cross. That was how this American institution, of which my father, General de Chambrun, was the volunteer manager, had escaped the greediness of the Wehrmacht."

Abetz was even better connected than the Chambruns. Described as a "man of some breadth but not enough character," he had been Hitler's translator and had worked for the Abwehr in Paris before the war. It was said that the Führer and the thirty-eight-year-old ambassador had a special relationship, that the Führer had designed Abetz's uniform, and that Abetz was always ushered quickly into the Reich Chancellery to see him one on one when in Berlin, a beautiful leather briefcase under his arm. The briefcase contained Parisian pornography, of which Hitler was particularly fond.

René de Chambrun, who was in fact Pétain's godson, and his wife, Josée, were often to be seen at Abetz's parties at the German embassy, in the Hôtel de Beauharnais, at 78, Rue de Lille. "Bunny," as René was known to family and friends, and Josée, with her dark complexion subtly accentuated by the best cosmetics, her bright eyes, her perfectly plucked brows, and her dark bob, did more than swap small talk over champagne and exquisite canapés. It would later be alleged that Josée, ever clad in the latest fashions of one of her favorite designers—Chanel, Hermès, or Schiaparelli—had spied for Abetz, passing him key intelligence that she had carried with her from America in a diplomatic pouch.

The Chambruns enjoyed excellent relations with Abetz and, just as crucially for the American Hospital, with several rich landowners around Paris. The general and René had arranged for one of them, a French aristocrat, to supply the hospital with his entire potato crop. Other mutually beneficial deals were struck. As a result, the hospital's ambulances often carried hidden food as well as patients, and even the odd few cases of wine. The authorities allowed each patient one half liter of wine per day, so the hospital soon had far more wine than even the most alcoholic could drink. Farmers by contrast were parched. "We took 500 liters of wine and bartered the wine for 5,000 kilos of fertilizer," remembered one of Sumner's colleagues, Dr. Otto Gresser, who was in charge of food provision—no easy task in wartime Paris. "One farmer gave us 10,000 kilos of potatoes for the fertilizer."

Meat was quite another matter. It was, it seemed to those without black market connections, literally worth its weight in gold. Still, Sumner managed at one point to acquire over 300 kilos of beef, a vast amount in wartime Paris. Nevertheless, the meat was quickly consumed and Sumner was soon imploring Dr. Gresser to somehow find more. "Look here," Sumner told him one day, "if we can't do any better, some patients are going to have malnutrition." Somehow more meat was found, but then several suspicious German officials made a surprise visit, having learned that a truck with German markings had made a large delivery. Sumner and his staff just managed to hide the meat in the hospital garden before the Germans could find it. General de Chambrun then had a word with the appropriate official and the nosy Germans promptly dropped their inquiries.

Sumner relied heavily on the general to keep the Germans at bay on an almost daily basis. As de Chambrun's American wife, Clara, recalled, the general "received visit after visit from German medical officers of high rank with no other object in view than to take over the whole establishment for the use of their army." But, due to the de Chambruns' superb connections, the hospital remained independent. Other Germans, namely the Gestapo, may not have been so easily deterred. Sumner assumed the Gestapo sometimes masqueraded as patients. Yet he believed the hospital was so chaotic, due to what he proudly called his "organized confusion," that none would be able to work out what was really going on. "They'll never figure out this madhouse," he told a colleague.

Sumner was not deluded. He carefully assessed risk. He was a master surgeon who made critical assessments—for example, whether a patient would live or die—all the time. And so he knew full well that he could be betrayed at any time. All it took was one patient, one nurse, one doctor, to turn informer, to be threatened by one of Knochen's French thugs, to talk too loudly in a bar, to confide in a traitor unknowingly, and it would all be over. Sumner knew what the Gestapo could do. He knew who his neighbors were. And he needed no reminding that if the Gestapo found out who Dr. Sumner Jackson, the grumpy hero of young English patients, really was, then he would, without a doubt, be faced with the devil's choice: work for the Gestapo, betraying others, as was their way, or be sent deep into the Third Reich, to a concentration camp.

Sumner's activities became even more perilous following the German invasion of the Soviet Union on June 22, 1941. Hitler's audacious attack proved a boon to the resistance as thousands of French communists responded to the call from Joseph Stalin to take up arms and defeat Nazism wherever it held sway. Attacks on German soldiers in Paris soared. Many French communists also began to join escape lines, helping downed Allied aircrews get back to Britain. In response, the Germans posted stark warnings throughout the country, marking a dark turn in Nazi occupation policy:

NOTICE

Any male who would aid, directly or indirectly, enemy air troops coming down in parachutes, or having made a forced landing, would facilitate their escape, would hide them, or would come to their aid in any manner whatsoever, will be shot on the spot. People who seize crews forced to land, or parachutists, or who contribute, by their behavior to their capture, will receive an award of 10,000 francs.

If caught, Sumner now knew that some of his neighbors, the Gestapo, would not hesitate to have him killed. Never had he had so much to lose. Why not play safe for a while? Why not join the vast majority of the French, hovering in the gray zone between heroism and collaboration? Was the risk really worth it?

IT WAS early on October 2, 1941, when the explosions awoke Paris. But there was no sound of planes overhead. At 2:30 a.m., in the Rue des Tourelles, a bomb went off. At 3:30 a.m. there was another explosion in the Rue Notre-Dame de Nazareth, and then just after dawn a massive boom on the Rue de la Victoire. Glass shattered, covering the street. In all, there were six detonations at synagogues around the city. A seventh failed to go off. It was the French who had left these bombs, surely, proving they really did despise the Jews, just as the Nazis did.

Helmut Knochen had in fact orchestrated the whole affair, hoping to set off a wave of spontaneous violence similar to that of Kristallnacht in 1938. He had ordered one of his men, SS-Obersturmführer Hans Sommer, to find the dynamite used in the bombs and to provide a getaway car for a group of hired French thugs. Unfortunately, there were two German victims: the explosions injured two German soldiers. The military authorities investigated and Sommer soon revealed that Knochen had been behind the bombings. The Prussian generals running Paris were outraged. There had so far been an uncomfortable truce between the Gestapo and the military, between the SS and the Wehrmacht grandees, who were perfectly happy to sit out the occupation in an elegant Parisian hotel, taking no part in Hitler's race war against the Jews. It was now time for the Gestapo, part of the ever-growing hydra of the SS, to be firmly put in its place and for the military to assert its power in dictating policy and the policing in France.

Five days after the explosions, General Otto von Stülpnagel, the military commander of France, finally learned of Knochen's role in the outrage. He despised Knochen and had worked hard to contain him, in fact ordering him to cease all intelligence gathering and communication with Gestapo seniors in Berlin. Now Stülpnagel pushed to have Knochen disciplined—at the very least, to have him sent back to Germany in disgrace.

Later that October, there was yet another explosion, caused by a stray bomb from the RAF that landed on the Avenue Foch and sadly missed all of the Nazi abodes. Nonetheless, it was a foreshadowing of sorts. Over the next two months, according to a German intelligence report, seventeen more bombs were set off in Paris by the resistance. By the time the last one exploded, Knochen was no longer residing at 72, Avenue Foch. Stülpnagel, it seemed, had won his fight with the Gestapo and Knochen found himself back in Berlin, his glittering career cut short just as he was about to reach his prime.

NOT LONG after Knochen's ignominious exit, a bitter cold spell settled over Paris. The Jacksons steeled themselves for a second winter under the jackboot. Phillip and Toquette were once again living mostly on Avenue Foch, spending weekdays there so that a delighted Phillip could return to his old school, the Lycée Janson de Sailly. It was at their home on Avenue Foch one evening that Phillip and his parents first learned from the radio that the Japanese had bombed Pearl Harbor on December 7, marking America's entry into the war in the Pacific. On December 11, four days after the Japanese attack, Hitler declared war on the United States, confident he could easily defeat the racially inferior Americans.

The greatest conflict in history had finally entangled Americans in Paris more than two years after Hitler invaded Poland and eighteen months after Paris was occupied. It didn't take long for the Germans to turn their attention to the estimated two thousand U.S. citizens who were still at large in the city. On December 18, 1941, the Germans arrested a total of 340 American men under the age of sixty. Notably, Sumner was "permitted to remain at liberty," undoubtedly due to General de Chambrun's influence. Sumner's fellow Americans were interned at a camp fifty miles northeast of Paris in Compiègne.

Another Christmas approached. There was so much snow that some Parisians, pining for the pistes of the French Alps, went skiing on the slopes of Montmartre instead. General de Chambrun's wife, Clara, busy most days running the American Library in Paris, remembered that there was a "feast" at the American Hospital that took months to prepare. "Under the Germans' very noses, clandestine pigs were raised and fattened, and the menu always included ham, bacon and sausage," she would later write. "The songs ran the musical gamut from 'My Old Kentucky Home' to 'My Country, 'Tis of Thee.'" Everyone tried to raise each other's spirits, she added, by stressing that the next Christmas France would be free.

Among those celebrating in the hospital were forty British wounded POWs. They could look forward only to grim incarceration when they returned to the POW camps from where they had been sent for treatment. Sumner apparently did what he could to help some of them fully recover in more hospitable climes by sending them, sometimes in the hospital's ambulances, along an escape line to sunny Spain. America's entry into the war had marked a point of no return. Just as he had in the last war, it was now his duty to do all he could to help the Allied cause.

EIGHT

AVENUE BOCHE

THE HEINKEL LANDED at Orly airport, about half an hour's drive from central Paris. Among the carefully selected entourage of SS officers and propaganda photographers waiting for the plane to come to rest and the doors to open was Helmut Knochen, back in Paris after a bitter Christmas exile in Berlin and for once in full uniform, his Iron Cross dangling from his left breast pocket. It was early on May 5, 1942, when a tall and slim figure, with an aquiline nose and piercing blue eyes, emerged from the plane. A few minutes later, Knochen was photographed on the runway, welcoming thirty-seven-year-old Reinhard Heydrich to France.

As a general in the SS and chief of the Reich Main Security Office (RSHA), Heydrich already pulled the key levers of terror, being in charge of the Gestapo, the Security Service (Sicherheitsdienst, or SD), and the Criminal Police (Kriminalpolizei, or Kripo). Tens of thousands had been murdered on his orders. Millions more would eventually die as a result of his carefully planned answer to the Jewish "problem" in Europe—the Final Solution, the greatest crime in human history. He now wanted to extend the reach of the SS so that it dominated every aspect and corner of the Third Reich, including France. Hitler no less called him, without irony, "the man with the iron heart."

Knochen was delighted to see Heydrich once more. Indeed, were it not for Heydrich, he might by now have been banished to some

Einsatzkommando in the East and be leading middle-aged Hamburg policemen, armed with cases of schnapps to deaden the disgust after a long day of rounding up shtetl Jews and filling pits with their bullet-riddled corpses. Instead, he was back, living in high style like some Prussian prince from the last century, on Avenue Foch. It was *glücklich Zeit* ("happy times") for Dr. Bones. Just a couple of months before, on February 27, he had married an attractive Aryan, Willerbel Ruth, in Paris. She had given him a son a year earlier to add to a girl, three years old, from his first marriage in 1935 when he had been busy helping organize the 1936 Olympic Games in Berlin. There had been a fancy wedding reception for Knochen and Willerbel at the German embassy, hosted by none other than Otto Abetz.

It was Heydrich who had made sure that Knochen returned to Paris earlier in 1942, after his sojourn in Berlin. Knochen's immediate superior, a slack libertine called Max Thomas, was made to pay the price for the synagogue debacle. Meanwhile, senior Nazis in Berlin had removed Helmut's nemesis, General von Stülpnagel. Seen as too effete and lenient, he was replaced by his own cousin.

Heydrich had arrived in Paris to set matters straight: to put the SS and Gestapo in their rightful place in the hierarchy of power, above the military. It was why Knochen was no doubt grinning from ear to ear that morning of May 5, slavishly fawning over Heydrich at Orly airport before joining his boss on the ride into Paris. They were soon in the southern outskirts of Paris and then crossing the Seine and entering the Place Vendôme, dominated by a high column, built to celebrate Napoleon's great victory of Austerlitz, with a veneer of spiraling bas-relief bronze plates made from the 133 cannons captured at the battle. A statue of Napoleon, bare-headed, holding a sword in his right hand, stood atop the column, directly opposite the entrance to the finest hotel in all of Nazi-occupied Europe: the Ritz.

A few adjustments had been made to the hotel since before the war in order to adapt to the new clientele. A small room, previously called the "writing room," had been converted to a checkroom where considerate Germans were requested by hotel management to please deposit their pistols and any other weapons. The formal dining room was reserved for the German command of Paris, but high-profile collaborators and the very rich could nonetheless be found discreetly seated at many tables. The famous Ritz croissants had alas disappeared from the room service menu, but there was plenty of caviar by the time Heydrich came to visit. Bertin the barman had served cocktails to Hemingway before the war. Now he mixed a mean martini for the highest ranks of the Gestapo. Bertin claimed to have invented the Bloody Mary in the twenties to help Hemingway recover from yet another hangover.

Also in residence while Heydrich was at the hotel were several notorious collaborators. René de Chambrun's most famous client, Coco Chanel, had lived there since August 1940 in rooms 227 and 228 on the same floor as Madame Marie-Louise Ritz, who owned the hotel and stayed in rooms 266 and 268. The actress Arletty, a dear friend of Josée de Chambrun who would later be famous for her role in *Les Enfants du Paradis,* shared one of the hotel's famous brass beds with Luftwaffe officer Hans-Jürgen Soehring, ten years her junior. *"Mon coeur est francais,"* Arletty would protest after the war. *"Mon cul est international."* ("My heart is French . . . [but] my ass is international.").

The following morning, May 6, 1942, Knochen was hard at work once more, introducing Heydrich to the men who really mattered in France, including thirty-three-year-old René Bousquet, Laval's appointment as head of the French police. Bousquet, a suave and persuasive operator, tried to convince Heydrich that German interests in France would be best served if he allowed Vichy to maintain control of the police. Knochen was inclined to agree, for he knew that if the SS wanted to solve the Jewish problem in France, only Bousquet's gendarmes could accomplish a large-scale deportation. The

SS did not have sufficient manpower. Bousquet managed to charm Heydrich into agreeing with him. "With men like him," Knochen would later stress, "we could prepare the future of Europe."

Heydrich's sojourn in Paris was not all about business. Knochen made sure of that. "Heydrich saw a lot of people and he loved Paris, parties and women," recalled Knochen, who helped introduce Heydrich to the city's many pleasures, and was also only too happy to provide entrée into its highest society. Knochen was by now very well connected, having attended several salons where, as he put it, *"la plus haute société"* gathered. One was held every Thursday afternoon at the home of the American-born Florence Gould, who lived just around the corner from Knochen's offices at 129, Avenue de Malakoff. Knochen also attended parties hosted by another American woman, Nina Crosby, who was married to Melchior de Polignac of the Pommery champagne dynasty. Then there was Madame Olga von Mumm, another rich champagne heiress and a friend of Josée de Chambrun, daughter-in-law of General de Chambrun.

On May 11, 1942, after a most enjoyable and productive visit, Heydrich bid adieu to Paris. He would never see the city or Knochen again. Just sixteen days later, on May 27, he would be fatally wounded after two Czech agents trained by the British Special Operations Executive (SOE) attacked him, rolling a bomb underneath his car in Prague. He died on June 4, aged thirty-eight, having told Himmler on his deathbed that the world was "just a barrel-organ which the Lord God turns Himself. We all have to dance to the tune which is already on the drum."

With Heydrich gone, Knochen could no longer count on support at the highest levels in Berlin. He would have to be doubly careful not to disappoint his SS seniors from now on. Heydrich's death was, however, of great benefit to Knochen in the short term. In the days before his assassination, Heydrich had believed that Hitler would shortly send him to assume total control of France. After Heydrich's death, the task of destroying all opposition to Nazi rule fell instead to none other than Knochen, who was promoted, and to a rotund SS general called Karl Oberg who would be the overall SS commander in France. A former doctor and World War I veteran, not once had Oberg shown hesitation when it came to eliminating enemies of the Reich. In the words of the mayor of Paris, Pierre Taittinger, he would soon prove to be "a demoniacal creature capable of doing anything for his Fuehrer. A perfect incarnation of the brute beast, he seemed to have taken on the task of making himself detested and in this respect he succeeded perfectly."

Knochen was quick to assert his new power. In late May 1942, his men took over the role of the German military police in France. With his full colonel's insignia—an oak leaf—on each collar, he now had real muscle, a status that the snobbish Prussian elites of the Wehrmacht could not challenge. All the hard work and his patience since 1940, when he had slipped into Paris in disguise, ironically as a military policeman, had paid off. He had lost his most important ally, whose patronage would be sorely missed, but as fate would have it he could now dance to an exhilarating new tune—as head of the Gestapo in Paris.

JUST BEFORE leaving Paris, Heydrich had given Knochen specific orders. The fight against terrorism was to be stepped up dramatically. In his efforts to destroy the resistance, Knochen was determined to employ all the Gestapo's considerable resources. But he knew he would also need to increasingly resort to more unconventional means, relying on the French criminal class to do much of the necessary torturing and murdering of select enemies. To this end, Knochen held a meeting at the end of June 1942 with one of his associates in the Parisian underworld, the gangster Henri Lafont, one of many career criminals whom the Gestapo had hired after releasing the most talented from prisons throughout Paris.

"You must devote yourself," Knochen ordered Lafont, "to the

battle against the English agents at large in Paris, the Gaullists and communists, and anyone who sabotages the friendship between Germans and the French."

The mustached, wiry, and always impeccably dressed Lafont had for some time tried to ingratiate himself to Knochen. For a wedding present, he had given him a white Bentley, three of which Lafont had acquired and famously prized. And for the SS-Standartenführer's fiancée he had found a diamond necklace. He had neglected, of course, to explain that he had stolen the jewels during a raid on a rival gang of black marketers. Such gifts were essential. Forty-year-old Lafont, whose real name was Henri Chamberlin, had made millions of francs from the black market under Knochen's protection.

"From today," stressed Knochen, "I want you to review your organization. Of course, you can carry on your black market activities, but they will from now on just be a cover and the source of your finances. Keep the men who'll be useful. Let the others go. I want a complete overhaul of your organization so it gives absolute priority to fighting espionage and terrorism."

Lafont tried to protest. He was very happy being a bandit. He didn't want to start a secret war against his own countrymen.

Knochen was not impressed. Lafont was the Gestapo's made man, the most powerful gangster in France. But there were plenty of other sociopaths vying to replace him. He would do as he was told and keep his mouth shut about it or else. Knochen was now head of the Gestapo in Paris, the new Nazi boss of bosses, and Lafont had better not forget it.

ALTHOUGH 72, AVENUE FOCH was a hive of activity early that summer after Heydrich's visit, no Gestapo offices were busier than those at number 31, less than a hundred yards from the Jackson family home. It was among the most imposing buildings on the avenue, once owned by Madame Alexandrine de Rothschild of the Jewish banking dynasty. That June of 1942 what happened inside was immensely ugly, for it became the epicenter of the Gestapo's efforts to annihilate the Jews in France.

The architect of the Final Solution, SS colonel Adolf Eichmann, had arrived in Paris from Berlin and set up an office beside his aide Captain Theodor Dannecker at number 31. His objective was simple: with Knochen's help he was to deport "all French Jews as soon as possible." Six groups were due to leave on July 6. Publicly, of course, no French or German official gave a hint of the mass genocide already under way throughout Nazi-occupied Europe. Instead, they propagated the fiction that a Jewish state in the East was being formed. In Vichy, Pierre Laval noted during a cabinet meeting: "It would be no dishonor to me if I were to send the countless number of foreign Jews who are in France to this state one day."

The question was: Who would take the Jews into German custody, the Germans or the French? On July 4, in Knochen's spacious office overlooking the flower beds along Avenue Foch, his colleague SS-Hauptsturmführer Theodor Dannecker insisted the SS round up the Jews. Knochen disagreed. René Bousquet's gendarmes should do so instead. Without their help, after all, there was insufficient SS manpower in France to remove the Jews en masse.

Dannecker snapped that Knochen should make sure the French understood they were the ones who were to take orders, not vice versa.

"Why the endless nitpicking?" replied an exasperated Knochen.

Wiser heads prevailed and Knochen got his way. The French themselves would clear France of its vermin. This was crucial for political reasons. In recent months there had been a rapid increase in killings of Germans in France, especially by the mushrooming communist resistance. In response, the Germans had devised a *code des otages*—law of hostages—that basically meant executing fifty to a hundred Frenchmen to avenge every dead Nazi. René Bousquet had made sure these hostages were mostly communists, Vichy France's best-organized and most violent enemies. The indiscriminate execution of so many French patriots had, however, only made matters worse. The German occupiers were now widely reviled. If they were seen to be rounding up women and children, there was serious risk of massive public unrest. So it was crucial that the French police, not the SS, be seen to be carrying out arrests.

That same day, July 4, 1942, Pierre Laval himself recommended during a meeting with Theodor Dannecker in Paris that children younger than sixteen also "be taken away" with their parents. Dannecker was delighted by Laval's unprompted offer and with Knochen's help he arranged for more than eight hundred teams of French police to move through five of the city's arrondissements, placing Jews they arrested onto fifty buses, painted green and white, that had been specially requisitioned from Paris's Compagnie des Transports. In all 27,388 names were selected from lists of registered Jews.

The Grande Rafle—the Great Roundup—began on the night of July 16 and lasted well into the following day as 13,152 Parisian Jews, including 4,000 children—thanks to Pierre Laval—were rounded up, with around half of them taken to the Vélodrome d'Hiver, or Vél' d'Hiv, a large velodrome beside the Seine. The medical conditions at the Vél' d'Hiv were atrocious. There were no lavatories. There was only one water tap for more than 7,000 people.

Sumner Jackson had been sending ambulances to care for the sick in internment camps since 1940 but was now barred from or unable to send staff to the Vél' d'Hiv. He had noted the flight of Jewish neighbors in 1940. He and Toquette had also been deeply dismayed when the Nazis introduced anti-Semitic legislation. Now their worst fears were being realized. The unthinkable was happening: French citizens were being seized at the very heart of what had once been arguably the most civilized city in the world. The screams of Jews committing suicide pierced the silence in some quarters. The famous German writer Ernst Jünger, serving in Paris, noted with matter-of-fact precision in his diary that he had heard "wailing in the streets" as families were torn apart, mothers separated from their children.

Knochen's staff worked hand in glove with the French police, some nine thousand of whom were involved in the roundups. According to one account: "It was a *rafle* conducted in keeping with the best of French conditions, for at noon the policemen returned to their posts to have lunch while higher-ranked and better paid set off to nearby restaurants. Only after the sacred *déjeuner* could the manhunt continue."

Women's cries could soon be heard throughout the Vél' d'Hiv. *"On a soif!"* ("We're thirsty!") they called out.

Only two doctors were allowed inside the velodrome, equipped with little more than aspirin. After five days of misery, those incarcerated were transferred in cattle trucks to camps at Pithiviers, Beaune-la-Rolande, and Drancy, a modernist high-rise development built in the 1930s also known as La Cité de la Muette—the City of Silence.

Meanwhile, along Avenue Foch and elsewhere, trucks loaded down with furniture and other Jewish possessions could be seen after deported Jews' homes were ransacked. The looters belonged to a special Gestapo task force, the Einsatzstab Reichsleiter Rosenberg, actually headquartered on Avenue Foch. Eventually, according to the Nazis, this looting saw 69,619 Jewish homes, 38,000 of which were in Paris, "emptied of everything in daily or ornamental use."

At the end of July, after more than 14,000 Parisian Jews had been rounded up, the Catholic Church in Paris made a belated appeal to Pierre Laval on the children's behalf. But the Vichy premier was adamant: they all had to go. And they did. Less than four percent of those sent east returned. Not one was a child.

Sumner and Toquette, like all well-informed Parisians, were aware of what had happened during the Grande Rafle and were appalled by it. According to one account, Sumner had done what he could, sending the American Hospital's ambulances to the deportation camps so they could fetch the seriously ill. But it had been impossible to make these patients disappear once they had recovered. The Germans had made certain that patients were returned to the deportation centers. It would have been heartrending for Sumner to watch. He had dedicated his life to healing and saving others. More than ever, he must have been determined to do whatever he could to defeat Nazism, to put an end to the reign of the mass murderers now living on Avenue Foch.

NINE

THE SHADOW GAME

WHAT SUMNER FEARED most would happen any day finally did: on the morning of Thursday, September 24, 1942, French gendarmes arrived, unexpected, at the American Hospital in Neuilly. They had come to arrest him.

Had Sumner been betrayed? It may have come as a relief to discover that the gendarmes did not want to hand him over to the Gestapo but rather were arresting him, along with hundreds of other American men under the age of sixty-five, so he could be placed in internment. Ironically, Jackson was about to take a vacation and had already packed a bag. Through General de Chambrun's maneuverings, he had avoided internment in the weeks following Germany's declaration of war on the United States in December 1941 after the attack on Pearl Harbor. But since then the authorities had become increasingly strict. Finally, he was going to have to join his fellow adult Americans in captivity.

News spread fast through the hospital, and several of Sumner's colleagues were able to talk briefly with him before he left, perhaps for good. Some handed him hastily prepared gifts as he made his way out of the hospital, including bundles of food and a few bottles of excellent wine, which he stuffed into the deep pockets of his overcoat. He was then escorted to a nearby police station, where the gendarmes placed tags around his neck and made him sign several documents. Then he and other Americans were taken in a bus to the Gare du Nord. Miraculously, Sumner spotted a railway worker at the station whom he had recently treated. Sumner asked him for a favor. Would he contact Toquette? He gave the railway worker the telephone number for 11, Avenue Foch.

Sumner arrived at the British internment camp of Saint-Denis, just outside Paris, at lunchtime. The camp was based in an old barracks that had once housed Napoleon's regiments and was home for the duration of the war to around two thousand British men. The conditions were surprisingly good compared to other camps in the Third Reich. Sumner noted that many of the internees received substantial aid packages from England. The gendarmes allowed him and his fellow Americans an hour and a half for lunch and also permitted them to buy provisions at the camp's store, where he purchased British-made suspenders; he had never been able to find a decent pair in Paris. He also bought a pipe cleaner. Then he was asked for his name and date of birth and to provide proof that he was a doctor before being taken that evening to the American internment camp at Compiègne-Royallieu, Frontstalag 122 B, some fifty miles northeast of Paris.

Frontstalag 122 B had been set up in January 1942. The barracks were surrounded by barbed wire and overlooked by control towers. To his surprise, Sumner was given a small room where he could enjoy a little privacy. It even had a rug on the floor. The meals were poor compared to Saint-Denis, but thankfully the thousand or so American men interned in the camp received regular Red Cross parcels. Sumner discovered there was a camp nearby called Sector C, run by the SS, where the Germans were holding Jews. It was from there six months before, on March 27, that the very first deportation train had left French soil with a thousand Jews bound for Auschwitz. Conditions were said to have been atrocious. He was appalled by what he learned. His contempt for the "damned Boche" was now absolute.

Sumner was in good company. Some of the men in the camp had served in World War I in the trenches. There were several proud doughboys, Jackson's favorite kind of Americans. He talked with them at great length, refighting key battles such as the Somme, which he had seen in all its horrors, but was no doubt careful not to mention his help for downed aircrews during these conversations. There were bound to be German spies in the camp. Several of the Americans interned with him had close dealings with the Germans, including a homosexual organist for the American Cathedral in Paris called Lawrence Whipp, who would soon be released, courted by the Gestapo, and then disappear in mysterious circumstances, allegedly abducted by the resistance. His corpse would eventually be found floating in the Seine.

Meanwhile, at the American Hospital, General de Chambrun was trying everything within his power to obtain Sumner's release. A word in the right ear was required. The general had his own high-level contacts but he also relied on his son René to help deal with the Germans. That summer René had already attended four or five official meetings with the Germans at the Ritz "for the purpose of defending the interests of the American Hospital." René also regularly visited the German embassy on Rue de Lille to speak with German ambassador Otto Abetz personally, and met with contacts in the Hôtel Majestic, headquarters of the German military command.

Sumner had been in Compiègne barely a week when, one morning early that October, he saw a car with official Red Cross markings pull into Frontstalag 122 B. The door to the front passenger seat opened. Out stepped General de Chambrun. He had succeeded: the German authorities had finally agreed to release Sumner. As the car left the camp, driven by the general's chauffeur, the general handed Sumner a sheath of press clippings. One included a report from the *New York Times* that included Sumner's name as among several Americans "released in France."

Sumner was happy to be a free man once more, but could not have been pleased by the very public mention of his name. It was crucial to retain a low profile if he was to continue to operate his escape line. By contrast, the general was delighted by the press coverage. What, he asked proudly, did Sumner think of it?

"It's free publicity," said Sumner. "Good for the hospital. Show 'em we're still in business. We need the money."

Chambrun agreed and went on to complain that the press had misspelled his wife Clara's name.

There was another aspect to Sumner's release of note: the Gestapo, his neighbors of two years now, had slipped up. Sumner was a notable citizen of an enemy nation and was likely, given his war record, to try to help the Allied cause. Unwittingly, by not monitoring the American expatriate community more carefully, the Gestapo had allowed a true threat, a "terrorist," to return to his double life and to his home—which, ironically, was just down the block.

Less than a fortnight after being arrested, a delighted Sumner was reunited with a much relieved Toquette and Phillip and then returned to work at the hospital. Thanks to General and René de Chambrun's connections, he found himself in a unique position, one he was determined to exploit to the utmost: he enjoyed official protection of sorts. Crucially, he was back in charge of a hospital, a safe haven, from which the Germans had been totally excluded—the ideal place to carry on his private war against the Nazis.

IT WAS a profound shock to learn of the invasion by Allied forces of Vichy-controlled North Africa. On November 9, 1942, the headlines in the newspapers in the kiosks around the Place de l' Étoile made bleak reading for collaborators: DIRTY ANGLO-AMERICAN ATTACK AGAINST OUR NORTH AFRICA.

The end of the fantasy came even for the most spellbound of Vichy courtesans after the last leaves had fallen in 1942. At dawn the previous day, more than 100,000 Allied troops had stormed ashore and seized ports in Tunisia, Morocco, and Algeria. "Now this is not the end," declared Winston Churchill in London. "It is not even the beginning of the end. But it is perhaps the end of the beginning."

A German embassy official, Helmut Rademacher, dined at the Ritz that evening of November 9. Also at his table was Knochen. Rademacher clumsily exclaimed that the war was surely lost. "[Knochen] was present," recalled Rademacher, "and though he was easily put into a rage, on that occasion he made no comment." After lunching at Le Fouquet's that same day, Josée Laval, René de Chambrun's wife, wrote in her diary: "The Americans have attacked Algeria and Morocco . . . I have the same sensation as in May and June of 1940 when life was suspended. It's the end of an epoch."

It certainly was. Even the most ardent collaborators knew they might have backed the wrong horse. There would be a price to pay. *Life* magazine in the United States had that summer already published a list of prominent Frenchmen alleged to be major collaborators. It had included the name of René de Chambrun. *Life* had also reported that some of these people were going to be "assassinated."

The headlines in the Paris newspapers got worse. On November 11 the Germans occupied Vichy France, their tanks rolling to the shores of the Mediterranean. Pétain was in effect reduced to a figurehead. Collaborators could no longer pretend to be cooperating with the Germans for the good of France. True friends were not in the habit of invading without warning.

From his offices at 72, Avenue Foch, Knochen wrote to Reichsführer-SS Heinrich Himmler about attitudes in the capital. Many people had "changed their position." The successful invasion of North Africa had created a "hitherto unknown Germanophobia" with the vast majority of the French, who now expected Allied victory. There was a "general rejection of all things German." Mass deportations of Jews to the East were no longer possible because of French bureaucrats' "lack of understanding." While German civilians were making great sacrifices to preserve the Third Reich, in

Paris German occupiers were being treated with "arrogance and disdain"—a sure sign of "insufficient volition."

On February 2, 1943, there was even more cataclysmic news, this time from the Eastern Front. The Germans had been defeated at Stalingrad. Although propaganda minister Joseph Goebbels did his best to minimize its damage, the story of the surrender to the Red Army of General Friedrich von Paulus with more than a hundred thousand Wehrmacht troops gave countless millions great hope.

The Nazis in Paris barely flinched. Their revolution would continue. As if realizing that time was now of the essence, they stepped up a campaign to purify French culture. The Louvre had long since been emptied. Cinemas mostly showed insipid Teutonic propaganda. On May 27, 1943, in the courtyard of the Galerie Nationale du Jeu de Paume in Paris, over five hundred works by Miró, Picasso, and other artists designated as degenerate were placed in a giant bonfire and torched, smoke and ashes spreading into the dusk. That same day Ernst Kaltenbrunner, who had replaced Heydrich as head of the RSHA, sent a twenty-eight-page report to Foreign Minister Joachim von Ribbentrop. Hitler saw the report in early June. It was a summary of all the latest intelligence that Knochen and his colleagues had gathered about the fast-growing "Secret Army"—the French resistance. There was no time to lose. Knochen and his fellow Gestapo must destroy de Gaulle's underground before it could threaten Nazi rule. Maximum force was required. Failure to annihilate the growing numbers of terrorists was out of the question.

TEN

NUMBER 11

IT HAD BEEN three long years since the Nazis had arrived, marching down the Champs-Élysées, ripping down tricolors in those early days and replacing them with lurid swastikas, plastering their ugly propaganda and warnings everywhere, casting a long shadow over the City of Light. By the spring of 1943, like so many Parisians, Phillip Jackson, now fifteen years old, had grown to deeply resent the arrogant men in field gray, many of whom continued to gather in the upscale bars and restaurants in his neighborhood.

Each morning, Phillip heard the sound of jackboots as the Germans stomped along the Avenue Foch for seemingly endless training in the Bois de Boulogne. After breakfast he said good-bye to his mother and the maid, Louise Heile, and set off for his school, the Lycée Janson de Sailly. Rarely did he venture west along Avenue Foch. It took a few minutes longer to get to school that way. But sometimes he did head along the avenue, toward the Bois de Boulogne, passing SS guards and sleek black Hotchkiss and Mercedes saloons parked outside several buildings before turning left where Avenue Foch met the Rue de la Pompe. His school's address was 106 Rue de la Pompe.

Most days, Phillip walked instead along the Avenue Victor Hugo. It, too, was popular with the Nazis. At number 72 was the Polo restaurant, a favorite with the Gestapo, as were the nearby Presbourg and Sports cafés, where beguiling Russian countesses dressed in Chanel and Hermès, with extravagant hats, conspired with their fascist lovers as they sipped chilled champagne. A few doors away, at number 79, were the offices of the Otto Bureau, responsible for the censoring of books. Even Shakespeare had been banned.

In Phillip's eyes, Paris had lost much of its gaiety under the Nazis. The news booths along Avenue Victor Hugo no longer sold sweets and spinning tops but instead copies of *Signal,* a German propaganda magazine, *Das Reich,* a dour Nazi newspaper, and phrase books for the "Fritzes" who massed at all the main tourist sites in Paris. Toy stores had closed. The pond at the Palais-Royal had no water. Boys could no longer play with sailboats there. Because of shortages, most children had wooden rather than leather soles on their shoes. It was hard to play hide and seek because of the loud clicking of wood on sidewalk. Those without access to the black market or food supplied by relatives with large gardens and farms were malnourished. Only the very rich were overweight, it seemed, and could find new clothes. Some infants wore dresses stripped from their sisters' largest dolls.

That spring of 1943, Phillip arrived at school on time and ready to study. He knew his father had high expectations. Sumner was determined Phillip would have every advantage he had not; above all, that meant a first-rate education. Before the occupation, Phillip had excelled academically. But after a year at the Catholic school in Enghien, he had fallen behind his brightest peers at Lycée Janson de Sailly, and his father was not happy about it. Sometimes, he made Phillip recite passages from the classics, expecting him to get every word right. It was as if he was making up for his own lack of early education.

Phillip knew his father had had a tough Yankee childhood—that he had grown up amid great beauty in Waldoboro, Maine, but with very little money, and had attended a small village school until, at age fourteen, he had left to help put bread on the table, joining his father in a quarry, breaking rocks. Sumner had been big for fourteen, almost six feet tall, and proven a good laborer. A year later, at Phillip's current age, he had begun to care for a local doctor's horses and was soon running errands for the doctor, who took a strong interest in Sumner and told him he could still get a good education. He, too, could become a doctor. He encouraged Sumner to return to school and even paid some of his tuition. Sumner worked every spare hour when not studying, tending to the school's playing fields, cleaning the toilets, with little time to socialize with other students, but was able to pay his own way through high school, Bowdoin College in Maine, and then he finally qualified as a doctor at the Jefferson Medical College in Philadelphia, where in a 1914 yearbook, at age twenty-eight, he chose the motto: "He doeth well who doeth his best."

Sumner expected Phillip to work as hard as he had. There could be no excuses for doing less, given how privileged Phillip's upbringing had been. According to a family friend, Sumner was not "light-handed" when it came to punishment. And he worried about his son's moral education. What was he to tell him about mankind? "Should I say to him: 'Men are good'?" Sumner asked a friend. "Or must I tell him: 'Men are wicked'?" He was also concerned that his son was too cosseted, unable to stand up for himself, and hired a former professional boxer to give Phillip a few lessons in self-defense. Phillip had quickly learned how to parry and punch in the living room at 11, Avenue Foch, the heavy carpet rolled back to give him a better footing.

The boxing lessons proved a good investment. Among Phillip's classmates that spring was the son of fascist forty-three-year-old Pierre Pucheu, the Vichy interior minister, a rabid anti-Semite who wanted France to be at the heart of a new Europe, crisscrossed by four-lane autobahns, united by anti-Bolshevism. For some time his son had bullied Phillip's classmates, among them Jews who had not yet been deported. One day Phillip caught him in the act, angrily punched him in the face, and made his nose bleed. Within a year the boy's father would also be punished. Pierre Pucheu would become the first leading collaborator to be executed under de Gaulle's jurisdiction in North Africa.

Lycée Janson de Sailly's motto was *"Pour la patrie, par le livre et par l'épée"* ("For the homeland, by the book and by the sword"). As with many of his classmates, Phillip took these words to heart. By this point in the occupation, his school was in fact a hotbed for Gaullist sympathizers, dozens of whom would soon join the resistance. A whole battalion of graduates would fight in the Vosges Mountains, bordering Germany, in late 1944.

Unlike communist youths in the poorer quarters of Paris, Phillip was not about to start throwing bombs at the Germans goose-stepping past his bedroom each morning on the Avenue Foch. But he had long yearned to do something to defy his occupiers, and so, as with so many of his peers, that spring he became a vandal. Sometimes he would filch pieces of chalk from classrooms when his teachers weren't looking. On his way home, as he walked along Avenue de la Grande-Armée to Place Victor Hugo, he would glance around to make sure no one was looking and then pull out the chalk and scrawl a "V for Victory" sign on a wall or the side of some building. Sometimes, he took a few seconds longer to etch the Cross of Lorraine, de Gaulle's chosen symbol for the Free French.

The BBC had first proposed the daubing of the V sign in public places as an act of resistance. On July 21, 1941, Parisians had looked toward the Eiffel Tower only to be greeted by the monstrous sight of a giant V hanging from it, a very public attempt by the Germans to appropriate the symbol, which proved a dismal failure. Despite severe penalties for those caught, young Parisians like Phillip still scrawled it everywhere, on dusty Wehrmacht trucks, shop windows, beneath posters of the grandfatherly Marshal Pétain, and across every swastika they could find.

One day that spring, Phillip's luck ran out. The family's maid, Louise Heile, found a piece of chalk in his trousers pocket while doing the laundry. A gentle and thoughtful woman in her thirties who had grown up in Alsace-Lorraine, she was utterly devoted to Phillip. But she thought she should mention the discovery to

Toquette, who was less than pleased. She forbade Phillip from scrawling any more V signs on buildings in the neighborhood. His father also admonished Phillip. There were to be no more childish stunts, nothing that might draw the Gestapo's attention to the family's presence on Avenue Foch.

THERE WAS in fact no more dangerous place to practice patriotic vandalism: by then more than a dozen buildings on Avenue Foch had been requisitioned by the Gestapo. Some Parisians had taken to calling it "Avenue of the Gestapo." The German criminal police, the Kripo, had taken over number 74. The great car manufacturer Louis Renault had long since departed number 88; it was now used by Knochen's men, who had also occupied number 19, a mansion that had belonged before the war to Baron Edmond de Rothschild.

At number 84 a former police detective working for the SS's counterintelligence branch, the Sicherheitsdienst, or SD, had set up a formidable organization under Knochen's watchful eye. Forty-two-year-old SS-Sturmbannführer Hans Kieffer had a thick mop of wavy black hair, deep-set eyes, and a slightly upturned nose, and had been an accomplished gymnast in his youth. He had the tenacity, it was said, of a stubborn bloodhound, and Knochen had formed a highly effective relationship with him, a near-perfect liaison. Knochen would naturally have worked with none less. That was why Kieffer, the Third Reich's finest spy catcher, had been sent to Paris to coordinate Knochen's counterintelligence efforts. Such a posting would have been given only to the very best.

As with his close colleague Knochen, with whom he was in daily contact, Kieffer preferred to blend into his surroundings, opting for tweed suits and plain trilbies when working the streets. He had no great love of the Führer, nor any intellectual pretensions like Knochen. He was a bluff policeman, priding himself in hunting down enemies of the state and then getting them to cooperate. If that meant playing the hard man, then so be it. But he preferred to use charm: sitting his British suspects down and having a friendly natter over tea and biscuits, or a piece of delicious *pain fantaisie* with hot black coffee, not the ersatz mouthwash favored by less effective Gestapo men. He had fine English cigarettes and real chocolate for those who talked.

By the summer of 1943, Knochen's own headquarters had expanded to include number 70, the large mansion next door. Number 76 was the base for a thirty-eight-year-old SS colonel named Hermann Bickler, a brutal Alsatian who led a unit of Frenchmen working for Knochen and specialized in infiltrating and tracking down the terrorists who belonged to the resistance. Neighbors kept their windows firmly closed that summer so they didn't have to listen to the piercing screams of Bickler's victims. His favorite technique was the "*bagnoire*" ("bathtub treatment"), which consisted of plunging a terrorist into a tub of ice water and then keeping the terrorist's head underwater until he or she almost drowned. Others on Knochen's payroll were even more inventive: they filed victims' teeth; slashed their feet with rusty razors; and used soldering irons and blow-torches when the standard softening-up routine of kicking, stomping, and punching failed to work.

Never had so many psychopaths and sadists been based on one street in Paris. Yet remarkably, even eighteen months after America's entry into the war, the Jacksons' presence at Number 11 had still gone unnoticed. Their home had not been requisitioned and turned into a Gestapo office or torture chamber. Dr. Sumner Jackson, the widely respected head of the American Hospital, was still at large, able to bicycle each morning, wearing an old WWI flying helmet for protection in the wind and rain, past his newest Gestapo neighbors.

ONE DAY early that summer of 1943, a man of medium height, aged twenty-three, with light brown hair, bright eyes, and fine features, stepped into the Rue de Traktir and walked north all of ten yards. He knocked on a door of the Jacksons' ground-floor home, located at the corner where Avenue Foch met the Rue de Traktir. He was just a few yards from the front garden where his younger sister Anne-Marie had played with Phillip Jackson before the war. The intense young man's name was Francis Deloche de Noyelle. The son of a diplomat, he had grown up as the next-door neighbor of the Jacksons at number 1, Rue de Traktir, right beside the Restaurant Prunier.

Since January, Deloche de Noyelle had worked for the resistance, moving around France from Montpellier to Grenoble in the lee of the Alps, recruiting for a major resistance network that took its ultimate orders from General de Gaulle. It was also his task to locate addresses that could be used as "drop boxes," where valuable intelligence in the form of photographs, blueprints, and stolen documents could be deposited before being ferried to de Gaulle's intelligence organization in London.

Deloche de Noyelle knew he could trust Toquette. She and Sumner were close to his parents. They were "good people." Inside number 11, Avenue Foch, Deloche de Noyelle explained to Toquette that he belonged to a resistance network, Goélette, part of a much broader organization called the BCRA (for Bureau Central de Renseignements et d'Action, or Central Bureau of Intelligence and Operation), commanded by a "Colonel Passy."

"We need a spot in Paris," Deloche de Noyelle told Toquette. "You are in exactly the right place—on the ground floor. There are two exits onto different streets. People know there's a doctor's office at this address. It's a place where a lot of people could go in and out without attracting attention like other places. Would you be willing to help?"

Over seventy years later, Deloche de Noyelle would remember that Toquette "did not hesitate for a second." Of course she would help.

De Noyelle explained that Goélette was based primarily in Vichy, where information about Pétain and Laval was being secured. It was also where Goélette operated a secret radio by means of which coded messages were sent to London. One of the network's key couriers was code-named Greenfinch. Toquette would never know his real name. Another important figure was thirty-eight-year-old Paul Robert Ostoya Kinderfreund, code-named Renandout, Goélette's head of intelligence in Paris. The Germans had seized several of his operatives in recent months, so he was especially careful about security. It was crucial to keep contact between members to a minimum to avoid betrayal. The Gestapo, headquartered on Avenue Foch itself, was prepared to pay large sums for the right kind of information.

Toquette had listened to the BBC and de Gaulle's speeches, like many others in France. She wanted to do her part in the fight against Nazism. But in joining the resistance she would be making a momentous decision, risking not only her and Sumner's lives but also that of their only child. They would be particularly vulnerable given their address. Unlike most of those working for Goélette, they would not be able to change their names and hop from one safe house to the next. If they were betrayed, Knochen's men had only to walk up the street to arrest them.

Having conferred with Sumner, who supported her fully, Toquette sat Phillip down and told him of the decision to join the Goélette network. She made it clear that, at all costs, he was not to talk to anyone about it. No one could be fully trusted. Even within the family, as much as possible was to be kept secret from each other. It was safer that way. For his own good, Phillip would be sent to the family's country house at Enghien, ten miles away, when Goélette agents met at 11, Avenue Foch.

Sumner and Toquette were concerned above all about doing what they could to protect their son, hoping that he would somehow be spared if they were caught. "What you can't see can't hurt you," Sumner told Phillip, determined like Toquette to hide everything they could from him, certainly their dealings with other members of the resistance, such as Kinderfreund, known to them and others simply as "R" or "Renandout," and Louis Joubin, code-named "Gustave," another leading member of the network. Given the importance of Avenue Foch as a network hub for Goélette and place where key intelligence would be deposited, no radio would be operated from the address. That would be too risky. It was just as well given that the Gestapo ran an elaborate radio detection operation on the first floor at number 84.

After recruiting the Jacksons to the resistance, Francis Deloche de Noyelle returned to Grenoble, where he continued to expand the Goélette network. He was able to report to his seniors that they had a superbly located "drop box" in Paris—on the Avenue Foch, no less—right under the Gestapo's noses. Early that June, Toquette got to work, turning her home into a place of maximum use to the resistance; placing potted plants in windows or a mop as signals to resistance members approaching along Avenue Foch; making it appear as if Sumner was again receiving patients. It wasn't long before Phillip began to notice strangers sometimes entering his father's office. One night he also accidentally saw a man placing banknotes into a briefcase in the hallway. The more he saw, the more fascinated he became by the secret goings-on in his home. He had an active imagination, which Toquette had nourished by reading him adventure stories every night as a child. Soon he yearned to become fully involved, to do something truly significant, yet he knew his parents would never allow it.

Toquette was the main liaison with Goélette, not Sumner, who still spent most of his time at the American Hospital in Neuilly. As her code name, she chose "Colombiers," the place where she had been born in Switzerland. She was fully aware of the enormous dangers she now faced, every moment of every day, by turning her home into a hub for the resistance. At any time, she knew, there could be an urgent knock at the door. When she answered it, would the man standing on the doorstep be a Goélette agent or one of Knochen's men? One thing was certain: nothing would ever be the same again.

THE JACKSONS had chosen the worst possible moment to join the resistance. The lights in the Gestapo offices all along Avenue Foch blazed late into the night all that summer as Knochen's men sought to crush the French resistance in Paris and beyond. Incidences of sabotage, particularly of critical railway lines, and of bombings had increased steadily as more and more French abandoned their *"attentisme"*—waiting game—and took up arms. Hitler ordered a swift and brutal response. By year's end, more than 80,000 people would be arrested. Thousands would be tortured and hundreds shot without trial.

Two hundred yards from the Jacksons' home, at 84, Avenue Foch, Knochen's head of counterintelligence, Hans Kieffer, worked tirelessly to destroy the French sector of Britain's Special Operations Executive, an outfit formed by Churchill in 1940 to "set Europe ablaze" by carrying out sabotage, espionage, and reconnaissance in occupied Europe and to help local resistance movements such as Goélette, which the Jacksons had just joined. Kieffer's first major breakthrough came on June 18. That night, a Westland Lysander plane came in low over the Norman fields, engine throttled back, and then touched down, bouncing across the rough pasture. Two SOE agents stepped down from the plane. They had not gone far when they were arrested.

The Gestapo had been waiting. The agents were escorted to Avenue Foch, unaware that a double agent had betrayed them, and not just any run-of-the-mill traitor—arguably the greatest of the war in terms of the damage caused to British intelligence and the French resistance, especially in Paris. He went by many aliases but was known to both his wife and the Gestapo as thirty-four-year-old Henri Déricourt, a brilliant actor and suave former French airline pilot logged in the Avenue Foch files as agent BOE/48. It was due to Déricourt that Knochen soon learned, as he put it, of "all [SOE's] landing sites and the means necessary to decode BBC messages" sent to the French resistance. Thanks to such treachery, hundreds of French resistance workers and dozens of British agents would be apprehended and tortured. Many would be executed in the dying days of the war.

The British continued to send new agents to fill out the ranks of a network known as Prosper. On June 20, 1943, two more landed in France. Again Knochen's men had been tipped off about their arrival and they were followed. As they tried to escape their tail in an underpowered Citroën driven by a female radio operator, the Gestapo gave chase in fast Ford cars, quickly closed to within a few yards, and then opened fire. Bullets smashed the windshield and tires exploded. The radio operator fell forward on the dashboard, hit in the head and shoulder, and the Citroën crashed. Inside the Citroën, later that day, Knochen's men found radio crystals and notes, one of which was titled *"Pour Prosper."* Three days later three more key members of the Prosper network were caught and also hauled to Avenue Foch by the Gestapo.

Knochen's interrogators worked hard on the captured agents, and on one occasion Knochen himself "engaged in the breaking" of their network. One of the agents, Francis Suttill, seemed most likely to talk and was tortured for several days. Finally he agreed to provide details of ammunition dumps on the condition that the men and women guarding them would not be killed. The Gestapo meanwhile had started to play what would be known as the "Funkspiel," a sophisticated "radio game." Knochen's radio expert, a bespectacled former schoolteacher called Dr. Josef Goetz, began to impersonate some of the seized agents, using their radio sets to communicate with SOE handlers, sending false messages, luring yet more agents to their eventual deaths.

Then came another remarkable victory in the war against the

resistance. Through informers, Knochen's agents in Lyon were able to locate the whereabouts of the legendary forty-four-year-old resistance leader Jean Moulin, code-named "Max," who, under de Gaulle's orders, that spring had succeeded in unifying several resistance groups and thereby formed France's first coordinated "army of the shadows." Seized on June 21 at a meeting with other resistance figures, Moulin was taken to Gestapo headquarters in Lyon, where he was brutally tortured. A week later, Gestapo officer Klaus Barbie transferred Moulin to Paris. But it was too late for Knochen to profit from any information that Moulin might be able to provide. Barbie had, it was alleged, lost control when beating Moulin in a cell in Lyon, and Moulin was no longer in a fit state to talk. In fact, he was barely alive. A fellow member of the resistance who was being held in Paris recalled his terrible condition: "Jean Moulin was lying on a reclining chair, and did not move. He showed no signs of life, seemed to be in a coma."

Knochen's colleague, fifty-eight-year-old Major Karl Bömelburg, who had been part of the group to arrive with Knochen on June 14, 1940, was present when Moulin was brought to his offices at 43, Avenue Victor Hugo, in Neuilly, a few hundred yards from the American Hospital. According to one source: "Barbie clicked his heels very loudly in front of Bömelburg, who stood chain-smoking. Bömelburg told Barbie in German: 'I hope he comes through this; you'll be lucky if he does.'" How on earth could "Max" be useful if he could not even communicate?

Moulin never did talk. It is thought that he died in custody, en route to the Third Reich, later that month. Although he had given nothing away, his arrest nevertheless dealt a body blow to the resistance movement, which the Jacksons had joined earlier that summer. The legendary "Max" had been eliminated—de Gaulle's underground army had been decapitated. All along Avenue Foch, Knochen and his Gestapo colleagues had cause indeed to celebrate.

ELEVEN

THE LAST SUMMER

PHILLIP COULD REMEMBER before the war when Bastille Day had been a joyous holiday and tens of thousands had lined the nearby Champs-Élysées, waving tricolors to commemorate the start of the French Revolution—the bloody storming of the Bastille on July 14, 1789. There had always been a great show of national pride and fantastic fireworks. But since the Germans had arrived, there had been no parade, no fireworks. Celebrations had been banned.

On this day, July 14, 1943, for the first time under the occupation, there would at least be a national holiday, with stores closed. However, due to "national circumstances," the Vichy government of Pierre Laval had decided that there would still be no official ceremony. The German authorities could do without a second storming of the Bastille.

That morning Phillip pulled out his bicycle and set off to see his father at the American Hospital in Neuilly, five miles of hard pedaling to the northwest. The massive chestnut trees along the Avenue Foch were heavy with leaves, casting shade onto the manicured lawns and flower beds. Paris looked more than ever like a city in the Orient, all of its avenues and streets filled with bicycles and elaborate velotaxis, some pulled by teams of four, among them Tour de France veterans who made sure, on the Avenue Foch, to get out of the way of the fast Hotchkiss cars that swept up and down, carrying Knochen and his colleagues to meetings, and the black police vans that delivered resistance workers and spies to number 84 for interrogation.

As Phillip pedaled north toward Neuilly, around the world there were celebrations by patriotic Frenchmen. In Algiers, de Gaulle reviewed a military parade. In London, thousands gathered at the statue of Field Marshal Foch, where a wreath was laid on behalf of de Gaulle. Then Phillip made his way onto the Boulevard Bineau, joining a steady stream of other bicyclists. He was carrying some hard-boiled eggs for his father. As usual, his father was busy, so Phillip decided to wait for him on the terrace of his office on the hospital's fourth floor, which afforded fantastic views of central Paris and the Eiffel Tower rising above the grandeur of Haussmann's boulevards.

After a few minutes, air raid sirens sounded. There was a piercing wail and then the bark of antiaircraft fire. Phillip heard the steady throb of Allied planes' engines in the distance. The sound got louder and then he saw American bombers approaching. He watched in awe as the silver-winged planes got closer and closer. Then there were smaller dots in the sky. They, too, got closer. They were yellow-nosed German fighters. Phillip watched as they began to attack several of the B-17 American bombers. Soon there was a full-scale air battle raging in the skies above. Pieces of shrapnel started to fall onto the hospital's roof.

A door leading onto the terrace sprang open. Phillip's father stepped onto the terrace.

"Don't stay here!" he cried. "There's shrapnel falling everywhere."

Phillip did as he was told and quickly scurried inside.

Meanwhile, twenty thousand feet in the air, a lanky and dark-haired nineteen-year-old New Yorker called Joe Manos was seated at the tail of a B-17 bomber. A wisecracking, utterly unworldly machine gunner, Manos wasn't as dumb as he sometimes pretended to be to get laughs—he knew now he would need all the firepower he could get, and he had in fact loaded the tail gun cans so full that he had not been able to fit the covers on.

Manos waited. Any second they would come for him, the bandits with their yellow noses, screaming down in almost vertical dives, streams of bullets fizzing toward him. Any moment they would come to test his nerve. He and the other nine men in his crew were especially vulnerable. Their plane had lost its position in the formation. It was alone, ready to be picked off, the weak straggler sacrificed by the herd.

Planes were in the distance. Manos aimed and pulled the trigger on his .50-caliber machine gun. It clattered as it fired. He soon had a good view of the battle. Black puffs were exploding all around from antiaircraft fire. Then he saw them: the German fighters, swooping down, screaming out of the sun. He shifted in his turret, tracking one of the fighters. It was in his sights. It had a black and yellow checkered pattern on its fuselage, tail, and engine cowlings.

Manos gave the bandit a burst but then his gun jammed. The bandit opened up with cannon fire, hitting two engines on Manos's plane. The right wing caught on fire. Manos stepped over to a small plywood compartment door. He opened it and saw two waist gunners trying to get an escape hatch open. A bell was ringing: the signal to abandon ship. Cut off in his tail turret, he had not heard it. Then a 20mm German cannon shell exploded, smack between the two waist gunners, blowing both their heads off. In great shock, Manos managed somehow to keep his wits about him. He grabbed a small oxygen bottle, placed it in the lower left pocket of his flight coveralls, attached it to his flight mask, and then pulled the release cable for the tail escape hatch. But only one of two pins came out of the hinges, leaving the door stuck. In exasperation, Manos tried to force it by sitting on top of it. That worked. The door gave way and he felt himself falling into space.

Manos pulled the ripcord on his parachute as soon as he was clear of the plane. The silk chute billowed from the pack on his chest. There was no jolt as it caught the air. He scanned the skies and saw three other parachutes. He guessed he was at around 16,000 feet. He watched his plane peel off, bank slowly to the left, then dive toward the ground, where it burst into flames, exploding near railway tracks.

He drifted down. He could see people in a village's streets. Then the ground was rushing up to greet him. He landed in a field of beetroot. His training again kicked in and he gathered up his chute, rolled it into a ball, and then quickly buried it in the soft soil along with his Mae West life preserver, glad that he had not landed on rocky ground.

He looked around. He was alone. He ran across a nearby road, down a steep embankment and into another field, along a hedgerow, and toward woods, hoping to find some of his fellow crew members. Before he reached the woods, he came across two Frenchmen who were trying to start a motorcycle.

One of them, his eyes wide with excitement, pointed down the road.

"Boche!" yelled the Frenchman.

Manos jumped into some nearby bushes and hid. A few seconds later he saw a German soldier on a bicycle, rifle slung across his back. The German passed by Manos but then stopped to look around. He was searching for downed flyers. He was no more than a hundred yards away.

Manos took off, crawling from under the bushes and then scrambling across a wheat field.

A young Frenchman ran into the field. "Comrade!" he cried.

Manos considered running away. The man reached him and began to pull him toward thick woods. Then he was in a clearing. The young Frenchman gave Manos a shirt to throw over his A-2 leather jacket and gestured for Manos to get into a truck parked close by. Soon he was passing through a town some five miles north of the outskirts of Paris. The truck stopped at a small house near some railway tracks. Inside, a middle-aged man took almost everything Manos was wearing or carrying, leaving him with only his underwear, two pairs of socks, his GI shoes, and dog tags. The Frenchmen with the truck provided Manos with some old clothes and told him to stay put. Manos decided to do as he was told.

Two days later Manos was taken in another truck to an office in a northern suburb of Paris where he met with a distinguished-looking man called Lucien Cazalis, who spoke English, to Manos's huge relief, and who soon took him to the apartment of a wine merchant and explained that Manos was to stay there for a few days until he could be moved again. The few days lasted almost exactly a month. Several times a young man called Maurice visited Manos with Cazalis. "I was taken to various places to be shown off or to make contact with the people who would be able to get me false papers," Manos remembered. He even visited several bars. One had a statue of Joan of Arc outside. He wasn't much of a drinker but Frenchmen insisted on placing large glasses of wine and spirits in front of him and he could hardly refuse. On another occasion Manos was driven around Paris in a small car. "The driver drove like he was half-crazy. I was worried and asked if [others] were concerned, and one of the men sort of nodded to the back seat and a fellow back there flashed one of those small machine guns that the Allies had made up for cheap and fast use by the troops." The gun was far from reassuring.

Manos's stay with the wine merchant ended abruptly on August 16, 1943. Someone in the apartment building where he was staying forgot to pull down the blackout shades and left a light on at night. The local gendarmes soon turned up and began to search the building. Before they got to Manos, an attractive English-speaking woman called Gladys Marchal hurried to the apartment, told Manos to accompany her, and then took him via the metro across Paris. Manos was feeling paranoid, as if he was "sticking out like a sore thumb" amid the other passengers. The dark-haired Marchal had divorced her French husband and described herself as a *telephoniste*—a telephone operator. In reality, she was a courier for an escape line and worked for the Libération resistance network.

The metro journey ended in Neuilly. Marchal calmly led Manos along a tree-lined street to the American Hospital and then to the fourth-floor office of one of the doctors. Manos looked around. The office was well furnished, "a nice place," he thought. He noticed a citation for bravery. It was framed on a wall. He thought it was the French Legion of Honor. There was a name on it: DR. SUMNER JACKSON.

THE STATION was busy. There were German soldiers everywhere Phillip looked. As usual, there was also tight security. Bags and parcels were routinely checked. At the entrance to the Gare Saint-Lazare, hundreds of bicycles were parked in long ranks. Men were using pushcarts to carry people's luggage to the velotaxis waiting where once cars had idled.

It was an August day, a couple of weeks after the Bastille Day raid, and Phillip was on his way to Saint-Nazaire in Brittany. His parents had decided he should spend some time in the country. Phillip boarded a train and took a seat. He was ever more eager to help his parents in some way and just as frustrated that he could not be involved in their resistance work. The train was full. There were German soldiers aboard. In the very seat beside Phillip there was a German soldier. Phillip did not hate him personally. But the man's presence right beside him was rather unfortunate, because Phillip had brought a camera with him, which was strictly forbidden.

The train was ready to leave. Then they were moving, out of the station, through the suburbs. The train was soon steaming through Normandy, past the ancient bocage, and through small towns and villages. Phillip looked at the rich Normandy fields as the train headed toward Chartres and then Brittany. Before the war he had vacationed in Normandy with his parents, spending precious days on the beach with his father, learning to fish, to swim, and to sail. Phillip had rowed with his father, each with one oar; combed the beach with him for driftwood; and watched him relax as he carved

miniature boats and other objects from wood with the skill of a surgeon who had, for such a big man, surprisingly nimble hands.

The landscape became less manicured, wilder. Phillip had arrived
in Brittany, where strangers were distrusted, the Germans detested,
and the resistance a fast-burgeoning and effective force—a region of
ancient hatreds and passions, with its long, craggy shoreline, mist-
laden moors, sunken fields, gorges, and pollarded oaks. In the glow
of full moonlight, Lysanders landed here regularly to drop off agents
who knew the locals could be trusted not to betray them. Allied sub-
marines often lurked off sheltered coves, ready to pick up returning
SOE agents and others carrying secret documents.

In Phillip's favorite books, boys were often transported to other
worlds where their mettle was tested, where they became heroes.
Perhaps in Brittany, far from his parents, he could finally do something that mattered—maybe even take some pictures that might help
the Allied cause.

AT THE American Hospital, Sumner met with Joe Manos in his office. Marchal proposed that Sumner hide Joe among a group of re-
tired British veterans who were being cared for in a nearby building.

Sumner was not keen on that at all. It was far too risky. "That's a
crazy idea," he said.

Instead, knowing that Phillip would be in Brittany until the end
of the summer, Sumner suggested Marchal leave Manos with him
for a few days. She could pick him up again once she had found him
false papers and send him along one of the escape lines run by the
Libération network. In the meantime Sumner himself would hide
Manos, not in the hospital's basement or in a safe house, but at his
home at number 11, Avenue Foch.

———

PHILLIP'S TRAIN pulled into the station in Nantes. Thankfully, German guards did not ask to search his suitcase. Possession of a camera was outlawed anywhere inside the "Forbidden Zone," which stretched fifteen miles inland all along the Atlantic Wall, Hitler's coastal defenses built from Norway to the Spanish border. Phillip was met at the station and then went to the home of Marcelle Le Bagousse, a friend of the Jacksons, who lived in Pontchâteau, some twenty miles north of the port of Saint-Nazaire.

Marcelle's husband, a large and affable man, worked for a railroad company and, because he had a special pass, was able to come and go as he pleased in the Forbidden Zone. One day he invited Phillip to accompany him on a day trip. He owned a house in Saint-Nazaire, which had been heavily bombed by the British. "I'm going to show you my house," he told Phillip, "or rather what is left of my house." From the central train station in Saint-Nazaire, they took bicycles to get around the port city. Phillip had hidden his camera in a panier on the back of his bicycle.

Saint-Nazaire was then the largest port in Europe, six miles upstream from the mouth of the Loire River, and of great importance to the Germans—large enough to harbor the Kriegsmarine's biggest ships, such as the *Bismarck* and *Tirpitz*. It had already been the scene of a heroic commando raid by the Allies in 1942 that had failed to destroy twenty-one U-boat pens, which the RAF and Eighth Air Force had since bombed repeatedly, but with little success.

When no one was looking, including Monsieur Le Bagousse, Phillip pulled out his camera. Seizing his chance to be something of a teenage spy, he snapped several photographs of bomb damage at the central train station and near the docks. Had the Germans spotted him, he would have been immediately arrested, interrogated at length, and handed over to the local Gestapo. And who knew then? By this stage of the war, youths in the resistance were being executed regularly.

Phillip returned from Saint-Nazaire to the Le Bagousse family's home, an old farmhouse that had a large basement with a workshop. He got on well with the Le Bagousses' son. They both liked to play around in the workshop, sharpening knives, making things using an excellent vise. Phillip enjoyed using his hands, just like his father. The basement had a small slit of a window at street level. One day that August, a German armored personnel carrier pulled up outside the farmhouse. Phillip was in the basement. He noticed the vehicle. Phillip couldn't help himself: he pulled out his camera and took another photograph. Fortunately, yet again, the Germans did not notice.

GLADYS MARCHAL walked to one of the two doors by which she knew she could enter number 11, Avenue Foch. Manos was waiting, dressed in his ill-fitting civilian clothes, looking remarkably French because of his dark Greek complexion, more than ready to get out of Paris and then France, as had been planned. He would never forget the kindness of Sumner, "clearly an undercover guy," and his equally brave wife. It was around August 20 when he left Avenue Foch with Marchal, headed for a train station, bound for southern France.

The Jacksons had taken an extraordinary risk in allowing Manos to stay in their home for even a few hours, let alone a weekend. They would never have done so had they known about Maurice, the foolhardy resistance agent who had stupidly paraded Manos around Paris. They had no idea that Maurice was a loose link in the Libération network, a bigmouth quick to boast about his work with de Gaulle's army of the shadows. Sooner or later the Gestapo were bound to track him down, for they had informers seemingly everywhere, and many Parisians, hungry and desperate, were only too happy to claim a reward on "Avenue Boche" for turning over the young men who were bombing France by day and night.

Gladys Marchal also knew far too much: where Sumner worked and where he lived. If the Gestapo caught her, would she talk when tortured? Those resistance members who survived longest moved address regularly and changed codes and their names as often as possible. Then they might stand a chance of staying a step ahead of Knochen and his men. But the Jacksons were not about to move. They would continue to live at number 11. And they were known by their real names. They were in fact extremely vulnerable, especially given their location so very close to Knochen's headquarters.

Hopefully, neither Marchal nor Maurice, nor any of the others who had helped Manos get as far as Avenue Foch, would be betrayed and taken to one of Knochen's torture cells at number 84. But what if Manos was apprehended trying to escape to Spain? Would he talk, giving them away, when Knochen's professionals attached electrodes to his testicles and yanked out his fingernails with a rusty pair of pliers? There was no way of telling how anyone would react when finally run to ground by the Gestapo, let alone the degenerate psychopaths like Henri Lafont, who would stop at nothing when it came to pleasing "Dr. Bones" at number 72, their paymaster and protector.

LATER THAT summer, once Manos was on his way south, Phillip returned to Paris by train. Again when he made his way through the Gare Saint-Lazare, he was not stopped and searched. After his exploits in Brittany, Phillip was more fascinated than ever by what his parents were doing, but they still kept everything from him, never discussing their secret lives. Strangers continued to turn up at odd hours at Avenue Foch. One day Phillip showed some of his holiday snapshots to a man who had visited a few times. Perhaps they might be useful? The man said they might be and took them from him. Phillip would never know if they were seen by British intelligence. One thing was certain: had his parents discovered that he had been playing the teenage spy, they would have been furious.

Phillip's images might not have made it to England, but plenty of other intelligence did pass through his home and did end up in London. By the fall of 1943, when Phillip returned to his school to study hard for his baccalaureate, his home was a critical "drop box," labeled "P2" by Goélette. When couriers could not be found to relay documents and photographs, Toquette may have carried the intelligence herself to Goélette contacts, some of whom operated in Brittany. According to Goélette records, information was regularly taken to a small village called Lannilis, where a priest called Père Lucq passed it on to an SOE contact. The SOE agent then arranged for the photographs and documents to be taken across the Channel, most often by motor torpedo boat.

One of those thought to have used 11, Avenue Foch, as a drop box was a remarkable forty-five-year-old engineer called Michel Hollard, one of the most effective spies of the war as far as the British were concerned. A senior Allied intelligence chief would describe him as "the man who literally saved London," because of the secrets he passed on about Hitler's "wonder weapon," the V-1 rocket, responsible for the destruction of more than 80,000 British homes.

British intelligence had learned that a pilotless plane was being developed at Peenemünde, Germany, in an underground testing facility. But no one had been able to work out where the weapon would be fired from or at whom. That summer of 1943, one of Hollard's many contacts, a young draftsman in a builder's office, managed to steal a blueprint from his boss's coat. The blueprint was for a launch site for the V-1 rocket to be built in northern France at Bois-Carré. London was clearly the target. The discovery was among the most critical for Allied intelligence of the war.

By the fall of 1943 the Gestapo had begun to penetrate Hollard's network. He lost several of his sources, one of them tortured almost to death by Kieffer's accomplices at 84, Avenue Foch. Hollard's oft-repeated journey from France to Berne, Switzerland, where he handed over diagrams and photographs to a British embassy official, was ever more hazardous. Instead of crossing the border, it is believed he began to use drop boxes in Paris instead, including the one at 11, Avenue Foch.

Just as daring as Hollard was a young Austrian aristocrat, Erich Posch-Pastor von Camperfeld, the son of the Austro-Hungarian Empire's last ambassador to the Vatican. Thin, dark-skinned, and according to one contemporary, "physically and socially supple," the twenty-nine-year-old spy had fought against the Germans in 1938 in opposition to the Anschluss. For that crime he was sent to Dachau, Hitler's first concentration camp. As further punishment, he was forced to join the Wehrmacht and serve on the Eastern Front, where he was wounded in late 1941. Through connections high up in the German command, he then managed to wheedle his way into a job with the German Purchasing Agency, headquartered in Paris, which acquired food and matériel to be sent back to Germany.

One of von Camperfeld's cousins worked for the Wehrmacht in Paris, and von Camperfeld was able to persuade him to pass him details of the V-1 rocket project: drawings of the rockets and maps of where they were going to be based along the Channel coast in anticipation of an Allied invasion. Von Camperfeld wisely avoided being seen anywhere near Avenue Foch, where the Gestapo might recognize him, so that fall he apparently began to visit the American Hospital, where he had several appointments with a certain Dr. Sumner Jackson, who knew him only by a code name, "Étienne Paul Provost."

From October 1943 onward, according to an official British report, von Camperfeld passed on "economic and military information of the highest importance, including some of the first designs of the V-1 rocket." Allied supreme commander Dwight Eisenhower later stated that this and other information about the most worrisome of Hitler's weapons was crucial to victory in World War Two. Without it the planned invasion of Europe—code-named Overlord—"might have been written off."

———

ACCORDING TO his identity card and other papers, he was thirty-five-year-old Victor Burnier, an architect living at 7, Rue du Lac, in Annecy. In fact, he was Squadron Leader Frank Griffiths, a thirty-one-year-old dark-haired Welsh pilot who had dropped SOE agents and supplies to the resistance for much of the war. Since August, he had been on the run from the Gestapo after he crashed his Halifax bomber in southeastern France after suffering engine failure. His crew had been killed, but although he was badly wounded and burned when the plane split in two on impact, Griffiths managed to get free of the crash site before the Germans could arrive. He then made contact with the resistance, who had helped him get to Switzerland. From there he made his way to Toulouse and the safe house, patrolled by a very large black cat called Mifouf, where he was now, late in October 1943, seated at a table eating his *petit déjeuner*.

A strange figure walked into the room. The man looked like a swarthy French peasant. Maybe he was the gardener? He walked over to Griffiths and grabbed him by the hand. His name was Joe, he said, and Griffiths was the first "English guy" he had set eyes on in months. His mother was Polish, Manos added, but the reason he looked like a local was because his father was a dark-skinned Greek.

Manos and Griffiths were in the home of an extraordinary sixty-two-year-old six-foot-tall woman called Louise Marie Dissard, more commonly known as "Françoise." She had joined the resistance in 1940 and ran an escape line from her home, the Villa Pamplemousse, in the city of Toulouse. By war's end she would help more than seven hundred evaders like Manos to safety. Her task was to feed downed airmen and prepare them for the arduous journey across the Pyrenees to Spain. It was no easy task and she was a tough disciplinarian, making Manos exercise before each meal, refusing to feed him until he had climbed a set of stairs twenty-five times on his toes.

Manos had been with "Françoise" for several days by the time Squadron Leader Griffiths arrived. They soon became friends and Griffiths would later recall Manos with great affection: "He was an amazingly relaxed person. Nothing ever disturbed him except, as I was to discover, rats and dogs. Germans, the Milice [Vichy anti-resistance paramilitary force], gendarmes worried him not at all. He was supremely confident in their company and was thoroughly enjoying his 'tour of Europe'!"

"Françoise" had soon arranged false identities for Manos and Griffiths. They then set off for Perpignan, where they met guides who would take them across the Pyrenées until they were within striking distance of Spain. Crossing the actual border would be the most dangerous part of the journey. Manos and Griffiths would do it alone. "However tired you are, never take the easy path and walk on a road," one of the guides warned Griffiths. "You're bound to be challenged there."

One evening in early November, Manos and Griffiths set off to hike the last few miles into Spain. It was so dark that Manos had to hold on to Griffiths' coat so they would not be separated and get lost. Near the border, they heard the sounds of a German patrol. They hid amid bushes and listened intently. Did the Germans have dogs? Luckily they did not, and after a few tense minutes the patrol moved away. Manos was wearing size eleven GI boots, which sounded terribly loud to Griffiths—"like a tank going over a corrugated iron shed"—as they walked on, finally making it to the Col du Perthus, high in the Pyrenées, where they rested amid some boulders. "It was thrilling," recalled Griffiths. "There below us were the lights of Spain."

Manos and Griffiths stumbled on through the darkness, crossed into Spain, and then headed to the town of Figueres, where they went their separate ways. Manos arrived in Gibraltar on November 28 and the next day left for Britain by plane. He was then extensively debriefed in London by the escape-and-evasion organization, MIS-X. He was hugely relieved that he had not been caught and tortured by the Gestapo. He had not had to betray any of those who had risked their lives to help him, including Sumner and Toquette Jackson.

TWELVE

THE LAST METRO

IT WAS A somber Christmas along Avenue Foch, the fourth the Jacksons had experienced under German occupation. Many in the resistance had hoped that by now the Allies would have landed in France and that Paris would have been freed. It was bitterly disappointing to contemplate another cold, seemingly endless winter under the Nazi yoke. Paris was gray, depressed, and increasingly tense. The weather felt especially cold, perhaps because ordinary Parisians had less and less fat for insulation. Families like the Jacksons huddled together in one room around a single fire if they were lucky enough to have found a source of wood or coal. Others, like the writer Colette, simply dressed in several layers and stayed in bed.

At the American Hospital, Sumner and his colleagues were determined to keep their patients' spirits up. The hospital's ingenious cooks made a superb Christmas dinner after slaughtering pigs that had been kept hidden from the Germans. At the Christmas party, General de Chambrun and his wife, Clara, mingled with doctors and staff. The festivities were cut short, however, because everyone had to leave by 10:00 p.m.: the strict German curfew began at 11:00, and it was crucial not to miss the last metro.

Clara de Chambrun recalled that she and the general walked quickly through the cold, empty streets of Neuilly that night to the nearest metro station, either Pont de Neuilly or Anatole France, having stayed too long at the hospital. Clara was scared that if they missed the last metro back into central Paris, they would be arrested and then be forced to spend the night in jail. It was widely known that the Germans took "curfew violators" to the headquarters of the Feldgendarmerie (Military Police). A common punishment was to spend the night shining Fritz's shoes. But if a German soldier had been shot or stabbed to death, as was increasingly the case, those caught in the roundup after midnight might suffer much worse. The Germans often selected curfew violators to be among "hostages" to be shot as a reprisal measure.

The Chambruns managed to get to the metro station in time to board a train. They crossed Paris, sharing their carriage with all manner of Parisians, rich and poor, the train rattling past the many stations that had been closed. They then walked through deserted streets in Saint-Germain, three blocks in all, to their home on the Left Bank, at 58, Rue de Vaugirard, overlooking the Jardin de Luxembourg. It was a frigid evening. Near her home, Clara saw a German soldier. He was standing under a streetlight, his sallow features illuminated by its pale blue glow. Clara felt panic surge inside her. Were they going to be arrested?

The German approached and, instead of arresting her, asked her directions to a nearby hotel set aside for German soldiers. He had lost his way. He was clearly scared to be alone on the streets of Paris at night. Clara indicated that the hotel was nearby. The German looked relieved and made his way quickly toward safety. Clara would remember the incident vividly. It had left her deeply troubled and she began to wonder what would happen to her and her kind, those with close connections to the Vichy collaborators, if the Germans lost the war.

ON JANUARY 10, 1944, Phillip Jackson celebrated his sixteenth birthday. Much of his time was devoted to studying for his baccalaureate. But when he didn't have his head in a book, he must have been aware of the strain his parents were under. Nothing could go unnoticed. They always needed to be alert, questioning things, on their guard. They knew their luck might only hold for so long. It was wise to be paranoid. Some days, given their location, it must have seemed that the men in trench coats walking past the house were actually watching them, sitting in local cafés and restaurants and pretending to read newspapers, waiting to pounce.

It was not just the Gestapo and Knochen's private army of criminals who were now hunting for the resistance. That January of 1944, the Vichy organization called the Milice arrived in Paris. They were paramilitary French fascists, trained and well armed by Knochen's immediate superior, SS general Karl Oberg. The Milice was headed by forty-six-year-old Joseph Darnand, a decorated World War I hero, who had been quick to realize who his real patrons were—Knochen and his colleagues on Avenue Foch—and eager to please given the enormous power they conferred. It wasn't long before Darnand's private army set about arresting, torturing, and killing more or less as they pleased. Their most famous victim was the politician Georges Mandel, a high-profile enemy of Nazism before the war who had been imprisoned by the Gestapo but was then actually seized from their custody and brutally murdered by the Milice.

Even the willfully blind Josée Laval, René de Chambrun's wife, busy most days visiting the Rochas and Schiaparelli fashion showrooms, began to worry about what might happen to her and her family given the murderous actions of the Milice. They would surely all be punished. One evening at Laval's official Paris residence, the Hôtel Matignon, she confided her fears to her father. "We'll all be hanged for what the Milice have done," said Josée. "I don't mind hanging but not with Darnand."

The resistance struck back, killing Milice and Vichy officials all across France. One bisexual American-born resistance agent, known simply by his alias, "Tom," worked that winter as an assassin, executing informers and their Gestapo contacts. His specialty was seducing homosexual Gestapo officers—easily picked up in various bars frequented by black marketers and gay gigolos such as the café Le Colisée on the Champs-Élysées—and then dispatching them with an ice pick that he'd concealed under the bed while they slept beside him. "The biggest problem and the greatest danger," he recalled, "was not the killing itself. It was the disposal of the body. I worked with a team of young men, powerful men. They could pick up a body like a loaf of bread and all but tuck it under their arms, wrapped up in sacking, or stuffed into an empty steamer trunk or a wooden crate."

Tom vividly recalled how dangerous it was to work in the resistance in Paris, particularly anywhere near Avenue Foch. One day he tried to make contact with a fellow agent in a street not far away. It was thick with Knochen's agents. Their black Citroëns were parked outside most cafés. They stood dressed in heavy trench coats, leaning against lampposts, trying not to be observed. Tom could always tell if they were Knochen's men because they were forever "reading" the same page of the same newspaper. It seemed that Knochen had informers in every café and restaurant. By some estimates, more than 30,000 Frenchmen and -women worked in some capacity for him, three times the number of French gendarmes in the city. He had apparently recruited every vengeful prostitute and jilted lover and then deployed a vast dragnet to watch for suspicious activity in every railway station, in every food queue and cinema.

Insurrection brewed all that winter. Passions rose as Paris began to starve. Boys could be seen stealing into the city's parks to cut blades of grass and stuff them into their pockets so they could feed the rabbits they reared for meat in their bathtubs. It was estimated that Parisians had lost on average forty pounds since the Germans had arrived. The most common after-dinner treat was a bitter-tasting cigarette to dull hunger pains. Cats had all but disappeared on Paris streets, as they had been cooked and eaten by the famished. Most of the city's bakeries were closed. In the poorest neighborhoods, far from the Avenue Foch, people were dying of hunger. Before the war,

Toquette had been able to buy a kilogram of butter for fifteen francs. Now, if she could find the money, it cost well over a hundred times that on the black market.

An American journalist called Alice-Leone Moats, who had slipped into Paris in disguise from Spain, was struck by the tawdry, depressed air in the city: "The avenues and streets were made ugly by the hundreds of German soldiers in their gray-green uniforms who crowded the pavements." She looked around and saw that "Nazi flags disfigured the government buildings and huge signs . . . defaced other buildings which had been turned into amusement centers for soldiers of the Army of Occupation. The fountains in the public squares no longer played, the streets were unkempt and dusty . . . Wooden sawhorses wrapped with rusty barbed wire hedged in the Hôtel de Crillon, the Ministry of Marine, the Place Vendôme entrance of the Ritz and every other place where the Germans were quartered."

Everything seemed to be slowly falling apart. The metro was not running properly, due to shortages of electricity. The projectors in cinemas on the Champs-Élysées, where Phillip sometimes watched movies, were powered by teenagers on bicycles hooked to generators, as were the printing presses of some resistance groups.

Early that February, Sumner came down with pneumonia. He also wrote to Elizabeth Ravina, a nurse whom he had befriended, about his "family's dire need of clothing." According to another friend of the family, Clemence Bock, "Sumner was drawn and careworn and went about in an old army sweater with a hole that showed his elbow when he took off his long surgical coat." Despite his pneumonia, he still rode his bicycle, specially constructed for his large frame, from Avenue Foch to the hospital and back each day, a First World War flying helmet squeezed onto his head to fend off the cold.

Like many Parisians, the Jacksons often listened to the BBC, gathering around a radio placed as far from the windows at 11, Avenue Foch, as possible with the volume turned low on General de Gaulle. So many other people were tuning in illegally—some had been executed for the offense—that a joke was making the rounds about a Jew who had murdered a German soldier and devoured his heart at 9:20 p.m. The punch line was: "Impossible for three reasons: A German has no heart. A Jew eats no pork. And at 9:20 everyone is listening to the BBC."

At the American Hospital, Sumner still struggled to keep patients fed and warm. On February 9, 1944, Max Shoop, one of the governors, reported that there were serious problems finding food as the winter got colder and stretched on. Yet, despite intensifying air raids, not a single window in the hospital had been broken. Shoop also worked closely as a spy for Allen Dulles, who was heading up the Office of Strategic Services, America's first international spy agency, in Berne, Switzerland. He was in fact OSS agent 284, a key liaison between the French resistance and the OSS. Through Shoop, Dulles supplied explosives and large sums of cash to the French resistance.

Did Shoop know about Sumner and his help for OSS agent Donald Coster in 1940? Was he aware that Sumner continued to help others to escape France? His Swiss colleague Otto Gresser, who helped manage the hospital's day-to-day affairs, recalled that Sumner "from time to time hid one or two [aircrew] who had been shot down but weren't killed. He would take care of them. Of course, it was very serious."

The stakes had never been higher. Never had Sumner been in such great danger at work and when he returned to his home on Avenue Foch. The latest gang of psychopaths to set up camp in the neighborhood, the Berger Group, was based just a hundred yards to the west of the Jacksons' home, at 180, Rue de la Pompe, almost within spitting distance of Knochen's office at 72, Avenue Foch. The previous occupant was thirty-seven-year-old Comtesse von Seckendorff, one of Knochen's most accomplished informers, code-named "Mercedes." She had since moved to an even more impressive address, 41, Avenue Foch, just around the corner.

The Berger Group was under the command of thirty-three-year-old Friedrich Berger, a veteran Abwehr agent before the war and an accomplished black market operator until employed by the Gestapo on Avenue Foch. Members of his band included Denise Delfau and Hélène Muzzin, sisters and both mistresses of Berger when not working as his secretaries. There was also Rachid Zulgadar, an Iranian taxi driver nicknamed "King Kong," a seasoned torturer who was especially creative when getting women to talk and had no problems keeping muscle-bound young communists' heads under water. Women were made to sit naked on ice until they broke down or passed out, shivering and screaming. Berger preferred to waterboard victims first and then beat them almost to death. He had no time for electrocution or sleep deprivation, both favorites of the Milice, opting to cause maximum agony as fast as possible.

No wonder the mental asylums in Paris that winter were said to be full of people who had gone insane after a visit or two to the torture chambers of the "Nazi Triangle," whose most notable addresses were 5, Rue Mallet-Stevens; 93, Rue Lauriston; and 180, Rue de la Pompe; and of course the Gestapo mansions all along Avenue Foch. The Jacksons were now living at the heart of Nazi evil, at the center of a vast web of informers, spies, and cold-blooded mass murderers. The enemy—Knochen and his men—were so very close by. Such was their reputation that Parisians talked fearfully of being "taken to the Avenue Foch," never to return.

It took immense sangfroid to maintain one's composure, to stay even-keeled when every ugly man in a gray suit and trilby was a potential killer under orders to fire if one decided to run. The stress for many within the resistance, not just for Toquette and Sumner—who were only too aware of the growing dangers surrounding them—became too much to bear. Every shrill of the telephone, every knock on the front door, every shifty look from a stranger, might herald the end.

Every time Sumner arrived home on his bespoke bicycle he knew he might have been followed. Knochen had "physiognomists" working for him, men who had previously prowled the lobbies of casinos on the lookout for cheaters, and who were now paid handsomely by the Gestapo to recognize fugitives who were most wanted by Knochen. They kept photos of key figures in the resistance concealed in their hatbands. That way they only needed to make a quick check of a photo and then make an arrest. In Sumner's case it would take no time at all to hustle him into an unmarked black Citroën idling a few yards away and take him to one of the many interrogation rooms now to be found on "Avenue Boche."

WINTER TURNED to spring. As the first daffodils and crocuses appeared in the gardens along the Avenue Foch, Sumner was one day contacted by a French police officer. The man had excellent sources. He knew a great deal about what was happening on Avenue Foch. For some reason, finally, the German authorities had woken up to the fact that an American family still lived there and had not been interned. "Be careful," the Frenchman told Sumner, "you're being watched."

There is no record of how Sumner reacted. But Clemence Bock, who had taught him French in the twenties and remained close to the family, later recalled that Sumner was not deterred. He was "very careful, very prudent" but he was not about to stop helping the Allied cause, and neither was Toquette. They were certain the Allies would arrive to liberate Paris soon. It was just a matter of keeping their nerve for a few months at most.

As the first buds appeared on the chestnut trees along Avenue Foch, all Paris was on edge, not just those who, like the Jacksons, were working in the resistance. On April 21 the city was badly bombed by the Allies. "The sky is alive with enormous stars, with multicolored tracers, signs of a human astrology none can yet decipher," recalled one Parisian. Number 11, Avenue Foch, had no basement for shelter. When his parents weren't paying attention, Phillip ran upstairs to the fifth floor, to the maid Louise's room, and in darkness looked up at the dramatic skies. Houses nearby shuddered from the shock waves. He had only to touch the window to feel the vibration—like a "bird's heartbeat" as one neighbor, the right-wing journalist Alfred Fabre-Luce, a friend of Josée Laval's living at 56, Avenue Foch, described it.

Remarkably, five days later, on April 26, Marshal Pétain paid his only visit to Paris during the occupation, shortly after his eighty-eighth birthday. There were massive crowds. His regime was deeply unpopular, with Laval universally loathed, but Pétain himself was still seen as the onetime savior of France. Around the same time, Goélette's head of Paris operations, Paul Robert Kinderfreund, contacted Toquette and warned her to be extremely vigilant. Fevered rumors were sweeping through the underground. It was said that the Gestapo was paying more than ever for information on airmen who had been shot down. Those who helped evaders were to be quickly executed along with their families.

April became May. The weather was glorious. Paris had never looked so beautiful, recalled the writer and painter Jean Hugo: "Without the stain of petrol fumes, the chestnut trees on the Champs-Élysées were a brilliant green." Lithe young Parisiennes, their bodies hardened and legs toned by four years of cycling, hopped out of velotaxis and strutted through the Tuileries Garden, smiling in the sunshine, wearing knee-length skirts, often in all-the-rage Scottish plaid, and large and elaborate hats—among the few garments during the war through which Frenchwomen were able to express their flamboyance.

Toquette also wore Scottish plaid but she seldom smiled. Nor did her husband. Clemence Bock noted how early that May "little by little [Sumner] became more and more tired, with an absent air."

Bock began to worry about the family. Not long after, she received a letter. It was not signed. "If you go to the Avenue Foch," it read, "don't think of visiting the people you know there." Bock ignored the warning and paid a visit to Toquette on Monday, May 15. They chatted and Bock gathered some lilies of the valley from the front garden that faced onto Avenue Foch. It was obvious that Toquette was anxious and she was clearly relieved when Bock went home.

The following day, May 16, 1944, the OSS in Berne sent a report to Washington in which it was noted that the French resistance in France was waging an ever more violent war against the Germans. In the first four months of 1944, 2,500 Germans had been wounded and almost 900 killed. Two thousand railway wagons had been damaged. In response, the Gestapo fought harder than ever to destroy the legions of ever more daring "terrorists" springing up across France. Knochen's assorted bands of criminals conducted indiscriminate sweeps, rounding up anyone remotely suspect. In Paris, every jail was soon full. To make room for even more enemies of the Reich, fifty members of the resistance were executed each week.

D-Day was just a couple of weeks away. Those like Toquette and Sumner who were heavily involved in the resistance as the invasion neared could not be told in advance its exact date, but everyone sensed it would be someday soon and they listened to the BBC, especially on the first, second, fifteenth, and sixteenth of that May for messages that would indicate if the invasion was imminent. If it was then they would hear the words *L'heure des combats viendra*. The hour of battle will come.

One of the most popular underground newspapers, *Defense de la France,* caught the mood of the resistance that May, calling for reprisals against the Germans, collaborators, and the hugely despised Milice: "Kill the German to cleanse our territory . . . Kill the traitors, kill those who betray, those who aided the enemy . . . Kill the men of the Milice, exterminate them . . . Shoot them like mad dogs on the street corners. . . ." One resistance activist was heard to comment that he had a long list of people he was planning to shoot and "there wasn't a German name on the list."

Avenue Foch had never been so dangerous. Just a hundred yards from the Jacksons' home at number 11, Knochen's head of counter-intelligence, Hans Kieffer, still worked long into the night at number 84, determined to utterly destroy the last remnants of Allied spy networks in Paris. He and Knochen's other spy hunters had continued to play the "radio game" with seized SOE radio sets. Tipped off by highly paid informers, Knochen had prepared "mousetraps" throughout Paris and had then ordered his men to arrest anyone seen entering or leaving them. The Gestapo had even had informers placed in concentration camps such as Buchenwald, Dachau, and Ravensbruck in case imprisoned spies and resistance workers revealed the names of colleagues still at large.

Knochen was so effective that SOE agents were recalled to London in the face of seemingly inevitable betrayal. He had finally won the spy game against the British. His spy hunters had destroyed Prosper and removed the SOE from Paris. In a final flourish that May, a last transmission was sent to SOE in London over a captured radio set: "Thank you for your collaboration and for the weapons you have sent us." The British replied: "Think nothing of it. These weapons were a mere bagatelle for us. It was a luxury we could easily afford. We shall soon be coming to fetch them."

It was around May 20, 1944, when Knochen's men claimed yet another victory. Finally, they penetrated the Libération escape line that Sumner had been a part of. The Englishwoman Gladys Marchal, who had in August 1943 escorted Manos to Sumner Jackson's office at the American Hospital, was arrested in Paris. It was later alleged that she was interrogated by Knochen's agents but then released after just twenty-four hours, which was highly unusual. Had she talked? Had she betrayed Sumner Jackson? Soon after, another member of the same escape line, a man named Gilbert Asselin, fell victim. He, too, had helped Manos reach safety and would have been able to name names, including the "underground" couple that lived at 11, Avenue Foch: Sumner and Toquette.

IN A SMALL MOUNTAIN TOWN called La Bourboule in the Auvergne, fifty miles southwest of Vichy, a group of Milice men dressed in blue jackets, brown shirts, and wide blue berets prepared to storm a building. They had been reliably informed that leaders of the Goélette resistance network were inside. It was in the early hours of May 24 when the Milice burst in and arrested seven agents, including two women and the group's leader, Claude Vallette, who were then handed over, along with incriminating documents, to Knochen's men in Vichy, commanded by thirty-six-year-old SS captain Hugo Geissler.

Geissler had led the SS war against the local resistance since the previous fall and employed a band of twenty-two Frenchmen, called the "Batissier Brigade," who had changed their names to sound more German and were mercilessly violent. He also worked closely with Joseph Darnand, head of the Milice. Geissler left a distinct impression, with his large oval face and a pointy nose, and because he had spent time as an interpreter in a casino in Nice before the war he was fluent in French. That had helped him penetrate several resistance networks in early 1944, but to seize so many terrorists in the operation in Bourboule, in one fell swoop, was good work indeed. A thorough search of the safe house yielded even more bounty: apart from an uncoded list of members of the network, there were several letters to a Madame Jackson. Her address was given as 11, Avenue Foch.

PART THREE

NIGHT AND FOG

It was a world composed of masters and slaves, in which gentleness, kindness, pity, the respect for the law, and a taste for freedom were no longer virtues, but inexplicable crimes. It was a world in which one could only obey by crawling, killing on orders, and dying oneself in silence if one could not howl with the wolves.

—JACQUES DELARUE, *The Gestapo: A History of Horror*

THIRTEEN

GUESTS OF THE REICH

AROUND 7:30 A.M. on Thursday, May 25, 1944, there was a knock on the front door at 11, Avenue Foch. Phillip Jackson was getting ready to go to school when Toquette went to the door, opened it, and found three Milice men standing outside in their blue jackets and berets, all of them armed.

Was a Madame Toquette Jackson at this address?

Toquette smiled at the men on the doorstep. Behind her, standing in the hallway, was Phillip. The Milice men noticed he was less at ease than Toquette.

One of the men was clearly the leader, "*le chef.*" He asked after Dr. Jackson.

"He's at the hospital," said Toquette, "seeing his patients."

Two of the men turned and left, headed for the hospital.

Toquette had hidden some documents under some pharmaceutical products in Sumner's home laboratory in the next room. Jauntily, she offered the remaining officer something to drink. He accepted and Toquette left him beside the telephone in the hallway, walked into the laboratory, gathered some letters, and carried them into the kitchen, where she found the maid Louise. "Take these," said Toquette. Louise immediately did so, quickly leaving by the door leading to the Rue de Traktir, then making her way to an address where a Goélette agent, code-named "Mr. Petit," could be found.

Meanwhile, at the American Hospital, the Milice arrested

Sumner, put him into their car, and drove fast south toward the Seine, finally reaching Avenue Foch. But they did not pull up in front of any of Helmut Knochen's offices. Instead they parked in front of the black iron railings at number 11, and then decided to place the whole family in the front garden, outside of Phillip's bedroom window, while they awaited orders from their seniors. They had clearly been told to arrest the family but not what to do with them or where to take them. It was a beautiful day and the lilies of the valley were in full bloom, the sweet-smelling bell-shaped flowers a glorious sight.

Two of the men went inside and searched the house, but they didn't find anything as they rifled through cupboards, chests, and wardrobes, leaving clothes and papers strewn in their wake. Then they told the Jacksons to pack a case. Phillip made sure to place his history book in a bag, determined to continue to study wherever he was going, because he was taking his crucial baccalaureate exam in just two weeks' time.

It was all rather civilized and polite. Sumner even invited the *miliciens* to have lunch and one of them assured him as they ate that there must have been some kind of mistake. Things would be worked out. After lunch, perhaps reassured, Sumner smoked cigars with the chief of the *miliciens* in the front garden. Every so often the telephone in the hallway shrilled. The *miliciens* were quick to answer it. Someone from the hospital was on the line, asking after Dr. Jackson, and later that afternoon the hospital called several more times, but the *miliciens* still refused to allow Sumner to talk on the phone, suspecting he might try to trick them or call for help.

Word spread fast through the Goélette network about the arrests of the Jacksons and the seven agents in Bourboule. Francis Deloche de Noyelle, based in Grenoble, learned immediately from contacts in his organization. He felt terribly guilty and blamed himself for their arrest. It was his fault. After all, he had been the one to recruit Toquette.

Toquette remained focused. Nothing could be revealed if she was questioned. Two days would be needed for agents in the Goélette network to disperse, change codes and identities or do whatever was needed to avoid being caught in the same trap. To warn off other agents, when the *miliciens* were distracted, she opened the windows overlooking the Rue de Traktir. It stayed light well into the evening, and when Louise returned she and Phillip were allowed to sit inside, near the open windows. When they saw someone they recognized walking toward the front door, they were able to wave the visitor away.

That night the *miliciens* even allowed Toquette and Sumner to stay together, alone in their bedroom. One can only imagine what they discussed. Toquette had been the driving force behind their joining the resistance and had agreed to Francis Deloche de Noyelle's request, but did she now regret doing so with all three of their lives in danger? They both had heard how brutal other *miliciens* could be, not to mention the Gestapo headquartered less than a hundred yards away.

The following morning, the *miliciens* informed the Jacksons that they were to be taken to Vichy, to their headquarters. Before the family got into a black Citroën under guard, Toquette had time to warn Phillip out of earshot of the *miliciens*: "If they question you, don't say a thing." Then they were leaving. Louise cried as she saw the Citroën head for the Étoile. For some reason the Milice did not think to arrest her, and for several days she would remain in the kitchen, looking onto the Rue de Traktir, and calmly wave away anyone approaching, even though she may have been watched.

The Jacksons sat in the back of the Citroën in silence as they made their way south along the upper Loire Valley toward the spa town of Vichy. The Citroën was a favorite with the Milice and Gestapo because it held the road well at high speed, essential for car chases. It stopped a few times for the Milice men to get out and urinate.

Phillip looked out of the window, recognizing the landscape from almost exactly four years before, when as an innocent twelve-year-old he had left Paris for a summer of fishing with his aunt Tat and mother. They were in the very same kind of car, passing through the same sleepy towns beside the broad, fast-flowing Loire: Nemours . . . Nevers . . . Moulins. It felt to him that the journey would last forever, but late that afternoon they arrived at the Château des Brosses, near Vichy.

The *miliciens* then split up the family. Phillip's parents were kept at the Château des Brosses, the Milice's main prison. Toquette, no doubt traumatized by her forced separation from her son, was placed in a room on the ground floor, while Sumner was escorted to another.

The next morning a *milicien* came to Toquette's cell.

"Would you like to have breakfast with your husband?" he asked.

Toquette was taken down to the château's garden, guarded by *miliciens*, where she and Sumner spoke in English, which their captors did not understand. They agreed on what they would say when interrogated: it was important to get their stories to match.

Meanwhile the *miliciens* had placed Phillip in a large white stucco building in central Vichy that had a prominent sign above the entrance: Le Petit Casino. The former theater was now the Milice's headquarters. Phillip and three other prisoners were made to sit down in a seat in the stalls, guarded by three *miliciens* with submachine guns who stood on the stage. Phillip was then taken to a cellar, where he was left alone in the darkness without food or water and soon became delirious, probably through dehydration and delayed shock. He dreamt at one point of the placid lake in Enghien, where he had boated so often with his parents.

Back at the Château des Brosses, Toquette and Sumner were still being treated extraordinarily well, and even allowed to have dinner one night together alfresco on a terrace. It was too good to last. One morning they were taken in a car to Le Petit Casino, where Sumner was placed in Phillip's cell. Phillip had been alone, utterly terrified, for more than two days, and it must have been a great relief to see his father, indeed for him to be at his side once more.

Toquette was put in another cell on a different floor. On May 31, she was able somehow to arrange for a letter to be sent to her sister, Tat, who was living in the Jacksons' weekend home in Enghien:

> *The weather continues to be good here but cooler following a storm. This is the third letter I have written you at intervals of two days. I have nothing new to say as far as we are concerned. Today is the day Pete should have taken his examination for the Baccalaureate and I haven't seen him since Friday [May 26, 1944]. I am beginning to feel really very dirty. I haven't undressed since the same day and even if I could undress it would be to put back on the same clothes and I have nothing to clean myself with. Happily, I am wearing practical clothes: my Scots skirt that doesn't get crumpled and gray sweater, flexible and comfortable.*
>
> *Jack [Sumner] is still here but on the first floor whereas I am housed on the second floor, better off than him, the poor fellow. If you get my letters you could telephone to . . . Miss Comte, the director of the hospital, to give her news of us.*
>
> *My courage is being tested to the extreme not so much for me as for Pete and also for Jack; if I knew that he was free my particular fate would be less painful.*
>
> *My sister, I hug you.*
>
> *Your Sister*

In his cell, Phillip pulled a ticket from his trouser pocket. It was for entry to his baccalaureate exam that day. He had studied hard for it, knowing his parents wanted him to excel. It was a tough exam, with only around fifty percent of students passing. That's why he had reviewed a great deal, wanting to make his father proud.

At least he no longer had to study. He tore up the ticket, thinking, *Good riddance.*

Several days later, on June 6, the Allies finally landed in France. D-Day, the greatest amphibious operation in history, had arrived. What the Jacksons had waited so long for had finally happened, just two weeks after their arrest. The Atlantic Wall had been breached and troops were streaming across the very beach, code-named Juno, where Phillip had played as a child. It was time, finally, for the French to take sides. From Vichy, Marshal Pétain called for all patriotic Frenchmen to remain neutral. French blood, he stressed, was too precious to be wasted in this fight. For Pierre Laval and other high-profile collaborators, the D-Day landings were an unmitigated disaster. He had already declared that an "American victory would mean victory for the Jews and the communists." In a speech broadcast on June 6, he went even further, imploring the French people to do nothing as hundreds of thousands of Allied soldiers fought an increasingly bloody battle to liberate them.

"You are not in the war," Laval emphasized. "You must not take part in the fighting."

The French were to play no part in liberating themselves.

"At this moment fraught with drama," Laval exhorted his listeners, "when the war has been carried on to our territory, show by your worthy and disciplined attitude that you are thinking of France and only of her."

THE NEXT day, June 7, 1944, the Jacksons were finally handed over to Helmut Knochen's colleagues in Vichy: the Gestapo. D-Day was of scant comfort now to Sumner and Toquette. What they had feared most was happening and there was no telling what the Gestapo might resort to, but surely they would try to play mind games, the kind they used with other families they arrested. A good start would be convincing one of the three Jacksons that another of them had talked.

Sumner and Toquette must also have asked themselves why the Gestapo had decided to get involved. Indeed, why had the Milice handed them over? Perhaps the Milice no longer wanted to be responsible for the Jacksons given that the Americans were fighting on French soil. Or maybe the Gestapo believed they had a potentially important source of information in the Jacksons.

Only one thing was certain; they could be executed at any time. The SS were increasingly trigger-happy and nervous as France spiraled downward into civil war, with the resistance fighting actual battles with the Milice in the mountainous regions of central and southern France. The German army was, meanwhile, rushing all available forces from the south to the Normandy front. But the pace of reinforcement was infuriatingly slow, because the resistance had blown bridges and rail lines. Atrocity followed atrocity as the SS struck back indiscriminately at any community thought to have harbored "terrorists." On June 10, men belonging to the SS Der Führer regiment entered the small town of Oradour-sur-Glane, 160 miles due west, and killed 642 people in the most notorious atrocity committed in France; 207 of the victims were children.

Around the same time, the Jacksons were moved to the Hôtel du Portugal, the Gestapo's torture house in Vichy, on a road somewhat ironically named Boulevard des États-Unis (United States Boulevard). It was not far from the shuttered American embassy in Vichy. Phillip and his father were put in separate cells, and Toquette was placed in a different building. The Gestapo officers in the prison were all French, and one of them tried to reassure Phillip that he and his father would soon be freed. He made no mention of Toquette.

Phillip shared his small, dark cell with three other men. The air was rancid. Prisoners had scrawled defiant messages on the walls.

For a bed, Phillip had a bunk the size of a door that was attached to a wall. One of the men in the cell belonged to the resistance and Phillip saw him taken away one day for interrogation. He was brought back two hours later, utterly traumatized, with all his nails pulled out, a bloody mess. Phillip looked at the man's disfigured hands in terror. Next time they would come for him. He would be tortured. But when? Tomorrow? Late at night? Not knowing was agony. Then Phillip witnessed true brutality for the first time when a guard whipped one of the other inmates twenty-five times just a few feet from Phillip. Neighbors were said to complain that the Gestapo played the radio too loud, day and night. No wonder. It was to drown out the screams.

One day, a guard entered Phillip's cell. Without warning, he struck out and hit Phillip with his whip. Phillip had apparently not stood quickly enough to attention. His jailers were clearly sadists looking for any excuse to lash out and vent their rage. One prisoner in his cell, a forlorn young man who came from Clermont-Ferrand, was also beaten savagely and later showed Phillip his back, which was covered in purple and yellow bruises and bleeding badly. Phillip did his best to care for him but there was not much he could practically do, and he had little strength anyway, feeling ever weaker through hunger because his rations were now just three small pieces of black bread per day and a bowl of so-called soup. He was always afraid, worried that something terrible had happened to his parents. One day he was taken from his cell to wash himself but given only a minute to get clean. No towel or soap was provided and he was allowed just thirty seconds to urinate in a bucket while a guard stood nearby with a whip in his hand.

Finally, the interrogations began. Phillip found himself standing facing a man called Nerou, a Gestapo interrogator—a man of average height, with black hair, maybe twenty-five years old at most. What had Phillip been involved with and what had his parents done? Phillip said he knew nothing about their activities, and to a great extent this was the truth. To his surprise, Nerou did not beat him and sent Phillip back to his cell after a short while. Both Toquette and Sumner were questioned extensively. Neither proved cooperative and, surprisingly, neither was mistreated. They were to be broken some other way, perhaps, but not now by Nerou. In the chaos and confusion following the Allied invasion, some Gestapo offices were stretched thin, overwhelmed by the sheer number of suspected resistance members who needed to be interrogated.

The Jacksons were then sent forty miles north of Vichy to a German prison based in an old castle in Moulins, where Sumner and Phillip were led down stone steps toward a dungeon. Phillip began to count the steps. He liked counting, had a way with numbers, and by focusing on the count he didn't have to think about what might happen next. He was glad he was still with his father. That was consolation. In all, he counted 118 steps, and then he and his father were placed in the same cell. Phillip grew even weaker from hunger until Sumner pleaded with one of the guards, an old German, stressing that Phillip was sixteen, growing fast, and needed extra food. The guard took pity, managed to get Phillip a double ration, and even allowed Phillip and his father to each send a letter to someone. Phillip wrote to his aunt Tat in Enghien, wondering if his friends had passed their exams.

Toquette also sent news to Tat in Enghien. She had lost her suitcase and had not been able to clean herself properly for six days, but she had not yet started to starve. She had been lucky enough to be given a food package from the Red Cross. Often, the Gestapo did not allow political prisoners like her to receive any packages whatsoever. They were instead to disappear into what the Gestapo called "Nacht und Nebel" ("night and fog"), becoming nonexistent victims, phantoms in the Nazi gulag to be shot and killed when deemed appropriate—certainly before the end of the war, when they could possibly be liberated and then testify at war crimes trials against Helmut Knochen and his kind.

Phillip spent the next three weeks in the same cell as his father, terribly worried about his mother. Father and son talked little but did share snippets of news about the invasion. Whenever new prisoners arrived, Phillip and others gathered around to hear what they knew about the Allies' advance. One day Phillip watched as his father was taken away for more questioning. Again Sumner said nothing of use and finally looked his interrogator in the eye and brazenly asked: "How are things in Normandy?"

Not long after, during a roll call, Phillip caught sight of his mother as she was being moved from one part of the prison to another. At least she was alive and close by.

In her cell, Toquette was somehow able to get hold of a pen and write a postcard and then send it, via the Red Cross, to her sister, Tat. It was dated June 22, 1944.

> *My Sister,*
>
> *You can write to me two pages written very clearly . . .*
> *I am well and my morale is good . . . I saw my son and*
> *husband the other day during an inspection. They are*
> *together and that makes me happy. I have nothing:*
> *toothbrush, etc. . . . . My comrades try to help but they*
> *have very little, too. Please try to send a few things but*
> *no food.*
>
> *Kisses,*
> *Your Sister*

Then they were moving again. At 7:00 a.m. on July 7, 1944, Sumner and Phillip were ordered out of their cell, handcuffed to each other, and—as the Allies fought fiercely to expand their beachhead in Normandy—were ushered out of their dungeon and into the light and taken into a waiting bus, where the guards placed Sumner, who looked all of his fifty-nine years, and Phillip. The bus was old and moved slowly, hour after hour, late into the night before finally coming to a stop beside a wheat field. The prisoners were told they could get off the bus and walk into the field to urinate. Phillip was seated, handcuffed, beside his father, and both agreed to get off and were soon shuffling into the wheat field. Phillip looked around. There was a slight chance of getting away. "Shall we run?" asked Phillip. "No," said his father. "It's no use." He knew they would not get far handcuffed together, and would probably be shot in any case as soon as they tried. So they wearily climbed back onto the bus and a few hours later, around 3 a.m., arrived in Compiègne, where Sumner had been interned in 1942, some fifty miles northwest of Paris. Then they were led to a very different part of the camp reserved for enemies of the Third Reich: a bare barracks that was heavily guarded and overcrowded with men waiting to be sent to Nazi Germany, and infested with vermin, fleas, and lice. But it was an improvement over Moulins: Phillip and his father received Red Cross parcels. They were not beaten, nor did they go hungry.

An SS officer called Captain Heinrich Illers, answering directly to Helmut Knochen and meeting on an almost daily basis with him at 72, Avenue Foch, oversaw and organized each day's deportations from Compiègne. Despite the repeated requests of the Red Cross, that summer he refused to free any of the prisoners or suspend the deportations, having been instructed to hold a firm line by Knochen, described in a British intelligence report that summer as being increasingly "brutal, often drunk, regarded as the most powerful man in France, arrogant, self assured."

As far as Knochen was concerned, prisoners such as the Jacksons were terrorists with whom he was "at war." "My job was to safeguard the security of the German army," he explained, "and I considered myself to be at war against the resistance, just as I was against the Allied armies."

Meanwhile, on July 14, 1944, Toquette was placed on a train headed north. She was determined to remain strong, to survive whatever ordeal lay ahead, and to notify her family of her plight. Again she somehow managed to find a piece of paper and wrote a brief note to her sister, Tat. She may then have thrown the note through the bars of the boxcar window. In any case, it landed near the tracks and, miraculously, someone found it and he or she posted the letter to Tat in Enghien, not daring to write their name on it for fear of reprisal. The letter arrived in Enghien on July 20.

> *My Sister,*
>
> *I am headed for Paris. Jack and Pete left here (Moulins) a week ago . . . I got your package with the small checked dress . . .*
>
> *Your Sister*

By the time Tat read the letter, Toquette had arrived in the outskirts of Paris, where she was taken to Romainville prison, a stone barracks built around a large courtyard surrounded by high walls, the last stop before Germany for many in the resistance. It was Bastille Day and there had been massive and forbidden demonstrations in Paris to celebrate, with more than 100,000 Parisians marching through the city. Notably, the French police had done nothing to stop the marchers, and German soldiers had been forced to fire into the air to disperse protesters.

Toquette was placed in a barrack with several other women, some of them American, all of them members of the resistance. She could hear a distant barking and the sound got louder the next day. It was Allied gunfire. Many of the women believed they would not be deported because the Americans were now so close. "Don't worry too much," the camp commander had recently told some of them. "I don't believe Romainville will be evacuated to Germany. You will be liberated here by your compatriots."

At Compiègne the next day, July 15, 1944, Phillip joined his father in a long line of some two thousand prisoners and walked, under guard, toward the railway station. As he crossed a bridge, Phillip looked down at the gray waters of the Oise River and again thought of escape; but then he saw that the river was not deep enough to jump into without breaking his neck, and so he trudged on. He and his father were placed in a wagon marked with a sign indicating how many cattle it could contain. Then the doors were closed and they were issued a small loaf of black bread and a piece of sausage for the journey. There was precious little water and the heat was oppressive. Then they were moving slowly east toward Germany.

The train stopped after a few hours when it was discovered that seventeen men had escaped from one wagon. Soon they were rolling again, crossing into Germany, passing through a long tunnel. Then came the heart-stopping sound of firing. One of the guards had shot randomly into a carriage of 103 men and killed a man. Others were wounded. To his horror and shock, Phillip saw German guards carrying the first dead man he had ever seen. The whole episode was surreal, something so brutal and inhuman it surely could not be happening. When he had learned that his parents were part of the resistance, it all seemed such a great adventure, an exciting game. No more. Not now. He had never imagined this. He watched, terrified, as the men dumped the corpse by the track, so much carrion for the buzzards and crows, a chilling introduction to the Third Reich.

There was talk that the train was bound for Dachau in Bavaria, Hitler's first concentration camp, erected in 1933, but no one really knew where the train would end up. Sumner remained stoic, making not a single complaint, as if he wanted to set an example for his son, who was by now desperately thirsty. The journey to the east continued—endlessly, it seemed—and in the corner of the boxcar, a pile of feces grew higher. Then the train halted. They had arrived at a labor camp called Neuengamme, ten miles southeast of Hamburg, established in 1938, and where more than 50,000 people would die by the war's end.

SS guards opened the boxcar doors. They were shouting, holding whips and leashes to large dogs, which snarled and barked loudly. Phillip saw the SS begin to whip and punch prisoners as if they were emptying the wagons of useless cattle, ready to be slaughtered, and he and his father were herded into a large basement and ordered to undress. A man wielding what looked like a pair of shears stood near a Slav who was so hirsute that he resembled an ape. The man with the shears held the Slav by his penis and tried to shave around it. They were issued odd clothes and wooden clogs for shoes; a man with a paintbrush splashed stripes down Phillip's and Sumner's backs to indicate they were "political" prisoners, and they were given numbers, to be stitched onto their jackets. Phillip's was 36461. His father's was 36462.

There seemed little chance of escape. Phillip saw that the camp was completely enclosed by high fences of electrified barbed wire. SS men stood in guard towers, manning machine guns. He walked with other prisoners, including his father, toward a barrack. He was wearing old rags and wooden clogs, his head was shaved, and everything he owned had been stolen, including his name; he was now just a number. However, all that he had left was all that he needed: he was in hell, but he was still beside his father.

The following day, July 19, 1944, from her barrack in Romainville, Toquette again wrote to her sister, Tat, in Enghien. Somehow, she managed to get the letter smuggled out of the prison—it would be the last Tat would receive from her:

My Sister,

> *Since the 14th, I am at Romainville camp. I hope to stay here . . . forbidden to write, have visits but I can have a package a month. If you send something be sure I am still here by giving [the prison gate guards]*

each package. . . . Jack and Pete must be together
at Compiègne since July 7, they left Moulins a week
before me. My health and morale are excellent. People
leave here frequently for Bitche in Alsace Lorraine—
a German transit camp . . . no one is sure of their
tomorrow.

FOURTEEN

THE COUP: JULY 20, 1944

KLAUS VON STAUFFENBERG, a tall and handsome thirty-seven-year-old German colonel, stood alone in a bathroom inside Adolf Hitler's Prussian headquarters—the so-called Wolf's Lair. It was 12:26 p.m. on July 20, 1944. Von Stauffenberg activated a bomb inside a briefcase, left the bathroom, and then walked down a long corridor and into a conference room. Hitler sat behind a table, toying with a powerful magnifying glass, his spectacles lying on a map. Stauffenberg placed his brown leather briefcase under the table, a mere six feet from Hitler, then excused himself, mumbling that he had to take an urgent phone call. He slipped out of the room and hurried down a corridor to make his escape.

At 12:42 p.m. there was a massive explosion. Smoke filled the room as splinters and plaster flew everywhere. Stauffenberg heard the explosion as he made his way through a security perimeter. Surely, this time it was all over. By later that afternoon he was in Berlin, where he set about ordering his fellow conspirators to secure the city. At 5:00 p.m. he called fifty-eight-year-old General Carl-Heinrich von Stülpnagel in Paris and told him that he had assassinated Hitler. Stülpnagel went to work carrying out his crucial role in the conspiracy, quickly ordering the 1,200 SS and Gestapo men in Paris to be arrested. The likes of Knochen were, it was assumed, prepared to support Hitler to the last breath. They had, after all, sworn "absolute allegiance" to him. Their motto was *"Unsere Ehre heisst*

Treue" ("Our honor is loyalty"). This "blood oath" was engraved on Knochen's dress dagger and his uniform's belt buckles.

All along the Avenue Foch, Major General Walther Brehmer's men of the 1st Guards Regiment surrounded buildings and hid in bushes in gardens. There was the shrill of a whistle. Trucks and cars moved into position, then another whistle. Hundreds of troops quickly overwhelmed sentries, some of them having fallen asleep that humid evening, and then stormed the Gestapo's headquarters. In his office, a shirt-sleeved SS general Karl Oberg, Helmut Knochen's immediate superior, was talking on the telephone with Otto Abetz, when his adjutant burst in. The adjutant said the commandant of the Paris Security Division, Major General Brehmer, was in the reception room nearby. He was very agitated and demanding to see Oberg.

Oberg carried on his phone conversation. Seconds later two doors into his office burst open. Brehmer stepped over to Oberg's desk and placed his hand on the cradle of the telephone, ending the conversation with Abetz.

Oberg put the receiver down. "What's this about, Mr. Brehmer?"

"Acting on orders of the Military Commander, I am here to place you under arrest."

There was no sign of Knochen at number 72. He had gone to have dinner at the German embassy with an old friend, Karl-Theodor Zeitschel, a specialist in Freemasonry and Jewish affairs in the embassy's political section. As the pair ate, one of Knochen's aides interrupted and told him he was required to return as soon as possible to 72, Avenue Foch.

Otto Abetz later recalled that only one shot was fired as Brehmer and his men arrested the 1,200 Gestapo and SS men in Paris: "An SS sentry had presented arms a little too energetically to Brehmer." One of Brehmer's men shot him on the spot. But, amazingly, there was no bloodbath. Knochen's colleagues on Avenue Foch, including his expert spy-catcher Hans Kieffer, were placed under guard with scandalously little protest. Theodor Dannecker, the "mad sadist" who had been based at Number 31, avoided the roundup, having been dispatched to Hungary that March to annihilate Europe's last remaining Jewish ghettoes. This spectacular lack of opposition to the Paris coup on the part of the SS would not go unnoticed by Himmler and others in Berlin.

Word spread fast through the great hotels of Paris: the reign of the SS "black bastards" was at an end. Political prisoners would be freed as the insurrectionists set about making peace with the Western Allies. Finally, there was real reason to hope. Everyone could breathe easier, including the collaborators, ever more paranoid about how they might be blackmailed or used as pawns by Knochen and his secret army of informers and enforcers. At the École Militaire, headquarters for the German 1st Guards Regiment, Wehrmacht soldiers were already preparing to shoot Oberg and Knochen the following morning: they were piling sandbags high in the courtyard to stop stray bullets.

"At last we're going to finish with the black bastards," said one soldier. "Then we'll soon have peace."

Meanwhile, Knochen, suspecting that something was amiss on Avenue Foch, decided to find his immediate superior, Oberg. It didn't take long for him to learn that Oberg was being held at the Hôtel Continental on Rue de Castiglione, close to the Opéra. He ordered his driver to take him there. As soon as Knochen entered the lavish hotel, its entrance lined with gold-enameled columns, he was placed under guard and led across the deep carpets and beneath several massive crystal chandeliers and taken to a similarly grand suite, where he found Oberg under guard.

A radio played in a corner. Knochen was still dressed in civilian clothes; he was the only man not in uniform. These days, wearing his gray SS uniform other than at formal occasions at the embassy and other protected places was to invite assassination. Clocks struck midnight throughout Paris. The radio continued to play. Then came a sound never to be forgotten. Hitler's voice could be heard on the radio in the hotel suite and throughout Paris, amplified by loudspeakers in other hotels and public places. Electricity had been found for a few minutes so that as many Parisians as possible could listen to the Führer.

Hitler's voice seethed with rage.

"A very small clique of ambitious, wicked, and stupidly criminal officers forged a plot to eliminate me and, along with me, virtually the entire leadership of the Wehrmacht," Hitler declared. But the plot had failed. Hitler had survived the explosion at his headquarters. Now he would carry out savage revenge: "We will settle accounts the way we National Socialists are accustomed to settling them." That usually entailed prolonged torture before being hanged to death from a meat hook.

Meanwhile, fifty-two-year-old Günther Blumentritt, a tall and pale Prussian who was chief of staff to Germany Army Command in the west, arrived at Gestapo headquarters at number 72, Avenue Foch. The first senior SS officers he saw wanted to know why they had been arrested. Clearly, there had been a colossal mistake. Hadn't there? Acutely aware of the immense bloodshed that might occur if the SS in Paris went on the rampage, as Hitler would want, Blumentritt eagerly offered to help reconcile senior Wehrmacht and SS officers. He was delighted when the SS officials at number 72 agreed to go along with his plan."Their attitude was very decent," he recalled, "and they showed a willingness to help in hushing things up."

At 1:30 a.m. Lieutenant General Freiherr von Boineburg-Lengsfeld, the garrison commander of Paris, ordered that the SS and Gestapo be freed, and then made his way to the Hôtel Continental to meet with Oberg and Knochen. He found the pair sitting in a suite, sharing a bottle of brandy, listening to the radio.

Oberg jumped up on seeing the fifty-five-year-old former Panzer division commander, a tall German nobleman in polished riding boots.

Boineburg-Lengsfeld made the "Heil Hitler" salute.

"What damned game is this you're playing?" shouted Oberg.

Boineburg-Lengsfeld said that General Stülpnagel would explain matters himself at the Hôtel Raphael nearby. The equally grand building, with immaculate black-and-white-tiled floors and polished wood-paneled walls, stood on the Avenue Kléber, less than five minutes' walk from Avenue Foch. From its wrought-iron fringed terraces matted in ivy, it was possible to see the Arc de Triomphe a few hundred yards away.

Oberg left with Knochen. They were soon passing through the large bar of the Hôtel Raphael. Expensive drapes hung at the tall windows; a lush red carpet stretched from wall to wall. At one table Stülpnagel was seated, deep in conversation with Otto Abetz, the German ambassador.

Stülpnagel stood up on seeing Oberg. Oberg looked furious, as if he might strike the general, but Abetz quickly intervened.

"What happens in Berlin is one thing," Abetz declared. "Here what matters is that the Normandy battle is raging and so here we Germans must show a united front."

Oberg grudgingly agreed. Although an ardent Nazi, he was also a pragmatist. He had forged excellent relations with several senior Wehrmacht generals in Paris and had actually served in WWI in the same regiment as Stülpnagel. Aides brought over wine and champagne. Glasses were handed around. Corks were popped. The French were good for one thing. Heavy drinking of grand crus ensued.

Knochen remained sober enough to realize that the arrest, without so much as a fistfight, of the entire SS and Gestapo hierarchy on Avenue Foch would not impress the most senior Nazis in Berlin. It would be best, as Otto Abetz suggested, if the SS and the military worked together to cover up their respective failings given that the common enemy was fast advancing on them. Over a million Allied troops were fighting in Normandy, headed toward Paris. There and then Knochen devised a plausible way for everyone to save face. It had all been part of some training operation, a mere "exercise."

No one in Berlin would be totally convinced, least of all Himmler, who was soon anxious to punish Knochen and others for their lack of resolve during the coup. Knochen would not know this, or that Himmler had viewed him as suspect for several months, or that someone close to the Reichsführer-SS in Berlin had turned him against "Dr. Bones." That April, on a visit to France, Himmler had confided his misgivings about Knochen to Oberg himself, complaining that Knochen was "not enough of a soldier and too much of a diplomat." Damning words indeed. Himmler had added that it was not the right time to replace Knochen, but Oberg was to "inculcate" in his urbane deputy a more "military attitude."

The failure of the July plot to kill Hitler had enormous repercussions. The Führer was convinced that he had been spared in order to save the Third Reich, and he began to plan an ingenious counterattack against the Allies that would that December erupt as the Battle of the Bulge, the greatest land battle ever fought by the United States. The coup's failure also removed what little trust Hitler had for the Wehrmacht's high command. More than ever, he would rely on the SS to perform crucial tasks. In Paris the change was immediately clear. Ordinary troops on the street had to give all officers, especially the SS, the Nazi salute. Loyalty to Hitler was all that counted.

The Gestapo and SS were now, without question, the masters of all Paris. Knowing their tenure would be short, they were as determined as every other German occupier to savor their last nights in the City of Light. Knochen and his colleagues were confined no more to the likes of the One Two Two brothel and a five-story nightclub run by Knochen's man Henri Lafont where Lafont's Jewish-German lover, a beauty called Carmen Palma, crooned "The Man I Love" by Gershwin. Le Tout-Paris belonged to the SS, as did Maxim's; La Tour d'Argent; Le Boeuf sur le Toit; Le Fouquet's; Sheherazade; the cabaret

Lesbos on Rue Sainte-Anne, where the sultry lesbian Suzy Solidor sang "Lili Marleen" in French; L'Amiral, where Django Reinhardt, a gentle Gypsy giant, played exquisite guitar; and Le Beaulieu, where Edith Piaf and Yves Montand filled the house every night. More and more of the unsmiling men in gray with the twin lightning bolts on their lapels could also be seen in the Ritz, perhaps the last great bastion of decorum in occupied Paris. The hotel's manager noticed how some senior Wehrmacht officers on the General Staff would "turn pale" when Knochen's colleagues entered the dining room.

To keep up appearances, following the aborted coup in Paris, the Gestapo began to investigate more than a thousand German officers in France. But neither Oberg nor Knochen, wanting to maintain good relations with the German military command, pushed hard for the revenge Hitler demanded. Maintaining security was critical, and the German occupiers could no longer afford to be divided. Ten of the July 20 conspirators based in Paris were eventually executed, hundreds jailed, but little was done to pursue most of the senior figures still at large. Both Oberg and Knochen, increasingly flustered by news of the Allied advance in Normandy, were much more interested in waging war on the last remaining threat to their power in Paris: de Gaulle's secret army, waiting patiently in the shadows for the right moment to strike.

FIFTEEN

AVE MARIA

A BLACK MARIA pulled up outside 84, Avenue Foch. Inside was a striking young British woman with a fierce intensity in her eyes: twenty-three-year-old SOE agent Violette Szabo, described by a colleague as a "dark-haired slip of mischief" with a cockney accent that made the five-foot-three-inch Paris-born F Section operative all the more impish. She was also the mother of a two-year-old called Tania, whom she desperately missed. She had been dropped into France on her second mission on June 8, the deadliest shot her training school had ever produced, just forty-eight hours after D-Day. In a fierce battle with SS soldiers on June 10, she had sprained her ankle while trying to escape and been captured and then handed over to the Gestapo. It was now August 10, 1944.

She looked through the small grille at the back of the Gestapo van, catching glimpses of the gardens, statues, and neat riding paths of Avenue Foch. She guessed where Knochen's men were taking her: the place where the Gestapo interrogated their prisoners. In London her SOE masters had told her all about the place. It was where Knochen's men tortured young women like her. The van moved along a smaller inner road that gave access to the large mansions on the northern side of Avenue Foch. It pulled up outside number 84. Heavily armed guards pulled back a black gate and the van swept into an underground tunnel and then emerged in a courtyard.

The courtyard had a door that led to an elegant central staircase.

On the ground floor were Knochen's agents in charge of Belgium. She was escorted up the stairs, past the first floor where his French agents worked, and then up more flights, to the third floor, where Knochen's radio experts had played the "Funkspiel" so brilliantly, transmitting back to London on seized radio sets. She was led through doors into a passage on the fourth floor. Here was Knochen's counterintelligence domain: Gestapo department IV E.

There was a large office directly to her right, next to a toilet. She was placed in a room nearby. A man entered. He looked to be in his twenties and was wearing an elegant suit. His attitude was unnerving, for he was assured and polite, a professional. She said nothing during the interrogation and was soon taken away, but not long after they brought her back from one of the small cells that had served as maids' quarters before the war, and the suave young man stood in front of her once more. He asked questions and still she said nothing. This time men brought in torture implements, the standard Avenue Foch equipment, including riding whips, truncheons, and pliers, which were shown to her.

"Will you answer now?" asked the well-dressed young man.

"I won't. I won't."

The German motioned to assistants, and she was soon in agony. Now would she talk?

"I won't. I won't."

They tried again and still she gave nothing away, and the more they tortured her, the less responsive she became, as if the pain sealed her lips tighter, until it was clearly a waste of time to inflict more. "I have given you your chance," the young German said. "As you won't speak, there seems to be nothing left but the firing squad."

One of Szabo's torturers offered to help her walk from the room. "Don't touch me," she hissed as she limped back to her cell. Szabo was the last known SOE agent to be interrogated at 84, Avenue Foch. She had no idea when she would be called back to be tortured again, or if she would leave her cell next time only to be taken to the nearby

Bois de Boulogne and shot. She was in agony but also elated, because she had not talked and had given no names.

Szabo was not called back to the torture room. She could sense that all was not well among Knochen's men: they were nervous, quick to anger, knowing the Allies were fast approaching and would soon be in Paris. But it was the French they feared most. Pent-up rage, long-repressed emotions of shame and humiliation, were set to explode to the surface. The resistance could smell blood, and not just German. Miniature coffins, small enough to fit through letter-boxes, were being delivered to high-profile collaborators on Avenue Foch and elsewhere. Even the most naïve knew that their days were numbered. They would soon become the hunted. Should they flee to the Reich with their German friends, or stay and risk the wrath of the vengeful?

Later that day, Violette Szabo was removed from 84, Avenue Foch, and taken to Romainville prison, where she was placed in a section with other women with just as much pluck and spirit as herself, including Toquette Jackson.

SINCE ARRIVING at Romainville, Toquette had become close to several other prominent members of the resistance. They included Virginia d'Albert-Lake, a spunky twenty-four-year-old American from Dayton, Ohio, who had married a Frenchman before the war and then, with her husband, helped more than a hundred Allied airmen escape France before being arrested that June. Another remarkable American was forty-eight-year-old Lucienne Dixon, who had worked at the Elizabeth Arden salon in Paris before joining the resistance. Then there was thirty-seven-year-old Maisie Renault, the strikingly attractive sister of Gilbert Renault, code-named "Colonel Rémy," arguably the most important figure in the French resistance. Her youngest sister, twenty-year-old Isabelle, had been arrested with her after they had been betrayed to the Gestapo in 1942. None of these women talked about their roles or actions with each other: they knew the Gestapo was more than likely to have planted spies at Romainville, and no one could ever be fully trusted, so they avoided all conversation that could incriminate anyone.

The day that Szabo arrived, these women had been told to gather in the courtyard and to get their bags packed. Then they were ordered to unpack and then pack again. Some of their fellow prisoners were understandably on edge, dreading the hour when they would finally be deported to Nazi Germany, but others were surprisingly buoyant and sang to keep their spirits up, as if their voices alone could speed the Allied advance so they could be freed.

As the women sang, an overweight sixty-one-year-old Swedish diplomat with a weak heart was doing all he could to save them. Raoul Nordling had been born in Paris, had attended the same school as Phillip Jackson, and, as Sweden's most senior diplomat in Paris, was working closely with the Red Cross to obtain the release of prisoners like Toquette and her friends in Romainville. Four days earlier, on August 6, he had visited Fresnes prison. The sight of so many brave men and women about to be deported affected him profoundly, and he was determined, with the help of contacts in German intelligence, to free them or at least prevent them from being sent to Germany.

At some point that day, August 10, 1944, Nordling met with two men who had agreed to help him in his quest to save the thousands crowding Romainville and Fresnes. One of the men was a veteran Abwehr agent who went by the name of Emil "Bobby" Bender, around fifty years old, fluent in several languages, always to be seen wearing tailored suits, close-shaven, with a youthful air despite his almost white hair. Bender was a good friend of the head of the Abwehr in Paris, a Lieutenant Colonel Arnold Garthe, based at the Hôtel Lutetia on the Boulevard Raspail. Thanks to such connections, Bender had acquired several identities, all of which were supported by superbly forged documentation, and moved freely around Paris in military and diplomatic circles. The only place Bender dared not venture was Avenue Foch, having had several "disagreeable" run-ins with Knochen's men at number 72 who believed the Abwehr had been fatally compromised and infiltrated by double agents, among them Bobby Bender.

Nordling's other contact that day was the Goélette agent Erich Posch-Pastor von Camperfeld, who was now also working for British intelligence, in all likelihood MI6, and still maintained excellent connections with senior German staff officers in Paris. "You met him everywhere," Nordling recalled, "among the most powerful Germans and the French high society." An Austrian colleague, Fritz Molden, recalled that Camperfeld, who insisted on being called Rickey, was a flamboyant and proud Austrian who sometimes would "place around his neck a green ribbon with a gorgeous Tyrolese eagle, which the lords and yeomen of the Tyrol were wont to wear on ceremonial occasions." In spring 1943, Camperfeld had helped Nordling secure the release of a French friend who had been arrested by the Gestapo. He had done so with the assistance of Bobby Bender. These days the pair was arranging for Nordling to meet various German officials who might be able to help in his quest to save political prisoners still in Paris.

It was also that day, August 10, 1944, that Toquette had a surprise visitor at Romainville, thanks to the intervention of the Swiss Consul in Paris who had somehow discovered that Toquette, who had dual American and Swiss nationality, was in Gestapo custody. Her sister, Tat, was escorted inside the fort and taken to a room where she found Toquette. Tat showed Toquette the letter that Phillip had written to her from Moulins. It must have been an intensely emotional experience, for Tat began to cry. Toquette told her to stop. Tat asked what had happened to Sumner and Phillip, and Toquette said she did not know. Tat would later recall her sister being "full of courage" as they parted.

That evening the women of Romainville sang once more.

———

IT WAS the eve of the Feast of Assumption, August 14, 1944. In Normandy, the fighting that had raged since June 6 was reaching a decisive stage at the Falaise Pocket, where the remnants of two of Hitler's finest armies, the Seventh Army and the Fifth Panzer Army, were about to be surrounded and then destroyed. This would finally open the way to Paris for the Allies.

Tomorrow would be a significant day in the Christian calendar: the commemoration of the death of Mary and her assumption into heaven, before her body could begin to decompose. It would mark the Blessed Virgin's passing into eternal life.

That evening, as the muffled boom of Allied guns grew even louder in the distance, Toquette and the other women gathered in Romainville's central courtyard. Some picked a few wildflowers growing amid the trampled grass and placed them on a makeshift altar, which would be the centerpiece for their celebration of the Assumption.

The German guard, named Kratz, was large and ugly. He spotted the women and loped across the courtyard toward them, nodding slowly, as if to some slow beat, shaking a large bunch of keys.

Kratz looked directly at the women.

"No Mass tomorrow morning, no Mass."

The women knew that the abbot of Lilas was supposed to celebrate Mass in Romainville the next morning. If there was to be no Mass, that could mean only one thing: they were headed for Germany tomorrow.

They looked afraid.

Kratz was delighted.

Here was the embodiment of Nazism, utterly unevolved, sociopathic, sadistic, taking perverse pleasure in women's terror. He reminded one of the women of an orangutan, with his huge hands and frame. When not patrolling the courtyard, he worked in the kitchens and, it was thought, as a torturer for one of Helmut Knochen's men.

He looked so very happy.

"No Mass," he hissed through clenched teeth. "Everyone will go on the transport to Germany. . . . All to die. . . . All to die."

He belly-laughed.

The Allies were only twenty miles away. And they were to leave tomorrow?

"Do you mock us?" said Maisie Renault. "The Allies are at Rambouillet."

Kratz came to a sudden halt and clasped his hands. He looked at the women. He knew what awaited them in Germany. He began to laugh, louder than before. For a few more seconds he stood and stared hard at the women before ambling away, jangling his keys like some Dark Ages jailer.

"All to die. . . . All to die."

Toquette and the other women returned to their barracks and began to sing once more. Few slept at all well that night. The following morning, August 15, 1944, they waited in their dormitory. They had been told they would be taken to the rail yards in city buses, but the buses were late. While they waited, they sang once more, their voices filled with intense emotion.

The morning was sunny and already hot when they heard the call to leave. Toquette and the other women who had become like sisters to her—Maisie Renault, Lucienne Dixon, and Virginia d'Albert-Lake—wanted to make sure they were not separated during the journey to Germany. It was crucial to be together. Older women stayed close to younger ones. Toquette, the eldest in the group, was right beside Maisie Renault, Maisie's younger sister, Isabelle, and Lucienne Dixon, and several other Frenchwomen.

They sang while they waited for the buses. It was a way to keep their spirits up. Then someone said they had to be quiet.

There was a narrow window. One of the women in Toquette's barracks looked through it and could see people walking on a hillside adjoining the fort.

The woman called out, "Hello over there! Listen to me."

The people walking stopped to listen.

"All the prisoners of Romainville are leaving," called the woman in a clear, strong voice. "Warn the Maquis [the resistance]. Stop the train. Do you hear? Stop the train."

There was a woman among the walkers outside. She waved a white handkerchief. She had heard. Perhaps she would act on her information.

In the barracks, it was quiet once more.

So this was it.

All to die. All to die.

A thin young woman, a Hungarian, leaned against a bunk for support. She could stand the silence no longer.

Her voice was beautiful as she began to sing the Ave Maria. It was August 15, after all, a holy day, the Feast of the Assumption, the day the Virgin Mary had gone to heaven. Other women prayed quietly to the Virgin Mary. It was as if they were sharing their fears with her.

The Hungarian woman continued to sing:

> Hail Mary, full of grace, the Lord is with thee.
> Blessed art thou among women, and blessed is the fruit
> of thy womb, Jesus.
> Holy Mary, Mother of God, pray for us sinners, now and
> in the hour of our death.
> Amen.

Many of the women were close to tears.

Others remained outwardly calm. They refused to feel sorry for themselves.

Nothing will prevent the certain advance of the Allies in the fu-

ture, thought Maisie Renault. *Nothing will prevent the Germans from being conquered.*

The women started to sing again. Then they heard the sound of buses' engines.

Kratz was back. His massive hands shook his bunch of keys.

Toquette and her friends left the barracks and climbed aboard the buses. They were soon being taken through the prison, formerly a fort. There was an exceptional view of Paris, parched and dusty, stretching toward the hazy horizon to the southeast. The women crossed the city, passing through familiar streets, faces pressed to the buses' windows, looking at women just like them waiting in food lines, about to be liberated. The buses stopped a few miles to the north of Romainville and the women realized they were at a freight station called Pantin. Before them was a train with cattle cars. They were escorted onto the *quai aux bestiaux*—the livestock platform. There were guttural cries, the sound of boots, shouting. Germans. Then Toquette was boarding a boxcar. The floor was covered in dirt. There was no straw. She was crammed next to her friends among ninety-two women, the number allotted to each cattle car. Then the door was closed.

The sun rose high above the city. It was another gloriously warm day. There would be thousands of young Parisians swimming once more in the Seine, the quays along the Île Saint-Louis and by the Pont Neuf filled with skinny, chattering sunbathers.

The sun began to beat down on the metal roofs of the cattle car, sending temperatures inside soaring. One window crossed with barbed wire served as the sole ventilation. Toquette and her friends were soon gasping for breath. There were 2,104 men and 400 women in the transport, also waiting for the train to move, for the waiting to end.

Women near Toquette began to take off their clothes. As the minutes passed, more garments were discarded. Many were soon down to their underwear, their bodies covered in a fine film of perspiration. When they moved, some women slid and slipped against each other's slick bodies. Others fainted. In some cars, they collapsed and died. In a wagon full of men, one prisoner could feel a dry tongue licking him. A fellow prisoner was sucking up the sweat dripping down the small of his back.

The Germans were walking up and down outside, their boots heavy in the heat. At one car where the door was still open, the women saw a large Ukrainian SS man, red-faced and sweaty. He was familiar to some of the women. He had supervised their torture, making sure they were roughed up good and proper. It was as if, re-membered one of the women, he had arrived at Pantin to wish them bon voyage—to see off a "herd of cattle on which he [had] stamped his brand, now being shipped to the slaughterhouse."

On a platform a few yards away, another man, his shoulders slumped, walked away and then out of the station and to a nearby café. It was silver-haired Bobby Bender, the Abwehr agent who had in recent days worked frantically with Raoul Nordling and Erich Posch-Pastor von Camperfeld to stop the deportation and have the prison-ers handed over to the Red Cross. Bender had just tried to fool the SS commander at Pantin into delaying the train. But the SS officer was having none of it. Bender knew that the only hope now was Raoul Nordling, due that evening to meet with Otto Abetz and Pierre Laval at Laval's official residence, the Hôtel Matignon, at 57, Rue de Va-renne. It was still possible to stop the train if both would agree to it.

There was another cause for hope, even at this eleventh hour: a teenage boy cycling frantically in the outskirts of Paris toward a village called Nanteuil-Saâcy. He had an important message for the head of the resistance in the village, which lay on the train line from Paris to Nazi Germany.

At any cost, by any means, cut the rail line.

It was around midday on August 15. From somewhere in Paris a resistance worker, huddled over a radio transmitter, tapped out an urgent message. He could not know that Knochen's radio experts were no longer at large, driving around in vans camouflaged as delivery trucks, loaded with tracking devices, and no longer walking the streets even on warm days wearing large overcoats that concealed their detectors.

The resistance worker tapped away on his radio set, sending a coded message. Thankfully, it arrived in London and was soon read by some of de Gaulle's intelligence staff.

Germans organized evacuation detainees Paris prisons . . . by rail via Metz Nancy. Fear general massacre during trip. Take all measures possible sabotage transport.

The afternoon stretched on endlessly, it must have seemed, to the men and women caged in the cattle cars at Pantin. Finally the light began to fade. At 9:30 p.m., while Toquette and the others still waited in the rail yard, Raoul Nordling walked into the Hôtel Matignon for his appointment with Pierre Laval and Otto Abetz.

The situation in Paris had completely changed in a matter of hours. The police had been on strike since the morning. There was no electricity or gas. Nordling could sense a fast-growing anxiety. After four years of increasing repression at the hands of the SS and Gestapo, uncontrollable forces were about to step boldly from the shadows to the barricades, to fight at last in the city's streets.

Laval's official residence, the Hôtel Matignon, just a few hundred yards from Josée and René de Chambrun's home, was in darkness. A few ushers groped around in the corridors holding candles. Nordling found his way to the building's antechamber with the aid of a flashlight. A dark-suited, chain-smoking Laval greeted Nordling and led him to his office where a paraffin lamp cast long, flickering shadows.

Abetz was not there yet and so Nordling and Laval talked politics for a while. Laval said he had wanted to reconvene the French parliament so that a new government could direct France once Marshal

Pétain had given up power. But it had not been possible to obtain agreement from the leader of the Senate.

Thirty-eight-year-old Otto Abetz finally arrived. He was also carrying a flashlight.

A few days before, Nordling had implored Abetz to show leniency toward the political prisoners, citing the case of the director of one of Paris's finest universities, arrested by the Gestapo for refusing to hand over names of students thought to have joined the resistance. At that meeting Abetz had revealed his true nature, dropping all pretense to diplomacy, and had ranted at Nordling, telling him the best thing to do with political prisoners was simply to shoot them.

"That college is a nest of assassins!" Abetz had shouted. "It should be torched. The Gestapo is much too soft on these types. I looked into the case of this director and you can rest assured he won't be released."

Nordling had persisted. He begged Abetz to release the college's director as well the thousands of other political prisoners held in Paris jails. But Abetz coldly turned Nordling away. "There is nothing left to do but kill them all," Abetz said.

Now, in the flickering gaslight of Laval's half-abandoned office, Nordling beseeched both men once more to show mercy. It was not enough to improve the conditions of deportation—to place fewer people in the cattle cars so prisoners could at least lie down. The transports should be stopped altogether. Nordling then gave his word that the SS guards at Compiègne, Pantin, and Romainville would be given safe passage and would not be prosecuted for war crimes.

Abetz was evasive, unwilling to give Nordling a straight answer. Nordling continued his entreaties, but both Abetz and Laval soon lost patience and told Nordling they had much more urgent things to discuss. The fate of the political prisoners, the women squeezed into a cattle car at Pantin, dying from dehydration, had nothing to do with them. It was entirely a Gestapo matter, not the concern of Laval or the German embassy.

Nordling pointed out that Abetz and Laval might want to consider their long-term futures. It might be a good idea to curry favor with the advancing Allies. They might want to gain a little goodwill or they could be punished severely.

"So you think Germany has lost the war?" asked Abetz.

"Whatever happens," replied Nordling, "I don't think it's going to turn out too well for your forces, Ambassador."

At Pantin the train still stood on the tracks. There was the sound of couplings clanking against each other. The cattle cars began to creak and shudder as the slack in the couplings was taken up.

The transport was leaving. Half a dozen women's bodies had been dumped beside the tracks. They had died of the heat.

Toquette heard singing. It was faint at first.

> Arise children of the fatherland.
> The day of glory has arrived.
> Against us tyranny's bloody standard is raised.

It was France's national anthem, "La Marseillaise."

The singing grew louder as it spread from one cattle car to another. Soon defiant voices could be heard from all the cattle cars as they clanked and jerked slowly into the darkness beyond the Pantin freight station, filled with heroes of France's resistance.

> Listen to the sound in the fields.
> The howling of these fearsome soldiers.
> They are coming into our midst.
> To cut the throats of your sons and consorts . . .

A railroad worker was watching. He was seen to be crying as the singing grew faint and the train finally disappeared into the humid night.

SIXTEEN

DAYS OF GLORY

THE PYRES WERE burning again. On the Avenue Foch, the men in gray SS uniforms and those in plainclothes, having received surprise orders from Heinrich Himmler to abandon Paris, were busy emptying filing cabinets, piling files onto the fires that sent smoke drifting across the sun-bleached lawns and riding paths. At number 72, where Knochen had been based for more than 1,500 days, vital documents were being destroyed lest they fall into the hands of Allied intelligence. Uncharacteristically, so rushed and stressed was Knochen, knowing the Allies were only a few days from Paris, he forgot about a cache of incriminating documents held at another Gestapo address.

That morning of August 17, although frantically busy, the Paris Gestapo still had time to ensure that the last remaining Jews at Drancy, fifty-one unfortunate souls, were sent to Auschwitz, joining 59,000 others sent to death camps from Drancy during Knochen's time in Paris. Fewer than 2,500 of that total would return. It was a deadly day for both Jews and patriots. In the Bois de Boulogne, a few hundred yards from the Avenue Foch, thirty-five resistance members who had planned to raid a German armory but instead walked into a trap, having been betrayed, were gunned down by Knochen's colleague Friedrich Berger, and some of the Rue de la Pompe gang of mercenary killers and thieves. Just to make sure they were dead,

Berger's men had tossed grenades at the bullet-riddled bodies, which were later found near a beautiful waterfall.

That same day, after learning that explosives had been placed at monuments, buildings, and bridges, Pierre Taittinger, the mayor of Paris, met with von Dietrich von Choltitz, the city's military governor. Just two weeks before, the stolid, gray-haired fifty-year-old Prussian general had been ordered by Hitler to crush all attempts at an uprising. When it came to destroying all opposition, Hitler had added, Choltitz would be able to count on all the military force that could possibly be provided. With around 20,000 men at his disposal, he was to hold the City of Light to the bitter end. There could be no retreat. All the great monuments and bridges were to be blown up, and Paris would be left as a vast ruin. Taittinger begged Choltitz to spare Paris. Was Choltitz to go down in history as a monster—the barbarian who had destroyed the most beautiful city in the world? Or would the world remember him as the good German who saved it?

The following morning, August 18, Knochen left Avenue Foch with suitcases hastily packed. The grand rooms he had occupied for so long—from the very outset of the German occupation—with their high ceilings and glittering crystal chandeliers and wonderful views were empty, the odd innocuous document strewn across the scuffed parquet floors. The only reminder of so much suffering was the desperate graffiti on the walls of the cells on the top floors at number 84, where SOE agents like Violette Szabo had been abused but not broken.

Knochen quit Paris after four years as he had arrived, surrounded by his most loyal cronies in a convoy of fast cars. His immediate superior, SS general Karl Oberg, had left his private residence at 57, Boulevard Lannes, a hundred yards from Avenue Foch, exactly as he had found it and had even insisted on handing over the keys to the concierge in person.

Knochen and his fellow Gestapo officers arrived later on August

18 at Vittel, a spa town some 250 miles to the east. It was an ignominious retreat for Knochen, along roads clogged with German
trucks and other staff cars also fleeing far from the onrushing Allies,
among whom General George Patton's Third Army was making as-
tonishing progress, covering sometimes fifty miles a day, hampered
only by ever-growing supply problems and shortages of gasoline.
Vittel was so very far from the action, and Knochen found it impossible to turn his back completely on Paris. It had gotten under his
skin, marked him, utterly seduced him, and was impossible to fully
abandon. On August 20, already wistful, he sent an elite group of
agents back the way he had come, ordering them to stay in the city as
long as possible. They were to send him regular radio reports, updat-
ing him on the progress of the Allies. One of Knochen's most trusted
men led the group, which comprised four cars of agents and a car
with a radio, eleven men in all, including five Frenchmen.

They found a city fast descending into bloody chaos. Fighting had
broken out between members of the French resistance and pockets
of Germans all across Paris. The resistance had strength in numbers
but was woefully short of weapons—a deliberate ploy of the Allies,
who had feared that the communists, if heavily armed, would ignite
a nationwide revolution. In fact, the resistance did not have the firepower to take a single one of the Germans' many heavily fortified
positions. The key question for all was how hard the Germans would
fight to keep the city. Would they battle to the last man, as Hitler had
ordered, or would they give up before all Paris was destroyed? It was
still anyone's guess.

THE SUN was blazing yet again. It was August 20, 1944, when the
cattle train pulled into a yard in Weimar in Nazi Germany. An exhausted and thirsty Toquette and the other women were let off the
trains and allowed to breathe some fresh air and stretch their limbs

for a while. Some women took the opportunity to question some of the guards.

"Will we be able to keep our own clothes, or will we have to wear uniforms?"

"You'll keep your own clothes."

"Do they shave women's heads in that camp?"

"Of course not. That's only for severe punishment."

"Will we have to work?"

"No, only minor chores."

The women were ordered back into the boxcars. The train moved slowly beneath a pitiless sun. Two days later it finally came to a halt.

A sign read: FURSTENBERG. They were around sixty miles north of Berlin. It was almost noon. Again the sun glared down on the women.

"This is our destination," someone said, "the camp at Ravensbruck."

It was the biggest of its kind in Nazi Europe, spread across swampy marshland, surrounded by high walls topped by electrified barbed wire, and had the dubious distinction of being the largest prison in history solely for women. When opened in 1939, it had been designed to hold around 7,000 women, and that late August of 1944, as with most concentration camps in Germany, it was vastly overcrowded. More than 40,000 women had been crammed into wooden huts, sleeping six to a bunk in lice-infested straw. Fewer than 12,000 of them would be alive at war's end.

The doors to the wagons were opened. Light streamed into them, blinding some of the women. Outside stood the SS with hard, angry faces, wearing the dreaded SS runes on their collars. Ordered from the cars, the women were made to get into groups of five as female SS guards, wearing jackboots and black uniforms, got to work, whipping, kicking, punching, welcoming Toquette and her fellow prisoners to the Ravensbruck regime.

Toquette was ordered to line up and then formed part of a long column that marched down a dusty road, past pine trees, over cobblestones, past neat homes, where German children and their mothers watched them from the gardens. It was very hot, an effort to walk, and then they were climbing a hill. Toquette could see large houses, long lawns, and yet more children playing. Some mothers alongside Toquette were reminded of their own children.

To Toquette's right was a large lake. She marched down a hill, past flower beds, neatly tended, to a green gate with high portals and beyond that to a long, low barrack, linked to others by a coal-dust pathway. Then she saw some of the inmates, their heads shaved, barely human, wearing blue-and-gray-striped skirts, few of them even half her age, so haggard, emaciated, open sores on their bare legs.

She was exhausted after a week of sleepless nights and travel, and weak from thirst and hunger, and now she was made to stand in a row and wait. Women cried out for water and an SS soldier walked back and forth, inspecting them, all that afternoon, forcing them to stand in the bright sunlight. She could smell death: there was a morgue close by beyond some barbed wire.

Finally, the women were taken into a brightly lit room. Everything of value was taken from them. Then Toquette was ordered to lie down on a table and examined between her legs to make sure she had not hidden anything in her vagina or anus. Next she had her head shaved and was taken to a shower block and made to stand in the nude, humiliated before leering SS men. Other older women looked acutely embarrassed by their nakedness.

The SS had taken everything from them. Toquette had nothing from her previous life: no hair, no clothes, no letters or photographs, not a single thing to remind her of Sumner or Phillip, whose lives she had risked for France.

———

PARIS WAS on the brink. On August 22, two days after Toquette arrived in Ravensbruck, General von Choltitz received an order from Hitler: "Paris is to be transformed into a pile of rubble. The commanding general [Choltitz] must defend the city to the last man, and should die, if necessary, under ruins."

Later that day Choltitz talked with General Hans Speidel, whose office had passed on Hitler's order to turn Paris into a vast charnel house.

"I thank you for your excellent order," Choltitz told Speidel.

"Which order, General?"

"The demolition order, of course. Here's what I have done. I've had three tons of explosives brought into Notre-Dame, two tons into the Invalides, a ton into the Chambre des Députés. I'm just about to order that the Arc de Triomphe be blown up to provide a clear field of fire."

Speidel sighed deeply.

"I'm acting under your orders, correct, my dear Speidel?"

Speidel hesitated.

"Yes, General."

"It was you who gave the order, right?"

"It wasn't me," Speidel replied angrily, "but the Führer who ordered it!"

Choltitz shot back: "Listen, it was you who transmitted this order and who will have to answer to history." Choltitz calmed down. "I'll tell you what else I've ordered," added Choltitz. "The Madeleine and the Opéra will be destroyed. As for the Eiffel Tower, I'll knock it down in such a manner that it can serve as an antitank barrier in front of the destroyed bridges."

Speidel suddenly realized that Choltitz was not being serious. He had no intention of being remembered by history as the destroyer of Paris.

Speidel sighed with relief.

"Ah! General, how fortunate we are that you are in Paris!"

The next day, August 23, several of Helmut Knochen's men returned to Paris on a reconnaissance mission. The Allies were now almost at the gates of the city in the west. The situation was so tense that Knochen's agents feared being lynched as they carefully approached the Port de Vincennes, in the eastern outskirts, but then dared go no farther and quickly retreated to a village outside the city.

There was even worse news for Knochen from Berlin. In Vittel, as he monitored events in Paris from afar, he received a communication from Heinrich Himmler, supreme head of the SS, a man whose father had like Knochen's been a strict bourgeois schoolmaster. Himmler was furious. He wanted to know why Knochen had let himself be arrested on July 20, the night of the attempted coup against Hitler. Knochen was a coward, a traitor. Worse followed: Knochen was informed that he was being stripped of his rank and would be posted to the Eastern Front as a private in a frontline antitank unit. It was a swift and utterly unexpected fall from grace. So long as Knochen had stayed in Paris, he had played a useful role. Having departed, it was obvious his superiors no longer had much use for him. The man who had so ably protected Knochen in the past, Reinhard Heydrich, was long gone.

Himmler may also have become aware of some of Knochen's off-the-record activities in Paris, including his use of a private army of criminals such as Henri Lafont. According to one intelligence report, Lafont had somehow survived the last few months of German occupation because he had been able, of all things, to turn the tables on his master and actually blackmail Knochen. He had then exerted a "special influence" over Knochen because of an incident in late 1943, around the same time that Lafont had been forming a Brigade Nord Africaine, which consisted of Arabs from North Africa who were to fight "terrorists"—the resistance—in central and southern France. Knochen had ordered Lafont to murder a French aristocrat, the Duke of Ayen, but Knochen was unaware that the duke's wife had approached no less than Himmler himself and pleaded with him to intervene. Knochen had sent the duke to his death in Bergen-Belsen anyway. Lafont had then been quick to warn Knochen that in case he had any ideas about also getting rid of Lafont himself, he had better think twice: Lafont would make sure Himmler knew what Knochen had done with the Duke of Ayen, whom Himmler had wanted to be spared.

Knochen had indeed fallen far. He was now to be dispatched to the Armageddon in the East, to confront the Red Army, which since June 22 had surged west, destroying three German armies— the greatest defeat for the Germans of the war. Most of the western Soviet Union had been freed. The Red Army was fighting toward Berlin itself, having reached Poland. German losses in the East, not to mention Normandy, had been staggering that summer: more than half a million men dead or wounded—higher than the losses at Verdun in 1916, where Knochen's father had fought and been injured. Now it would be Knochen's turn to see actual frontline combat. He knew he would be lucky to come back alive. Indeed, serving on an antitank crew on the Eastern Front, which would undoubtedly make Knochen's father proud, was tantamount to signing his own death warrant.

AT DAWN, the bells had started to ring out across Paris. The sun seemed to rise in a rush. There was not a cloud in the sky. Parisians looked at their watches, counting down the last minutes of living by Berlin time. Women pulled out their best dresses; others retrieved handcrafted tricolors and bottles hidden from the Boche. It was August 25, the feast of Saint Louis, patron saint of France. The Allies could not have chosen a better time to arrive.

Around five thousand German troops remained in central Paris, manning key strongpoints, but far too few in number to hold up the Allies for long. More than five hundred Parisians had died in recent days in street fighting that had forced the Germans to retreat into bunkers and other fortifications at the heart of the city. At the Hôtel Meurice, General von Choltitz now waited anxiously to surrender to uniformed representatives of the Allies—not the resistance, who might deliver swift justice.

At nine o'clock, French troops passed through the Porte d'Orléans. Minutes later a dense crowd swarmed around the first Frenchmen to have fought their way into the city, waving bouquets of flowers. Women climbed aboard jeeps and kissed their liberators passionately.

"Vive de Gaulle!" they cried. *"Vive Leclerc!"*

Others shouted over and over again, *"Merci, merci, merci!"*

For many, it was the most joyous day of their lives. All the bottled-up emotions of the last few years flooded out. No one was ashamed to weep.

It was around 11:00 a.m. when troops with Lieutenant Colonel Paul de Langlade's spearhead from the 2nd Armored Division rolled in tanks, followed by jeeps, past the Lycée Janson de Sailly, Phillip Jackson's old school, and then north along the Rue de la Pompe, where Friedrich Berger had committed his many crimes, to the Avenue Foch.

Crowds all along the route swarmed around the tanks, marked with the Cross of Lorraine. Children clung to the Shermans' cannons as young women in summer dresses draped themselves around beaming young Frenchmen, their cheeks soon checkered with bright lipstick. There were none of Knochen's men standing guard outside numbers 84 and 72. There was no resistance as the Shermans trundled toward the Place de l'Étoile on the 1,525th day of German occupation.

At the Étoile a group of Germans were soon taken prisoner. One of them threw a grenade at his captors. Soldiers took cover around the Arc de Triomphe and then the German prisoners were machine-gunned to death in retaliation. Their bodies lay in the open, beneath the hot sun, as far in the distance, down the Champs-Élysées, French soldiers and Americans from the 4th Division fired on German holdouts around the Place de la Concorde.

In the Place du Palais Bourbon, just across the Seine, there was also heavy firing. A French officer waved his men forward as he headed past René de Chambrun's home at number 6 and then liberators entered the Chambre des Députés, the seat of French democracy before 1940.

At his headquarters almost a thousand miles away, in Rastenburg, Hitler received an urgent report.

> *The Allies are in the heart of Paris, attacking strongpoints with artillery and infantry.*

Hitler turned on General Alfred Jodl. He had demanded that Paris be defended to the very last bullet. The jewel of the Third Reich, which he had visited that glorious, unforgettable sultry June morning in 1940 more than four years ago, was being stolen from him. Beyond Paris lay the Third Reich. Berlin would be the last prize.

"Jodl!" shouted Hitler. *"Brennt Paris?* Is Paris burning? Jodl! I want to know—is Paris burning? Is Paris burning right now, Jodl?"

Jodl had no answer.

Back in Paris, a fireman called Captain Lucien Sarniguet was soon racing up the 1,750 steps of the Eiffel Tower. He had last made the climb on June 13, 1940, to lower the flag from the top of the tower. Two other men were now trying to beat him to the honor of putting the tricolor in its rightful place once more. Almost at the summit, Sarniguet passed his competitors, heart racing, pulled out a flag and then raised it on a flagpole. It was made from three old bedsheets. But no one in the joyous city below cared. After 1,532 days, the tricolor was back where it belonged.

Shortly after noon, a carbine-toting Ernest Hemingway and colleagues arrived at the Arc de Triomphe. A French captain invited "Papa" to get a better view of the liberation from the monument's roof, which provided a splendid vista. "One saw the golden dome of the Invalides," recalled one of Papa's men, "the green roof of the Madeleine, Sacré-Coeur. . . . Tanks were firing in various streets. Part of the Arc was under fire from snipers. A shell from a German 88 nicked one of its sides."

Hemingway and his party took cover, popped the corks on several bottles of champagne, and then drove at high speed down an almost deserted Champs-Élysées. They carried on through joyous throngs in the Place de l'Opéra and on to the Hôtel Ritz, where the manager welcomed Papa and his merry band—a group of perhaps a dozen—at the entrance. When asked if they required anything other than lodging, Hemingway's party promptly ordered fifty martini cocktails.

A mile away, Lieutenant Henri Karcher of the 2nd Armored Division entered the Hôtel Meurice armed with a submachine gun, accompanied by three men. He spied a massive portrait of Hitler, opened fire and riddled the Führer with bullets.

A German officer appeared. His hands were in the air. Karcher leapt over to him.

"Everybody, one by one, hands up and arms thrown away!"

The German shouted an order and others dropped their weapons.

"Where," asked Karcher, "is your general?"

General Dietrich von Choltitz was a floor above, seated at a table, his pistol placed nearby. Just nineteen fateful days before, he had been sent by the Führer to turn Paris into a fortress and then destroy it. He was proud that he had not done so.

A corporal appeared at the door. *"Sie kommen, Herr General."*

As Karcher entered, Choltitz got to his feet.

"Lieutenant Henri Karcher of the Army of General de Gaulle."

"General von Choltitz, commander of Gross Paris."

Was Choltitz ready to surrender to the Allies?

"Ja."

"Then you are my prisoner."

"*Ja.*"

On the Avenue Foch, groups of euphoric and vengeful Parisians from less affluent neighborhoods entered numbers 72 and 84 and started to explore Knochen's former residences. The offices, as captured hauntingly on film by a young photographer called Henri Cartier-Bresson, still looked surprisingly elegant given that Knochen and his colleagues had made sure to send all the best furniture and paintings east, ahead of the Allies, to the Reich.

Later that afternoon, Charles de Gaulle stepped onto the balcony of the Hôtel de Ville before an ecstatic crowd and made the best speech of his life. "Paris!" he cried. "Paris outraged. Paris broken! Paris martyred! But Paris liberated! Liberated by itself, liberated by its people with the help of the French armies, with the support and the help of all France, of the France that fights, of the only France, of the real France, of the eternal France!"

By evening most of the Germans left in Paris had surrendered. As darkness fell and the sound of gunfire faded into the distance, the City of Light was again lit up for the first time in four years, and the tricolor and the Stars and Stripes were raised side by side over the Eiffel Tower. Parisians sang "La Marseillaise" from windows throughout the city. "[It] was like a champagne dream," remembered one war correspondent. In the words of an ecstatic young American private called Irwin Shaw, "it was the day the war should have ended." By contrast, at 11, Avenue Foch, home of the Jacksons, there was only silence. By the time the Allies had liberated their neighborhood, they were at the heart of the Third Reich, struggling to survive, paying the price for having dared to defy Hitler.

THE JACKSONS had not been forgotten amid the heady euphoria of liberation. As soon as Sumner had been arrested, his colleagues and General de Chambrun tried to find out what had happened to him. According to one source, the general contacted the Red Cross in order to trace Sumner. Asking the Germans for help was no longer possible. Like many of those who had been close to Laval, the general and his son René de Chambrun could no longer pull strings. They could not save the Jacksons no matter how much they might have wanted to.

Sumner's and Toquette's relatives had also done their best to help. Toquette's family had pressured the Swiss embassy and along with Sumner's relatives had contacted the State Department in Washington. The day that Paris was freed, the U.S. secretary of state, Cordell Hull, sent a telegram to the Swiss authorities in Geneva: "Telegraph exact location Moulin [*sic*] and request Swiss to report urgently latest known whereabouts of Jackson family." Three days later Hull learned that the Jacksons had in all likelihood been deported to Nazi Germany.

A fortnight later, on September 6, 1944, a story in the *Waldoboro Press Herald*, near Sumner's hometown in Maine, gave a few further details. It was reported that "scores of Waldoboro residents, especially brother, Daniel Jackson, were keenly interested in [an] Associated Press dispatch from Paris telling of the efforts to trace Dr. Sumner Waldron Jackson, noted surgeon, Spruce Head native and Bowdoin graduate who had disappeared after he and his wife were interned on the grounds that he and his wife had harbored American fliers . . ." But there was no other source for either Sumner's relatives in the United States or Toquette's in Switzerland. All they knew for certain was that the Jacksons had disappeared like millions of other Europeans into the vast gulag of Nazi death and work camps: an unimaginable world of *Nacht und Nebel*—night and fog.

THE KNOCKING they had long feared had finally come, an urgent rapping on the entrance to the grand home of Clara Longworth and her husband, General Aldebert de Chambrun. It was September 9, 1944, when they were then taken from their home at gunpoint to a local jail. Its entrance reminded Clara of a famous picture from the French Revolution: *The Last Victims of the Terror.* Anxious hours followed. Through the de Chambruns' maid, news of the general and Clara's whereabouts had reached Miss Elisabeth Comte, the head nurse at the American Hospital. Comte quickly contacted the American embassy. But an official there was unmoved and could see no reason to help out. Comte stressed that "gangsters" had seized the de Chambruns.

"Gangsters or not," the official replied, "the French are free to do what they please."

Comte gave up on the embassy. She soon managed to contact General de Chambrun's high-ranking brother, Pierre, who in June 1940 had been the only one of eighty French Parliamentarians who voted against the granting of special powers to Philippe Pétain and the creation of the Vichy regime. General de Chambrun's brother was now influential, given this lone show of integrity, and threatened to end the career of a member of de Gaulle's cabinet if his brother and Clara were harmed. Sure enough, the de Chambruns soon learned they would be spared. "Our first impression of freedom was conveyed by the sight of the camionnette belonging to the American Hospital," recalled Clara. "Miss Comte, her charming face beaming with pleasure, was [there] to greet us."

They were not out of danger yet, and both wisely decided to keep a low profile and spend as little time in Paris as possible, as did their son René and his wife, Josée, who assumed false identities and hid with rich friends in the country. To Clara it seemed that de Gaulle's supporters wanted collaborators' heads to roll across the Place de la Concorde as they had by the thousand in 1794, at the height of the Great Terror. Hundreds of Parisians would be executed, shot on their doorsteps, and gunned down in the streets in the weeks after liberation, and an estimated 10,000 across France would be murdered. By contrast, thanks to their connections, Clara and her husband, General de Chambrun, would pay a small price. Both would soon be quietly eased from their roles at the American Library and the American Hospital, tainted in the eyes of Paris's American liberators by their close relationship with Pierre Laval. Their only child's father-in-law had on August 17 been arrested in Paris by Knochen's men and then escorted, along with the utterly discredited Pétain, to a fortress at the heart of Nazi Germany, where their fates, like those of so many millions, were now dependent on the whims of Adolf Hitler.

Dr. Sumner Jackson, left, serving as a combat surgeon in World War I.

Massachusetts General Hospital archives

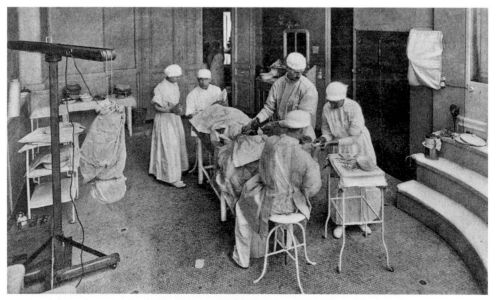

Dr. Sumner Jackson, seated facing camera, operating in the
American Red Cross hospital of Paris in 1917.

Massachusetts General Hospital archives

Toquette and Sumner Jackson, Paris, 1920s.

Sumner, Phillip, and Toquette Jackson, Normandy, 1930s.

LEFT: Phillip Jackson with maid Louise Heile, 1930s.
Phillip Jackson via John Snowdon
RIGHT: Sumner Jackson cutting wood with Phillip, winter 1939–40.
Phillip Jackson via John Snowdon

The Jackson country home in Enghien-les-Bains.
Phillip Jackson via John Snowdon

General Aldebert de Chambrun and wife, Clara, 1936. Author's collection

René de Chambrun and wife, Josée, 1930s. Author's collection

Gestapo officer Helmut
Knochen, based at 72
Avenue Foch, 1940–44.
Bundesarchiv

OSS spy Donald Coster.
Mudd Manuscript Library

Otto Abetz, the Nazi
German ambassador to
Vichy France, 1940–44.
Bundesarchiv

Bomb damage at Saint-Nazaire train station, photographed secretly by
Phillip Jackson, summer 1943. Phillip Jackson via John Snowdon

Women inmates at Ravensbruck concentration camp. Bundesarchiv

Toquette Jackson arriving in
Malmö, April 1945. Loraine Riemer

The *Cap Arcona,* sunk by the RAF, Lubeck Bay, May 1945; photographed by Phillip Jackson. Phillip Jackson via John Snowdon

Phillip Jackson on motorbike, Germany, summer 1945.

Phillip Jackson via John Snowdon

Phillip Jackson, right, while testifying in Hamburg at the war crimes trial, 1946. Phillip Jackson via John Snowdon

SS General Karl Oberg, left, and Helmut Knochen, on trial in Paris, 1954. Bundesarchiv

"She didn't hesitate for a second." Francis Deloche de Noyelle, Goélette agent who recruited Toquette Jackson to the resistance, photographed in Paris seventy years later, December 2013. John Snowdon

Phillip Jackson at Les Invalides, January 2013.
John Snowdon

SEVENTEEN

NIGHT AND FOG

THE CHILL OF WINTER was already in the air, the nights colder, the dew heavy on the grass each morning. On September 11, 1944, Toquette and the other women in her barrack were led to the shower rooms and made to stand naked once more while being examined by SS guards. All they knew was that they were to be taken to a subcamp of Ravensbruck somewhere in Nazi Germany, where they would be put to work. Every personal item they may have acquired since arriving at the camp was stripped from them. Then they were issued new clothes: flimsy cotton summer dresses. By candlelight Toquette and others hastily sewed on new prison numbers. Then a siren sounded. The women were marched back to a train at Fürstenberg. They climbed into boxcars, fifty women to each one. A female SS guard and an armed Wehrmacht soldier sat on boxes near a half-open door.

Three days later, having passed through the shattered outskirts of Berlin, Toquette arrived in Torgau, about 150 miles due south of Ravensbruck. As she and her close friends marched from the train yard to their new barracks, they encountered some French POWs who told them the Allies had reached the German border around Aachen. The women trudged on through open country and finally arrived at a munitions factory where a drunken SS officer gave them a choice. Work in the factory making weapons for the Nazis, under a roof, or return to hard labor outside at Ravensbruck. "Ravensbruck is slow death," one of the women argued, out of earshot of the SS. "We must avoid going back there, at any price. We have parents and husbands and children in France who need us."

Toquette and several of her friends were ordered to form into a work detail. However, they would not spend each day making fuses in the munitions factory. Instead they would work in a kitchen, peeling potatoes for eleven hours each day. They counted themselves extremely fortunate to have been given what amounted to a lifeline, a way to stay alive. It was hand-numbing work but the women could eat as many potatoes as they wanted and would therefore fend off starvation, and they would be together, able to care for each other every hour of every day.

A week after arriving at Torgau, Toquette somehow managed to smuggle a message out of the camp on a four-by-four-inch piece of paper, hoping it would be passed on to the Red Cross: "Madame Jackson, No 57 855, American, would be grateful if you would write to Touvet Barrelet de Ricou [her brother] to say to him that she is well and has been here for a week after 15 days at Ravensbruck. Tell him simply that the message is from 'Toquette.' Many thanks." The Red Cross received the note and duly sent it to Toquette's brother with a covering letter: "We have been able to pass a message from Mrs. Jackson to you. [Toquette] is interned at Torgau (Germany) . . . We advise you not to write to her. The message was transmitted to us in a confidential manner."

Each evening Toquette and her friends returned to the barracks, where they slept close to each other in a corner. Violette Szabo, the brave SOE agent, lay curled up only a few feet from Toquette in a rickety wooden bunk. Virginia d'Albert-Lake vividly recalled how Szabo would "stretch her limbs like a cat" and chatter about her young daughter Tania back in London. "To me that stretch expressed a love of life and desire to be back in the world of dancing and danger," d'Albert-Lake added. "Violet was always planning to escape and, night after night, her plan was to be culminated. Somehow, it never worked and, although she spent hours waiting for her chance, it never came."

All too soon, that November of 1944, the work detail ended and Toquette and her friends were sent back to Ravensbruck, where the increasingly cold weather began to take a dreadful toll on women working outside. Each morning Toquette stood for two hours in the darkness, shivering, before being sent to a nearby forest to clear ground for a planned landing strip. The next ten hours were a battle against the elements as well as malnutrition. "Unselfish gestures were becoming more and more rare," recalled d'Albert-Lake. "No one wanted to die, especially in Germany, and the war would soon be over, we knew that. To resist the cold, the hunger, the deprivations, until then was our only aim."

The women had no coats or blankets, nothing to protect them from the cold. In late November the first snow arrived. They could never get truly warm, not even as they clung to each other in their lice-infested bunks at night. Some of the Polish women, 40,000 of whom passed through the camp during the war, had stolen all the blankets, leaving none for Toquette and her group of friends.

Some mornings Toquette looked out of the barrack window and saw to her relief that it was raining, not snowing. Clear skies made the women afraid, for they meant even greater cold. Most days it seemed that time no longer existed. The line between reality and nightmare had blurred. Hope was the most precious thing, far more valuable than bread. All of Toquette's friends these days looked like the emaciated wraiths whose appearance had so shocked her upon arrival, with dull eyes, hollow cheeks, and gray skin. A Swiss woman called Mina, half Toquette's age, had lost her will to live and become a haggard old lady who had to be led around like a troubled child.

As Toquette trudged, bone-tired, between the barracks and various workplaces, the black cinders of the paths crunching in the cold silence beneath her feet, sores itching, lice bites spreading across her neck, dysentery forcing her to the latrines several times a day, she understood that there was a fate worse than death: the annihilation of people's souls, the single purpose of Ravensbruck. But she was also determined not to be defeated. She would not lower herself like other women, elbowing their way to the soup bowl, stealing others' food, or simply giving up, lying in a corner in their feces and the dirt, utterly humiliated, broken by Nazism.

Christmas approached. Those women with children ached for their families more than ever. Toquette had not seen Sumner and Phillip for almost six months. Where were they? Were they together? Were they still alive? There was no way of knowing, but it was impossible to stop asking.

Toquette tried to celebrate Christmas as best she could. Some women decorated their bunks with pine branches. A few foraged during work details for pieces of wood and then, at great risk, hid them beneath their blouses and smuggled them back into the barracks. They wanted a real fire for once on Christmas Day. Women in several barracks also decided to try to make Christmas cakes with whatever scraps of food could be found.

On Christmas Eve, the women visited friends elsewhere in the camp and admired their decorations. A tall fir tree stood a few yards from one barracks. Some Russian women had decorated the tree with brightly colored paper and the SS had not pulled it down.

For most women the absence of loved ones made that December 25, 1944, one of the saddest days of their lives. On New Year's Eve, the mood in the camp was much different. Some women were so eager and delighted to put the year behind them that, for the first time since arriving at Ravensbruck, they laughed as they light-heartedly argued over whose turn it was to rub their callused hands for a few seconds over the stove. Everyone was eager to heat water to wash with. They all wanted to scrub off a little grime to welcome the first day of a fresh year.

The cold returned. One morning, at roll call, it was so cold that the very marrow in the women's bones seemed to freeze. Some collapsed in the snow. Terrible huddles of defeated women soon formed, shivering and sobbing before being hauled to the infirmary where most would die before long. "It was a fearful sight to see them huddled there," recalled Virginia d'Albert Lake, "one against the other whimpering and moaning—such grey, haggard, shrunken things they were, half alive, half dead."

By contrast, for the most part that endless winter Toquette appeared remarkably upbeat, an inspiration to all around her. Virginia d'Albert-Lake recalled that she had never met "a woman with such courage, will power and vitality." Toquette's close friend Maisie Renault noted that Toquette was "short and light, very gentle, of joyful appearance and striking bravery. She was very secretive concerning the reasons leading to her arrest."

Staying alive was harder every day as the temperature dipped further and the work got more draining. Toquette and the other women had never performed hard physical labor, let alone in freezing conditions and living on starvation rations. "Clad in scanty summer clothes we were near dead with cold and hunger," recalled d'Albert-Lake. At roll call, more and more women fell unconscious. If no one was able to pick them up and take them to the infirmary, they simply were left in the snow and ice, their limbs turning blue. Some of the corpses were then stored temporarily in a washroom but then quickly incinerated when it was discovered that ravenous inmates had resorted to cannibalism.

Women like Toquette with children lasted longer than those without. But sooner or later that winter, everyone would succumb to malnutrition, cold, and disease. Toquette would have known that the Soviets were fast approaching from the east. But would they arrive in time to save the women of Ravensbruck? Or would the SS liquidate Toquette and her fellow prisoners in a final spasm of barbarism?

A stark indicator of the women's possible fate came on February 5. The SS took twenty-three-year-old Violette Szabo from a cell in the punishment block. She was to appear before the camp commandant, redheaded thirty-six-year-old SS Major Fritz Suhren. That morning he stood wearing his black SS cap with a silver skull, the infamous death's-head insignia, and watched as Szabo and two other women were brought before him. Szabo was able to walk unaided. It is thought that her fellow British spies from SOE, Lilian Rolfe and Denise Bloch, were carried to the execution spot on stretchers.

Violette had suffered so greatly, had been beaten and assaulted so often, yet she stood tall, back straight, and looked at Suhren and the execution party with withering contempt as he read out the execution order.

It was around 7:00 p.m., after dark, on a grassy patch in a yard beside the crematorium. Each woman was made to kneel down. A corporal called Schult then shot each in the back of the neck with a pistol. Szabo was murdered last. "All three were very brave and I was deeply moved," recalled bystander Johann Schwarzhuber, Suhren's deputy. When the camp doctor had pronounced them dead, their corpses were taken to the nearby crematorium and burned along with their clothes.

IT WAS also a long winter for Helmut Knochen, stripped of his rank and assigned to an antitank unit as an SS-Schütze, a private, the previous summer, just before Paris had been liberated. He had then learned that he would serve with the 1st SS Panzer Division, which in December 1944, at the height of the Battle of the Bulge, became notorious for the Malmédy Massacre, in which more than a hundred American POWs were killed in cold blood in Belgium. But then Himmler, apparently realizing how effective Knochen could still be, relented just days before Knochen was to be sent to the front. He was recalled to Berlin, which that January was a fast-spreading ruin, bombed day and night by the Allies.

According to a British intelligence report, the notoriously brutal alcoholic Ernst Kaltenbrunner, Knochen's new boss, hoped that

Knochen "would be acceptable to [Walther] Schellenberg [head of the SS's foreign intelligence service] and that through Knochen he would be able to obtain a better insight into Schellenberg's work. However, Schellenberg refused to accept the appointment and Knochen, after a short time. . . . became [SS general] Winkelman's liaison officer at the headquarters of Army Group Rendulic in Hungary." Knochen could have fared far worse. He was not being bombed around the clock in Berlin. He was safely behind the lines. If he could stay out of the clutches of the Red Army, who would without doubt kill him as a member of the SS, he would surely survive the war.

While Knochen had managed to avoid frontline combat, his former associate in Paris, Henri Lafont, had been run to ground on a farm just outside the capital. Early on December 27, 1944, in a prison cell, he had told his lawyer: "I don't regret a thing. I've had four years surrounded by orchids, dahlias, and Bentleys—that was worth it. I have lived ten lives so I can afford to lose one. Tell my son not to go to nightclubs. . . ." At 9:50 a.m. that day, his head uncovered, a cigarette plastered as usual to his lips, Henri Lafont was executed by a firing squad.

EIGHTEEN

NEUENGAMME

IT WAS A bitterly cold day. Phillip Jackson was beside his father as he marched into the central square in Neuengamme. It was early January 1945. He could see a brass band made up of some twenty men. The conductor was a small man who stood on a stool. He raised his baton and martial music began. Four men arrived carrying two posts and a crossbeam—a gallows. Soon a long rope with a noose was dangling in the frigid air.

The band played and the gallows was made ready. Then the music stopped. Phillip watched as a young man in a striped uniform climbed and stood below the gallows. He looked like a teenager, almost Phillip's age, thin and pale, as his sentence was read out in four languages: German, French, Flemish, and Dutch. He was going to be hanged because of sabotage he had carried out during his work, an SS officer explained, which could have led to the death of German soldiers.

An order was given. The man did not fall far, just two feet. His neck was not broken but he was barely alive, and the SS soon took him away. Phillip later heard that such cases were carried to a blockhouse, where a particularly vicious *Kapo* then strangled the "mistakes" using his bare hands. Darkness had fallen by the time Phillip and Sumner were back in their barrack that day. They could no longer see the yellow smoke that streamed without letup from the chimneys of the crematorium.

Phillip did nothing to celebrate his birthday that January 10 of 1945. It was just another cold day in a world drained of color and humanity. He did his best as usual to stay warm and avoid being beaten by an SS guard called Adolf Speck, one of the *Blockführers* who derived the greatest joy from striking men in the face with a riding whip. Phillip had seen him do so several times. Speck was just one of several SS officers who had shown themselves to be exceptional sadists, encouraged in their indiscriminate cruelty by thirty-seven-year-old SS major Max Pauly, the camp's commandant. Upon his arrival four months before, Phillip had learned quickly to stay clear of all of them. One day, however, Pauly had spotted Phillip washing a pair of trousers that had been covered with filth and lice. This was strictly forbidden. "Bash him in the face," Pauly casually ordered a guard. "Give him a couple clouts." The block guard did not hesitate to do as he was told.

By that January of 1945, most inmates had come to recognize Dr. Jackson, the "big American" towering above most others in the morning lineup at 5:00 a.m. At first, the previous fall, he had worked in a forge with a welding torch. He had no face mask and the sparks from the torch had soon hurt his eyes. Not long after, he was sent to the infirmary suffering from acute edema—swelling of the legs and arms caused by malnutrition. Although he was seriously ill, he started to look after other inmates, and the authorities took notice. He was not officially recognized as a doctor by the camp administration, but he was permitted to leave the forge and work instead in the infirmary. However, his health continued to fail and he came down with a serious chest infection. A lifetime of smoking had weakened his lungs.

Sumner carried on regardless, doing his best to save lives in appalling and insanitary conditions. When operating, he could not sterilize equipment, and one day he cut a finger while treating an inmate. The cut became infected and got steadily worse. Finally, a

Czech doctor in the infirmary had to operate on him, removing part of his finger. Still there was no improvement. During a third operation, it was necessary to "disarticulate"—remove—his middle finger, a grave loss for a master surgeon. Indeed, there was little hope of him working at the highest levels in his profession ever again.

THE INCENDIARY bombs fell in their thousands, whistling down, exploding all across the city, turning parts of Hamburg into a vast inferno. Three hundred and sixty-two B-17 bombers had been sent to destroy key strategic targets, including oil refineries. It was one of 214 raids on the city during the war, and by no means the most destructive. The worst had occurred the previous July, when unusually dry weather and concentrated bombing had created a tornadic inferno with winds of up to 150 miles per hour, with temperatures of up to 1,472 degrees Fahrenheit. Lasting a week, "Operation Gomorrah" killed more than 40,000 civilians, many of whom had died as they vainly tried to find shelter from winds that swept them off the streets like dry leaves.

In Neuengamme that night of February 24, 1945, the inmates could hear the bombs explode and the crackle and roar of huge fires raging twenty miles away. After the raid, it was decided that a work detail from Neuengamme would be used to clear rubble and remove bodies from the worst-hit areas of the city, half of which had been leveled. "We need a thousand pieces," the SS declared.

The pieces were Neuengamme prisoners.

Sumner hoped Phillip would not be among those selected. He knew that within a couple of weeks most men succumbed to exhaustion and exposure. But during the evening roll call, with the camp's 15,000 "pieces" arranged in perfect rows, the SS selected a thousand and Sumner soon learned that Phillip was among them. He immediately found an inmate named Jacques Sauvé, one of the

Prominenten, the so-called special prisoners being held as hostages in Neuengamme, whom Sumner had befriended during the journey the previous July from Compiègne to Neuengamme.

"Pete's been called for the commando," Sumner explained. "I'm afraid he won't survive. Can you do something?" Sauvé managed to locate a *Kapo* named André, and late that night André found Phillip, took him to a nearby building, and told him to change back into his camp clothes and then return to his own barrack. The next morning, at the roll call for the Hamburg work detail, there were exactly 999 people. At the last minute, another inmate was selected to take Phillip's place. Most of the detail would soon be dead.

Sumner had managed to save his son, but he knew he would have to do more if he was to keep him alive until the Allies arrived, hopefully in a matter of weeks rather than months. Through connections in the camp administration, he arranged for Phillip to be given one of the best jobs in Neuengamme. One morning Phillip was told to report for work in the kitchen. He would be inside where it was warm, but more important, he would also have the opportunity to steal food. His job consisted of preparing large vats containing four hundred liters of so-called soup. He and another inmate were responsible for three of the massive containers, and had to fill each one with cabbage and beetroots, heat the vats until the liquid boiled, stir it, and then scoop it into large kegs, which they then had to push to a distribution point.

One day Phillip was pulling one of the vats through the kitchen when the boiling-hot liquid spilled, some of it splashing over his foot. In agony, Phillip took off his wooden shoe as fast as he could but saw to his horror that he had suffered a third-degree burn. He was taken to the camp infirmary, where his father treated the burn—which soon blistered badly—with a thick brown paste. Although Phillip was in great pain, at least he was able to see his father several times each day.

Phillip learned that the SS had decreed that no inmate who was a doctor could formally work as such in the camp. So although Sumner should clearly, in a rational world, have overseen the infirmary, it was in fact a taxi driver from Berlin who did so. To Sumner's surprise, the taxi driver had become quite a skilled surgeon. The taxi driver answered to the SS officer who was formally in charge of the Neuengamme medical facilities: the chief physician of Neuengamme, Dr. Alfred Trzebinski, a bloated, ugly man who always wore polished boots, an immaculate uniform and cap, and carried out live-or-die inspections solely by glancing at patients' legs. If they looked bad, his victims were sent to their deaths. Dr. Trzebinski had learned his foul trade in Auschwitz, where his fellow SS had by now murdered well over a million Jews. Other SS doctors in Neuengamme also utterly revolted Sumner. One called Kurt Heissmeyer had since the previous November performed medical experiments, injecting twenty Jewish children, aged five to twelve, with tuberculosis before having removed their lymph glands. All the children would be hanged before liberation.

Other SS monsters who stalked Neuengamme included thirty-two-year-old Anton Thumann, dark-haired, bushy-browed, three silver pips on his uniform's collar patch, an utter sadist. Thumann never used a whip. He liked to use his fists instead. It made him feel more powerful, Phillip observed, giving him greater pleasure. Phillip also saw him kick people almost to a pulp many times. It appeared Thumann could never get his fill of violence, and he loved to see people die. Phillip noted that the man was always present, reading the death sentences, when inmates were hanged.

Then there was SS sergeant Wilhelm Dreimann. Phillip often saw him riding around the camp on a bicycle with a leather whip, beating the prisoners as he went on his way. He also loved to watch the prisoners take off their clothes and stand nude, shivering with cold and terror, before being killed.

"Get a move on," Dreimann would shout. "The quicker you are, the quicker you will be dead."

———

PHILLIP NEVER knew how much his father was suffering, how agonizing his ordeal was, for Sumner never exhibited a moment of weakness before his son. There were to be no tears, no self-pity. Only the most determined, the most positive and focused, could hope to stay alive.

Among Phillip and Sumner's fellow inmates at Neuengamme was forty-six-year-old Michel Hollard, founder of the Agir resistance network, who had provided crucial intelligence about the Germans' V-1 rocket program. Hollard remembered Dr. Jackson as being "very upright, with white hair, strong features, and a stern, almost hard, expression—he appeared as a person of great energy and forcible character." That winter Hollard became part of a tight-knit group that included Jackson. He recalled that Jackson never spoke about his activities in the resistance, nor why he and his family had been deported. He was no doubt afraid, as was Toquette, that the Gestapo had placed spies in the camp and that any information he revealed would endanger other captured members of the Goélette network.

Sumner was determined to contact his family and Hollard was able to help, managing after several attempts to smuggle a postcard from Sumner to one of Toquette's sisters in Switzerland. At least her relatives would learn of his and Phillip's fates.

What about Toquette? Was she still alive? Sumner knew better than anyone that she had immense inner strength, but in the end she was, like everyone else at the mercy of the Nazis that winter, very much human. There seemed little chance of her having survived.

NINETEEN

DELIVERANCE

A SIREN HOWLED, waking Toquette and the women of Ravensbruck. Aching from the cold, the women stirred in their bunks, spooned together, sharing each other's lice and body warmth. It was three in the morning, the time of the daily wake-up call. Near the kitchen, forlorn parties of emaciated women waited for the doors to open. A couple of them soon returned to Toquette's barrack with tureens filled with the bitter-tasting liquid they called coffee. Meanwhile SS soldiers arrived in the camp's central square. Some were holding the leashes to snarling dogs. Whistles blew and another day began with the formal roll call.

This morning, late in March 1945, Toquette Jackson was feeling terribly weak. She knew she had a high temperature. Perhaps, if she was lucky, it would be high enough to avoid work. She found her block senior, a brutal Polish woman, asked if she could report sick, and was allowed to go to the infirmary, where she joined a line of women waiting to be inspected. Only a temperature of 102 degrees Fahrenheit would allow Toquette to escape the fatal cold. Thankfully, hers was more than high enough. She was indeed fortunate: the doctor on duty that morning was not Dr. Benno Orendi, a Romanian who had volunteered for the SS and despised the French-speaking women in the camp and usually barred them from treatment.

The cold and hunger had taken its toll. Toquette's upper body was covered in countless lice bites. She had open sores and was suffering badly from dysentery. In the infirmary, through early April, her condition grew steadily worse. There was no adequate medical care, little water, and a pitiful ration of watery soup. The bunks, which patients were forced to share, were infested with lice. The infirmary was in fact a giant incubator of disease. But at least Toquette did not have to work in the numbing cold, watching young women freeze to death. Her last strength was no longer sapped by hard labor, clearing a nearby forest, cutting down trees in the icy darkness wearing just a summer dress and thin shawl.

Even if she survived the brutal conditions, it seemed highly unlikely that the SS would spare her life. Indeed, around the same time that Toquette was admitted to the infirmary, the head of the SS, Heinrich Himmler, issued an order to all concentration camp commanders: "Surrender is out of the question. Camps are to be evacuated immediately. No prisoner is to be allowed to fall into the hands of the enemy alive." All across what was left of Nazi Germany, death marches began, with thousands dying each day as the inmates in camps closest to the Soviet advance were herded west and the survivors then crammed into already overcrowded camps such as Ravensbruck and Neuengamme in north-central Germany.

The Red Army was advancing so fast that, just a fortnight later, on April 15, 1945, a rumor began to circulate in Neuengamme that the camp would also soon be evacuated as Himmler had ordered. But where would the inmates be taken? What other camp could absorb them? Most of Germany had been overrun.

Sumner had by this stage gained considerable sway within the infirmary at Neuengamme. He also had excellent contacts within the broader camp through his friendships with *Prominenten* such as Jacques Sauvé, key *Kapos* like André, and others within Neuengamme's administration. When he learned of the pending evacuation, he again acted decisively, arranging for Phillip to be readmitted to the infirmary as a patient so that he could watch over him. For all he knew, he was Phillip's only surviving parent, and he was determined to be right beside his only child come what may. It was all that Toquette would have asked for.

IT WAS a special date in the Nazi calendar: April 20, 1945—Adolf Hitler's birthday. At Ravensbruck the SS allowed each woman to have a small piece of meat in their daily soup to mark the occasion. In Berlin the fanatically loyal propaganda minister, forty-eight-year-old Joseph Goebbels, urged his fellow Germans to greater feats of resistance, to fight harder than ever to defeat the vast armies storming across Germany from east and west. A miracle was at hand. One just had to believe: "Our Führer has not deserted us. This is our victory."

That same day, fifty-year-old Swedish nobleman and diplomat Count Folke Bernadotte, chairman of the Swedish Red Cross, arrived in Berlin. He had a long, serious face, thin lips, and unnervingly wise eyes. He knew the Nazi capital well, having visited many times during the war. In previous years, the twentieth of April had been a time for massive celebrations by Berliners, an opportunity for full Führer worship, but now the rubble-strewn streets were deathly quiet.

Bernadotte met with Himmler at a hospital north of Berlin the next day, April 21, at 6:00 a.m. The bespectacled forty-five-year-old Himmler with his neat little mustache looked like a rather portly schoolmaster, not the monster who had overseen the systematic killing of millions of enemies of the Reich. "The Head of the Gestapo was a very tired and weary man . . ." recalled Bernadotte. "Himmler ate with a good appetite. Occasionally he tapped his front teeth with his finger nail . . ." This was a sure sign he was feeling extremely stressed. They did not talk about the end of the war, or the fighting, or whether Bernadotte could help broker a peace agreement between the Western Allies and a Nazi Germany run by Himmler. "This time our talk was entirely about humanitarian measures," recalled Bernadotte.

Himmler agreed to some of Bernadotte's requests. Crucially, a number of prisoners could be transported to Sweden with the help of the Swedish Red Cross. Among these fortunate souls were to be the women "interned at Ravensbruck concentration camp," recalled Bernadotte, who remained pokerfaced, wanting to wring more concessions from Himmler, who continued to tuck into his breakfast.

"The military situation is grave, very grave," Himmler confided before Bernadotte left to make arrangements for Toquette and other women at Ravensbruck to be rescued.

That same day, Phillip and Sumner were marched together out of the gates of Neuengamme under heavy SS guard to a rail siding where they boarded a boxcar. It was loaded with sick and dying men. When Sumner asked for water for his new patients, an SS guard lashed out and beat him. Sumner took the blows stoically. Along with some 15,000 other Neuengamme inmates, Sumner and Phillip were to be transported to the Baltic port of Lübeck, where they were to be placed on prison ships. What would happen then was anyone's guess. Some feared the SS would sink the ships, killing all aboard, while others hoped that they were bound for freedom in Sweden.

The train left Neuengamme and passed through Hamburg, making its way the hundred-odd miles to Lübeck, the windswept city of some 150,000 whose historic center, dating back to the eleventh century, had been severely damaged by the first large-scale RAF bombing of a German civilian target in 1942. Conditions on the transport were atrocious. There was no food or water, and soon men began to die. Sumner did what he could for them in their last moments and also tended to Phillip, who had developed a worrying abscess on his leg. Somehow he obtained a small penknife. From his time working in a quarry in Maine, he knew how to sharpen blunt metal, and he opened the abscess and let it drain as Phillip lay down amid his other new patients in the boxcar at a siding on the docks at Lübeck, thirty-five miles northwest of Hamburg. The able-bodied on the train were then taken to a ship anchored nearby called the *Thielbek*, while Phillip remained with the sick and his father in the boxcar, whose doors were left open so they could smell the Baltic Sea air. They knew the Allies were advancing fast into Germany. The war would soon be over.

The next day, April 22, 1945, SS-Obersturmführer Franz Göring arrived at Ravensbruck, met with the commandant, Fritz Suhren, and ordered him to evacuate the camp. The women were to be marched to another site where the Swedish Red Cross would then take them into its care.

Suhren refused to do as instructed. Himmler had ordered him to kill the women as the enemy neared the camp. That day had not yet come. There was to be no last-minute reprieve for Toquette and her friends.

Göring found a telephone and reported the situation to an associate of Himmler. It wasn't long before Suhren received a telephone call from Berlin. He was to release the women. Suhren reluctantly agreed, but what about the fifty-four Polish and seventeen French women who had been the subjects of gruesome medical experiments? Surely Himmler didn't want them to be found by the Allies? The answer came later that day: even these women, so-called *Versuchskaninchen*—experimental rabbits—were also to be freed.

Meanwhile, Phillip and Sumner's wagon still stood on the quay in Lübeck. Three SS prison ships—the *Athen*, the *Thielbek*, and the *Elmenhorst*—lay at anchor close by. The ships had been loaded with prisoners from other convoys as Phillip and his father tended to the sick and dying around them. Those still alive were in a pitiful state, lying in their own feces, unable to even crawl to a small barrel to defecate.

One of the able-bodied men taken on board the *Thielbek* spotted the ship's captain. He was reading a newspaper that had a thick black border all around the front page. The headline exclaimed: OUR FÜHRER HAS FALLEN.

Hitler was dead. The war was surely over. Some inmates who

were taken into a hold below celebrated. Others did not trust the SS. They might still be killed.

Deep in the bowels of the *Thielbek*, resistance leader Michel Hollard, the forty-six-year-old founder of the Agir network, was crammed amid hundreds of others. Men were barely able to breathe, corpses beneath their feet, the stench of human waste and rotting corpses lacerating their throats, forcing some to vomit, others to scream as they lost their senses.

Hollard would never forget how he was saved. He heard a German cry from above: "All French-speaking prisoners on deck!"

Hollard heard something being lifted above him. It was a hatch.

"French speakers up!"

For some reason, the SS were allowing men who could speak French to leave the hold. The Swedish Red Cross had apparently arranged for the French to be spared. Hollard didn't think twice, didn't hesitate to wonder why the SS were letting some men leave the ship. All that mattered was getting off the *Thielbek*. He quickly joined a group of Frenchmen and climbed up a ladder and out of the hold. Soon he was back on the quayside, walking with others past a stationary train. Hollard spotted his friend Sumner and called out to him.

"Come on, come quickly!" Hollard urged. "We're getting out."

Hollard approached Jackson.

"Dr. Jackson, you are not French but you speak French. You're a Westerner. You are eligible for being taken out by the Swedes. Come with us."

Sumner faced the most difficult choice of his life, far harder than when he had been forced to decide between spending the future in the United States or with Toquette. Should he go with Hollard or should he stay with his patients?

"No," replied Jackson. "I've got my patients and son here."

Phillip was also French-speaking. He too could have chosen to leave with Hollard but instead decided to stay where he was, beside his father. Being together was all that mattered.

Hollard begged them to reconsider.

"Jackson made no answer," recalled Hollard, "but, raising his arm wearily, pointed to the prostrate figures covering the floor of the wagon. They were the bodies of his dying patients."

The column of prisoners selected for Sweden was moving on. Hollard ran to catch up with it. He joined the last rank and then turned and took one last look at his friend, Sumner, the "devoted American."

TOQUETTE WAS dying. The end would come in a matter of days, not weeks. It was April 25, 1945. Swedish Red Cross buses and trucks had for three days been ferrying women to Padborg, on the Danish border, and now officials were trying to evacuate hundreds more women, listed as "political," from Ravensbruck. The SS denied that any Americans or British women were in the camp. It looked as if Toquette would be left behind in the squalid horror of the camp's overcrowded infirmary. But then one of the inmates, a fifty-year-old British-born nurse called Mary Lindell, produced a list and was able to persuade the SS to allow those on it to board a white bus belonging to the Swedish Red Cross. Lindell had been deported to Ravensbruck in 1943 for organizing an escape line.

Among the women saved at the eleventh hour was Toquette Jackson, skeletal, wracked by dysentery and covered in open sores, boils, and lice bites. She was barely able to stand as she joined other women and then sat down in the clean Red Cross bus. Two days later, on April 27, she and the other women traveled north on a train guarded by several Gestapo agents wearing trilbies and long overcoats. Spring had finally arrived. There were bright green buds on the trees. They were bound for freedom—Sweden. Shawls wrapped around their shaved heads, they held tight to each other and staggered or were carried onto a boat docked in Lübeck. Toquette had no idea that her son and husband were now so close, in fact in the very same port, less than a mile away. Then, finally, the Gestapo men who had guarded her reluctantly departed.

On April 28, the *Lillie Matthiessen* left Lübeck with 225 women aboard, including Toquette Jackson. Incredibly, from the deck it was possible for her to see the *Thielbek*, the prison ship in whose hold her husband and son had been placed that same day. She of course had no idea that Sumner and Phillip were still alive, let alone that they were so very close, aboard a blacked-out ship across the swelling waters of the Bay of Lübeck, which Toquette and her fellow survivors were so glad to be leaving behind.

The *Lillie Matthiessen* crossed the gray Baltic to Malmö, arriving several hours later. There were no more Germans. No more Gestapo men in heavy overcoats and stained fedoras. Finally, the women of Ravensbruck were free. Yet, most were too tired and traumatized to feel much more than profound relief.

It was a beautiful spring day as the boat docked in Malmö. The women were seated on pathetic little bundles of belongings. Red Cross officials announced that they would have to discard the bundles because of fears of contagion. Out of habit, many women hid small items of sentimental value. Their long ordeal then ended as it had begun at Ravensbruck: they were taken to a building and disinfected in large shower rooms. This time there were no leering middle-aged SS men but there was, remarkably, a film cameraman who recorded the women as they lay and shivered in severe shock and trauma at the touch of the water.

Toquette and her friends were then taken in groups and placed on a white bus that wound through the streets of Malmö, neat and prosperous, untouched by war, utterly surreal. The bus stopped in heavy traffic. The women looked out of the windows, some staring in wonder at a bakery. In the shop window were beautifully iced cakes and cream puffs.

One woman spoke up. "Who'll trade me a cream cake for four potatoes from Ravensbruck?"

Civilians in the street gathered and began to stare at the women, not knowing where they had come from. The Swedish shoppers looked scared, as if they were encountering ghosts.

Toquette should have been long dead. Of the 550 women deported with her from France on August 15, 1944, she was one of just seventeen who had survived—an extraordinary victory over Nazi bestiality. But what about her husband and only child? Later that day she summoned the strength to write a letter. Her hand was shaking, she was so weak. She had to know if Sumner and Phillip had lived.

The letter was to her sister, Tat, in Paris.

> *Malmo, 29 April 45*
>
> *My Sister,*
>
> *I know nothing about you since we saw each other at Romainville. Do you have any news of Jack or Pete?*
> *If my handwriting seems to tremble it is because I have open wounds on three fingers and no eyeglasses.*
> *I also have otitis and my ears run—I can't hear on one side, my feet are swollen and I have terrible dysentery.*
> *But after all that my morale is good.*
> *It is a miracle I am not dead; and to think that I will see you soon.*
> *No time for more.*
>
> *Kisses,*
> *Your Sister*

Glen Whisler of the American Red Cross reported on April 29, 1945: "Mrs. Jackson is being hospitalized today for draining ears and ulcerated sores on her hand and legs. She is little more than a skeleton." Most of the other women, he noted, were also in a very "nervous" condition and severely malnourished. Hardly any of them were older than forty. It was incredible that Toquette, at age fifty-eight, had survived.

PART FOUR

AFTER THE FALL

It was a world where people exterminated for pleasure and where the murderers were treated as heroes. It already seemed far away, like a nightmare one would prefer to forget. And yet the poisoned yeast is still ready to rise. Men have not the right to forget so quickly. They have not the right. Never. . . .

—JACQUES DELARUE, *The Gestapo: A History of Horror*

TWENTY

ONE DAY IN MAY

DAWN ARRIVED SLOWLY on May 3, 1945. There were low clouds and a thin drizzle. In the *Thielbek*'s hold, Phillip felt the ship begin to move. The British were less than twenty miles from the Bay of Lübeck, and the SS had ordered the prison ships to leave the port of Lübeck and head out into the Baltic before they could be liberated.

Since being placed in the hold, Phillip had seen several men die. Now their bodies were piled up at one end of the hold. The SS opened a hatch, flooding the inmates with harsh light, and then lowered a rope with a hook at one end. The corpses were pulled up to the deck and thrown overboard. At the bottom of the hold, meanwhile, Phillip and others watched, barely able to move, it was so crowded. There were, in fact, more than 2,500 inmates crammed beside Phillip and his father. Almost 8,000 more were being held in nearby ships.

It was dark, cold, and damp. There were no toilets and no water. It was obvious that the Germans were going to kill them all, but how and when?

FIFTY MILES away, at Ahlhorn air base, young men in dark blue uniforms, veteran Hawker Typhoon fighter-bomber pilots, arrived sleepy-eyed in their mess for a breakfast of bacon and eggs. Twenty-three-year-old squadron leader Martin Rumbold of the RAF's 263 Squadron joined his men at the breakfast table. Not long after, he briefed them on that day's mission. They were to "destroy a great number of ships assembled in the Baltic Sea." For weeks they had been shooting at pretty much anything that moved in Germany, meeting very little resistance from the Luftwaffe. Later that morning Rumbold received more specific orders. The squadron was to sink all "enemy naval formations" in the Bay of Lübeck.

ABOARD THE *Thielbek*, conditions were ever more horrific. Hundreds of people had acute dysentery. Yet more dead bodies had piled up, so many that Phillip felt as if he were in a slaughterhouse. It was around midday when he made his way to a metal ladder leading from the hold to the deck above. He was desperate for fresh air, determined to fill his lungs with something other than the stench of feces and decaying flesh. He began to climb the ladder. Near the top he saw a guard. He looked old and haggard and was armed with a Mauser rifle.

"Be a good man," Phillip begged. "Let me breathe some clean air."

To his surprise, the guard did not strike him as Phillip stepped onto the *Thielbek*'s main deck. He filled his lungs with sea air and looked up at the overcast sky. He breathed in again. Then he saw several planes far in the distance. Their pilots had been given orders to sink any German boat still afloat in the Baltic. Some had also been told that the *Thielbek* and the other ships in the bay contained thousands of SS soldiers trying to flee justice.

Pilot John Byrne remembered that he and his fellow British pilots were flying in close formation until they arrived over the Bay of Lübeck.

"There they are," cried one pilot.

Byrne looked down and saw the *Cap Arcona* making out to sea. There were two other vessels that were also quickly visible. One was the *Thielbek*.

"Come on," said Byrne. "Let's get it over."

The Typhoons banked toward the targets.

"Okay, down we go," ordered the squadron leader. "Going down, going down, now."

The pilots concentrated hard, determined to hit one of the boats. Antiaircraft fire exploded around them as they dived at around 500 miles an hour. They had been ordered to sink the ships and then to strafe any survivors they saw in the water. At about 3,500 feet, they opened fire.

Squadron leader Derek Stevenson was leading the first wave of attackers. "We had been in action for days blowing up railways, refineries and ships," he recalled. "For us this was just another job, but knowing the SS were on board made us all the more determined to destroy the ships. We came in at 9,000ft, dived to 3,000ft and I fired all eight rockets and every cannon round at one ship."

PHILLIP SAW one of the planes swoop down and fire a rocket. He watched as it screamed toward him, trailing white smoke. It was mesmerizing. Phillip was certain it was slightly off target. He just knew it. It exploded fifty yards away but a second followed and did not miss. The next thing Phillip knew, the deck below shifted violently. In shock, stunned by the explosion, he was then dimly aware that the ship was sinking. Amazingly, he had managed to get on deck just before the RAF's attack. He was not trapped below.

Water began to flood the *Thielbek*'s hold, where Sumner was surrounded by a pressing, hysterical mass. Men screamed and begged for help as more water flooded in. The only way out was the metal ladder Phillip had earlier used and now men fought furiously to get to. Some placed a foot on the ladder only to be knocked down by others as men started to tear planks from the decking. The water kept rising and men started to drown as others used the planks to keep themselves afloat.

On deck, Phillip tried to make his way to the hold to find his father. The boat was listing badly. Then there was a loud bang. Blood and brains splattered across the deck. An SS guard had shot himself in the head.

Phillip looked around, hoping to catch sight of his father among men scrambling out of the hold. Where was he? More rockets exploded nearby, so Phillip began to strip, casting his clothes aside, knowing he had a better chance of making the shore if he were free of the rags that would weigh him down once he was in the water. When he was naked he made his way to the edge of the deck.

Hell . . . the ship . . . It's going down. . . . I'm going to go down too. . . .

The ship was listing so badly that the ocean was just a couple of feet from him, lapping at the edge of the deck. The boat would soon sink and those still in the hold would surely die. But where was his father? Should he wait a few seconds longer before jumping in the water? There was no sign of his father wherever he looked. He called out for him. Still no sign.

Death was nearby now, closer than ever. Phillip couldn't wait for his father any longer. So he made his way to the edge of the deck and dropped down into the water. It felt ice-cold as he began to swim away from the boat. He wasn't in bad shape, had some muscle, and was not too thin, because he had worked in the kitchen, where he had been able to scrounge extra food.

Phillip knew he was a good swimmer. He had learned the breaststroke and the crawl in the choppy waters of the English Channel, thanks to his father, and now he struck out confidently for the shore, about three miles away. He had to get away from the boat before it sank. There would be a cavitation effect as it went under. He could remember a scene from a book his mother had read to him in his bedroom on Avenue Foch. In *The Swiss Family Robinson*, a boat had sunk, pulling people down after it, sucking them into a whirlpool. He didn't want that to happen to him. So he swam hard, away from the boat, toward a beach near a small town called Neustadt.

The water was not rough, but it was much colder than the English Channel in August. He kept swimming, focused on the beach far off, unaware that as many as nine thousand men were dead or dying in the waters of the Bay of Lübeck, five thousand from just one boat, the *Cap Arcona*. The RAF Typhoons were making strafing runs now, their bullets zipping through the air, jolting bodies in the water. Men who had survived years of hell were being slaughtered just four days from the war's end.

Phillip was aware of boats closing on him. They were powerful, fast, and well armed. The Germans had sent out several launches from the port of Lübeck. One came close to Phillip and then a German sailor was pulling him into it. He was shivering badly. A motor roared and the launch began to return to the shore. Phillip had been among the first to escape the *Thielbek* and was the first survivor, he realized, to be pulled into the launch. The German sailors quickly spotted other survivors in the water and pulled some of them into the boat too.

Phillip watched, seated on the deck beside an antiaircraft gun, as the Germans noticed that other survivors in the water had shaved heads. They were not Kriegsmarine men, Germans in the navy. The men in the water were Neuengamme inmates, vermin from the camps. The sailors stopped trying to save people and the boat turned back toward the shore, its antiaircraft gun firing away, the steady bark leaving Phillip almost deafened. Elsewhere in the bay, other German boats rammed men in the water and some Germans opened fire as survivors begged and screamed for their help.

Phillip was extraordinarily fortunate. He was not thrown off the boat. He was not shot, and he was brought back to the shore. Then he heard harsh voices. They belonged to the SS, men in black uniforms, their eyes blazing with hate and insatiable rage, who had already killed about 150 men on the beach nearby, gunning them down with undisguised glee, determined that there would be no survivors even among those who had made it to dry land. Elsewhere, navy cadets and even German locals joined in the killing, pulling out old rifles and double-barreled shotguns and then carrying out a cull along the nearby beaches, which were soon covered with thousands of washed-up corpses and bodies riddled with bullets.

Phillip was not killed on the beach like so many others. He was herded through the town of Neustadt with some two hundred survivors. The SS made him and others line up against a building. Phillip stood shivering, naked, in shock. Then the young men in black were setting up an MG42 machine gun, placing it in on a tripod, and aiming it at Phillip.

TWENTY-ONE

HIS MAJESTY'S SERVICE

PHILLIP COULD SEE the machine gun. Two Germans manned it. There was the sound of tank fire. The Germans looked worried. The firing continued. They abandoned the machine gun and beat a hasty retreat. Phillip stood, in complete shock, barely registering events, knowing only that he was still not dead. He saw a green tank, its treads clanking. Soldiers in wool uniforms followed close behind. He had been saved. The British had finally arrived.

Phillip was alive, one of around 50 people out of 2,750 who survived the sinking of the *Thielbek*. At some point that afternoon of May 3, 1945, another of the fifty, a Frenchman, told Phillip he had seen his father around a hundred yards from the ship, supporting himself with a plank but "in difficulties." There was a chance that his father might have made it to shore.

By evening, as the British soldiers began to take traumatized survivors to nearby hospitals for medical care, according to another survivor "an eerie hush" had fallen over the Bay of Lübeck, which had been the scene of one of the greatest maritime disasters in history. The odd wave could be heard crashing on the beaches strewn with bodies. For weeks, corpses would continue to wash up, and as late as 1971 human bones could be found amid less macabre flotsam and jetsam after storms.

Phillip was taken to a hospital in the nearby town of Neustadt to get some rest and receive medical attention. The next morning he found a blanket, draped it around himself, and wandered into the town. Maybe there was a chance of finding his father. It wasn't long before he came across a British officer who was with a patrol. It was around 10:00 a.m. on May 4, 1945.

The officer had a friendly face.

"Can I do anything for you?" asked Phillip. "I've escaped and I'm alone now."

"You speak German?"

"Yes."

"Then come with us."

The British captain told Phillip he needed an interpreter. Although he was still in shock, numbed by his ordeal, he was taken to a barrack nearby. By afternoon he had been issued a uniform, billeted in a sergeant's mess, and even given a cigarette ration. He was told where he could send and receive mail if he needed to contact relatives. Then he was put to work. A couple of nights later, Frenchman Maurice Gacheny was surprised to see Phillip approach him with the British captain.

"This officer is inquiring for Michel Hollard," said Phillip. "Some of the others said you might know what had become of him."

"Do you know Michel Hollard?" asked the British officer.

Phillip translated.

"I knew him better than anyone in camp," said Gacheny.

"But not as well as we do," said the British officer.

"How can that be?" asked Gacheny.

The British officer explained that Hollard's intelligence about Hitler's rocket program had been of vital use to the Allies. They wanted to find and debrief him, but it was a futile search. Unbeknownst to them, Hollard had already returned to France.

Over the next few days, including May 8, when victory in Europe was declared, Phillip was kept busy with the unit from the British Eighth Army, commanded by Field Marshal Bernard Montgomery of El Alamein fame. After the deep and protracted trauma of Neuen-gamme, not to mention the sinking of the *Thielbek*, Phillip was at least distracted from feeling or thinking too much about being an orphan—about the loss, he believed, of both his parents. He was proud to be wearing a uniform. He asked another soldier to take photographs of him in it. That May 8 he sent a letter to school friends in Paris explaining what had happened to him since his arrest in May 1944. He was just seventeen but in some ways felt like a grown man. He had learned that "being brave" does not come easily to most of mankind. The cosseted child was gone.

When not helping the British to interrogate German prison-ers, Phillip looked for his father's corpse, cutting a pathetic figure as he traipsed along the local beaches, moving from one washed-up victim to another. There were hundreds of corpses on every beach. Some were around Phillip's age. A few were children who had been clubbed to death using rifles. The SS had clearly run out of ammuni-tion. The faces of many corpses were bloated beyond recognition, so Phillip began to examine their hands; he was looking for one with a severed finger.

Meanwhile, Toquette was making a slow recovery in a hospital in Malmö, in Sweden. That May, she received a letter from a good friend in Paris:

> *Your husband and son in Germany safe and free and looking for you/Paris relations all well/will attend [to] money matters. . . .*

Her son and husband had, apparently, survived. At least 27,000 of their fellow deportees from France had not.

Before long, Phillip's letter of May 8 to school friends was for-warded from Paris to Toquette, who received it late that month in the hospital in Malmö. She must, of course, have been delighted that her son had survived, as earlier reported. And she was eager to get in touch with him as soon as possible.

But as she read Phillip's letter she also learned the truth about her husband:

> *I am working with H.M.S. forces, living with them and sharing their life.*
> *My father is dead.*
> *I do not know if I shall see my mother.*
> *It is likely I shall still spend a few weeks here.*
> *This life is fine.*
>
> *Phillip Jackson*
> *O.H.M.S.! [On His Majesty's Service]*

A month later, in a room near Toquette's in the hospital in Malmö, her close friend Maisie Renault opened a letter from a relative. Inside, she found a copy of Phillip's letter to his school friends in Paris. She would never forget reading it. "Dear friends," Phillip had written, "you probably wonder what's happened to me since a year ago—this is the truth, and it is tragic." He had then told the story of the day he lost his father before writing: "I think my mother died in a concentration camp . . ."

Maisie would later remember that she was "struck by the tragic tone and the resignation with which a boy of 17, who had been through such a trauma, believed his whole family had died." She was also glad to have received the copy of Phillip's letter, for it gave her hope. If Phillip had survived the tragedy in the Bay of Lübeck, then her brother, Philippe, who had also been imprisoned in Neuengamme, might have also escaped death. Tragically, within a few weeks she would learn that he had not.

Toquette grieved as she continued to recuperate that June in Malmö. In early July, after sending a letter to Phillip confirming she was alive, she returned to France, to the empty apartment at 11, Avenue Foch.

On July 18, 1945, she wrote to Sumner's sister, Freda, in Maine, passing on what she had learned from Phillip's letter of May 8 that had been forwarded to her:

> *Sumner didn't have a bad heart, but he was very short of breath since he had pneumonia a few years before the war. It was the third finger of his right hand that had to be disarticulated. He had been working in the infirmary of the camp, taking care of his fellow prisoners. Of course, hygiene was very bad and he got an infection. They were always together, father and son, at the camp of Neuengamme, which they never left. It seems his morale was always good, he was so courageous, never knew what fear was.*
>
> *We were all three arrested on May 25, 1944, not because we were Americans but because we were working for the underground liberation movement that we call the "Resistance." We were therefore political prisoners and much worse off than regular prisoners of war.*
>
> *As soon as my health permits, I am going to look for a job. Life is very expensive in France and we have not the means to live on our income.*
>
> *I want you to know that I never ceased to be in love with Sumner, for whom I had moreover a great admiration and respect. He had such big qualities.*
>
> *Best remembrance, Freda.*
>
> *I hope you are a happy wife and mother.*
>
> *Affectionately,*
> *Toquette*

IN GERMANY, meanwhile, Phillip Jackson did his best to live in the moment, to escape the past. He focused totally on his new role, not as a victim of Nazism, but rather as a proud member of the British Army. There were moments when he was consumed by rage and wanted to avenge his father's death, which he had only slowly come to accept. But he was mostly too busy with his new duties, helping the British run a prison camp for German soldiers, millions of whom languished behind barbed wire that summer as the Allies searched among them for war criminals. In his free time he went hunting, roaming a nearby peninsula, on the lookout for rabbit and other game. Amid a stash of weapons he had collected and kept under his bed, he treasured a Belgian .16-caliber side-by-side shotgun. He hunted hares with it, then gave them to a delighted mess cook. "One day," he recalled, "I was in a wheat field when I saw something reddish. I started aiming and then I saw it was a redheaded boy who was lying on top of a girl—making love to her. He was lucky, very lucky. . . . That was the closest I got to killing a German."

He would get much better revenge by helping the British track down the perpetrators of the crimes he had seen in Neuengamme. "The British knew they were going to find horrible things in Germany and they had prepared for it," he remembered. "They had organized war crimes commissions—a high-ranking officer, usually a colonel who had legal training, often a former barrister, went out with the troops when they arrived in a camp." Phillip provided detailed written testimony for a British colonel who was leading an inquiry into thirteen members of the SS who had been responsible for the atrocities in Neuengamme.

The summer stretched on. Phillip was in no hurry to return to the past—or to Paris and his widowed mother, no matter how much he missed and loved her. He needed more time to "readjust from the camp to normal life." Facing his mother would mean confronting the past and the reality of his father's loss. He was not ready for either just yet. The older men among the 14th Light Field Ambulance Unit, to which he was attached, looked after him as if he were their own son. He felt protected. It was almost as if he were part of a joyful family again. "I think they liked me," he recalled. "I certainly liked them. I was able to decompress. Going home too soon would have been like going from zero to infinity."

Phillip traded his cigarette ration for a Leica IIIb camera and photographed the Bay of Lübeck and the surrounding area. He visited the nearby city of Kiel with a group of British soldiers to celebrate King George VI's birthday. He had left Paris as a sheltered child. For the first time he was expected to behave like an adult and was treated as one. He bought a motorcycle in Neustadt and posed proudly beside it in his British uniform for a photograph, one of several images from that long summer that he would prize for the rest of his life.

As the fall approached, Toquette became ever more anxious to see her son again. It had been over a year since she had last set eyes on him in Moulins before he and Sumner were taken to Compiègne. She wrote to Phillip, asking what was keeping him in Germany for so long. He was to stop playing the soldier and come home to her. School would start again soon.

Phillip duly arrived back in Paris in late September at Le Bourget airfield in a French military plane, a Junkers Ju 52 with corrugated metal on its sides, the same kind that had brought Hitler to Paris in June 1940. When he stepped onto French soil, he was still proudly wearing a dark green British uniform, not yet ready to be a schoolboy again. He had brought a suitcase with him. It was full of guns he had acquired in Lübeck.

Phillip took a bus into Paris and then the metro to the Place de l'Étoile. He walked along the platform, up the stairs, past the advertisements on the tiled walls, into the light, the Arc de Triomphe before him, just as he remembered it. The thickets of road signs in German were gone. He walked along the Avenue Foch. There were no more black Citroëns parked outside the grandest homes. Tricolors had replaced swastikas. His mother, looking far older than he remembered, was waiting for him at number 11. Never had she been happier to see her son. Her only child was no longer a boy. He was as tall as his father had been. At long last he was home.

Phillip put his suitcase, full of guns, in his bedroom. It was just as he had left it in the spring of 1944. Nothing, it appeared, had been touched. Nothing had changed.

TWENTY-TWO

JUSTICE

WHEN THE WAR ended, like all senior SS officials, those who had controlled the apparatus of terror in France quickly went to ground. SS general Karl Oberg disappeared on May 8, 1945, in the Austrian Tyrol. He then assumed the name Albrecht Heintze but in July 1945 was captured by American investigators and handed over to the French. His deputy, Helmut Knochen, was typically more cunning. He hid in Göttingen, south of Hanover, and managed to stay a step ahead of Nazi hunters for several months. At one point he was seen in Madrid, a popular refuge for collaborators and the SS. In a British intelligence report he was described as "having a large head and brutal German face. Cleanshaven. Blue eyes. Always carries a briefcase. Wears camel hair coat with leather pockets."

It was January 16, 1946, when "Dr. Bones" was finally run to ground near Kronach in the American zone of occupied Germany. First he was incarcerated at Dachau, site of Hitler's first concentration camp, and then he served as a key witness in the Nuremberg trials of senior Nazis such as Ribbentrop and Kaltenbrunner. "It was a harsh year—at Nuremberg," Knochen recalled. "My cell was below that of Göring." Unlike his former Gestapo colleague at 31, Avenue Foch, Theodor Dannecker, Knochen chose not to commit suicide, even though he knew it was highly likely he would, when it was his turn to go on trial, be found guilty and executed. He would not take the coward's way out like Dannecker, who had hanged himself in his cell under American custody. He was proud of his war record. He had served his country with honor. He would defend his actions to his last breath.

HAMBURG WAS still a city of ruins. Remarkably, however, one building in the old center had survived with very little damage: the Curiohaus on the Rothenbaumchaussee. One day in March 1946, eighteen-year-old Phillip Jackson entered the building and made his way to a courtroom. As soon as he stepped inside, he saw SS men lined up in the dock, numbers hanging from their necks. His heart began to race. "The terror came back to me," he later recalled. "I was back in Neuengamme, at night, standing on a parade ground, and the SS in the dock were there, holding whips, with dogs and guns."

Phillip had been called to testify at the trial of fourteen SS officials who had been primarily in charge of Neuengamme. They were now seated in the dock, dressed in shabby suits, looking thin and gaunt, much older than when Phillip had last seen them just two years before. Each of them knew they were going to die if found guilty of crimes against humanity. The camp's commandant, thirty-nine-year-old Max Pauly, was tagged as number one.

After several months back in Paris, Phillip had started to recover from the immense trauma of Neuengamme and the tragedy of the Bay of Lübeck. He was one of the prosecution's key witnesses. He had agreed to testify in English. As he took his place on the witness stand, he managed to control his fear so he could face the men whom he had last seen in immaculate black uniforms, barking orders as 15,000 people stood at attention at Neuengamme. Blessed with a superb memory, able to describe in great detail the crimes he had witnessed, Phillip quickly proved to be a highly effective witness.

During his first day of testimony, Phillip was asked if he had witnessed any cruelty in Neuengamme.

"Did you see people beaten by the SS?" asked a prosecutor.

"Yes, I did," Phillip replied calmly.

"Can you point to any particular SS man or officer who you saw beat a prisoner?"

Phillip turned to look at the SS who had murdered and terrorized thousands. "I saw number three, number five, number nine, and number ten."

On Thursday, March 21, 1946, the fourth day of the trial, a lawyer for Max Pauly named Dr. Curt Wessig began to cross-examine Phillip.

"I want to ask a question in the interests of my client, Pauly," he asked.

Pauly sat nearby in the dock. Phillip did not look at him.

"You said that Pauly said 'bash him in the face' or something like that. My client, Pauly, denies this phrase and he would like to ask you whether you have really seen [him] when he uttered this phrase?"

Phillip remained focused. "I am very sorry that he does not remember," he replied. "It was a daily happening. I remember distinctly. I saw Pauly when he said it."

"You said that your father was drowned," Wessig continued. "Did that happen in the camp, or do you attribute any sort of responsibility to the accused Pauly?"

"This was not actually in the camp," replied Phillip, "but still in captivity because we were guarded by the SS on the ship, *Thielbek*. I do not know in what measure the accused Pauly may have been responsible for the placing of the prisoners on the ship."

The trial continued. The catalogue of crimes was long and numbing. Finally, Wessig called upon the court to recognize that "Pauly had simply been a tool of a system that stormed through most of the countries of Europe in hate and fury, and that this system was bound to flounder because it refused to acknowledge and live out an ethics that called for the love of all that is human."

None were convinced that Pauly had been a mere "tool"—far from it. On May 3, 1946, a year after Phillip's father had perished in the cold waters of the Bay of Lübeck, Pauly was sentenced to death. He wrote to his son from his cell while waiting to be executed: "Always be proud of being a German, and detest with all your might those who acquiesced in this absolutely false verdict. . . . Please remember my favorite dish—pancakes and chocolate pudding. If I could only eat my fill once more!"

On October 8, Albert Pierrepoint, Britain's last official hangman, placed a rope around Pauly's neck. The iron grate on which Pauly stood was pulled away and he dropped to his death. Others followed Pauly, including the doctor Alfred Trzebinski, responsible for murdering more than two dozen children upon whom he had experimented at Neuengamme, and whose last words showed not a hint of regret as he waited to drop: "Lord, forgive them, for they know not what they do."

HELMUT KNOCHEN was sentenced to death in March 1947, along with his close colleague Hans Kieffer, his head of counterintelligence, but not for crimes against humanity, nor his role in sending almost 80,000 Jews to their deaths. Instead, both he and Kieffer, his chief spy hunter, were condemned to hang because of their involvement in the murder of several British soldiers in early August 1944, just before they quit Paris. In the dying days of Nazi occupation, Knochen had received orders from Berlin, which he had then passed on to Kieffer, to execute five members of the Special Air Service, the SAS.

During his trial, Knochen had skillfully argued: "Neither I, nor one of my subordinates, could have acted otherwise, without being condemned to death immediately." In the aftermath of the failed July 1944 plot against Hitler, Knochen added, it would have been suicide to disobey any order coming directly from Berlin. He had even managed to persuade no less than senior general Günther Blumentritt to plead for his life. "I am not able to mention all examples but I remember that Dr. Knochen and his office in *many* instances acted in the *interest* of the French population," stated Blumentritt, who would play a key role in forming Germany's postwar military. "Dr. Helmut Knochen," he concluded, was a "decent man without a brutal disposition."

Hans Kieffer, too, argued that he had simply been carrying out orders when he passed on Knochen's specific instructions to Gestapo executioners, three of whom worked at 84, Avenue Foch. Like Knochen, he was also condemned to die. While awaiting execution, forty-seven-year-old Kieffer was interrogated at great length by Vera Atkins, head of SOE's French Section, which he had brilliantly destroyed under Knochen's watch. When told that SOE agents including Violette Szabo had been viciously treated just before being executed, Kieffer looked surprised and began to cry.

"Kieffer, if one of us is going to cry," replied Atkins with contempt, "it is going to be me. You will stop this comedy."

Just before being escorted to the gallows from his cell, Hans Kieffer pulled down a photograph of his daughter, Hildegard, and asked if it could be sent to her. He had placed a note on the back: "Moggele, I bless you in my last hour." Albert Pierrepoint then placed a rope around Kieffer's neck and made sure he was quickly dispatched to Valhalla, one of around two hundred Nazis he personally accounted for after the war.

Kieffer had been neither as calculating nor as well connected as Helmut Knochen, who was spared the noose when in 1950 his sentence for the SAS killings was commuted to twenty-one years in prison. But he was then extradited to France, where he finally appeared in court along with Höherer-SS und Polizeiführer Karl Oberg, head of the SS in France, in February 1954. While awaiting trial, Oberg was questioned 386 times by the French, who collected ninety kilos of documentary evidence. On October 9, 1954, a gray-haired Knochen and haggard Karl Oberg were sentenced to death for crimes committed in France. "The French government was severe," Knochen recalled. "My case was linked to that of Oberg. . . . [René] Bousquet [former head of the French police during the mass deportations of Jews from France] testified at my trial: he arrived by plane, tanned from a trip made to the Bank of Indochina—he was my counterpart in the war!"

To Knochen it seemed incredible that Bousquet, an old rugby chum of René de Chambrun, had escaped justice after the war for his role in the deportation of French Jews. As the head of the French police, he had, after all, helped organize the mass roundups of 1942. Bousquet still clearly had many powerful friends in high places and in fact would in the 1980s be photographed dining with one of them, no less than President François Mitterrand. But unlike Mitterrand and so many other former Vichy officials, he did not live to a ripe old age. He was sensationally killed in 1993, just weeks before he was finally to be tried for war crimes, by a fifty-one-year-old man who then pled not guilty to murder, arguing that Bousquet had so obviously deserved to die.

By the time Knochen was sentenced to death for a second time, the Cold War was raging and, to cement close relations between Germany and other Western democracies, many convicted Nazis had their sentences dramatically reduced. This was the case with both Knochen and Oberg, whose death sentences were commuted to life imprisonment. Knochen was finally pardoned and released along with Oberg on November 28, 1962, by none other than the French Fifth Republic's first president, Charles de Gaulle. Knochen then returned to Germany, settling in Baden-Baden, where he worked as an insurance agent before dying in April 2003 at the ripe old age of ninety-three, apparently weary of life and very much embittered by his treatment at the hands of the French. "Let me say that the greatest crime in history was the extermination of the Jews by Hitler," he told one interviewer, a skilled fabulist to the very end. "And the greatest tragedy of my life was the fact that in an indirect way, and quite without being aware of it, I was mixed up in it. At no point did I know, or even suspect, that the Jews of France, deported to the East, were murdered."

LES INVALIDES

AS WITH COUNTLESS Europeans, Toquette Jackson tried her best to put the war behind her. She would rarely talk about the past and only ever discussed her time in Ravensbruck with the women who had actually shared the trauma with her.

One day not long after the war, the remarkable Maisie Renault arrived at Toquette's home in Enghien. Renault remembered that it was a beautiful day. Phillip greeted her at the front door. Maisie had been eager to ask him questions about the Lübeck tragedy, in which her brother Philippe had been killed, but when she had seen how young Phillip still was, just seventeen, she decided not to ask him.

Renault looked through a window and saw a lush lawn leading down to a lake dotted with sailboats. Toquette spoke little about her own suffering but became very emotional when she described what had happened to Sumner. Renault was reminded of what Toquette had so often told her in Ravensbruck: how much her husband was admired and loved, and what a good father and doctor he had been, committed to helping others to the very last minutes of his life. Toquette said she was working again as a nurse. She showed a picture of herself, taken just after liberation, that had been used in a magazine. From her upper neck to her chest, she still bore the scars of countless lice bites.

Toquette and Phillip both struggled to overcome their loss. "Everyone we knew had lost something or someone in the war," Phillip recalled. "We were lucky to still have each other." The bond between them grew stronger than ever. They had survived the greatest of tests but both had been deeply scarred. "I skipped adolescence," explained Phillip seventy years later. "I was a kid until I was arrested and then spent time in a concentration camp, which made me into an adult, but I had no adolescence. I had skipped from child to adult."

A bleak future appeared to lie ahead. "My father had been killed," Phillip recalled. "There was no source of money. We were living in a very expensive apartment in one of the most expensive places in Paris or in the world." There was no life insurance. For a while Toquette took in lodgers but still could not afford the home on Avenue Foch, and decided reluctantly to live full-time in Enghien instead. She also, sadly, had to part ways with Louise, her ever faithful maid for over a decade.

To make ends meet, Toquette then found a job in a small business making jellies. It was still a struggle to get by. Phillip felt he had to do his share as soon as he could, but he was determined first to finally pass his baccalaureate, so he returned to his old school, the Lycée Janson de Sailly. One day a teacher ejected him from a classroom because he was talking. Phillip couldn't help but laugh. The punishment seemed so insignificant compared to what had happened daily in Neuengamme.

Phillip eventually passed his baccalaureate and then looked for work. College was out of the question. He had to support his mother. Then Toquette's brother, Tuvette, who had survived two world wars fighting in tank units, found him a job as a junior draftsman in an engineering company. His first month's paycheck was all of sixty francs, and he gave every centime to his mother. Phillip had always had a good head for numbers, was bilingual, and became quickly irreplaceable. He worked hard, just as his father had at his age. He would eventually spend thirty-five years with the firm, retiring as a vice president, having enjoyed "Les Trentes Glorieuses," France's thirty great years of postwar boom.

In his spare time Phillip still went hunting and fishing, losing himself in nature and the quest for game. As the years passed and he gained promotion, he could afford to travel the world in search of ever bigger trophies, several of which hang to this day in a home he built himself on the site of the house his parents once owned beside the lake in Enghien. The hobby that had begun as a child, bagging an owl with a 9mm rifle his father had given him, ended with him on a grand safari in Africa, tracking rhinoceros and water buffalo, aping the "great white hunters" he'd read about as a boy at 11, Avenue Foch.

In the early 1950s, Phillip married a caring young Swiss woman, Suzie, to his Swiss mother's great delight, and went on to have three children, one of whom chose in her late twenties to make her life in America. As a grown man, he looked very much like his father, who had been posthumously awarded France's highest award for valor. Phillip remained extraordinarily close to his mother, Toquette, to the day she died at the American Hospital in 1968. Like her husband, she had served both France and America with great distinction in two world wars.

In late 2013, Phillip Jackson was reunited for the first time since before the war with Francis Deloche de Noyelle, the man who had recruited his mother to the resistance in 1943. De Noyelle, aged ninety-four, visited Phillip at the Hôpital des Invalides, where Phillip had lived following a serious accident in the late 1990s. After the war, Deloche de Noyelle had gone on to enjoy a distinguished career as a diplomat, and in a truly extraordinary chapter had become a member of the French mountaineering team that first conquered Annapurna in 1950, then the highest peak, at 26,200 feet, ever reached by mankind. He had braved the Gestapo and frostbite high in the Himalaya. But even after seventy years Deloche de Noyelle had not come to terms with the death of Sumner Jackson, his former neighbor on Avenue Foch. He still felt responsible. He had, after all, asked Toquette to join the resistance.

Deloche de Noyelle had never been able to face Toquette after the war, so great was his guilt. His father had, however, made sure to visit Toquette to commiserate with her. Toquette had told Deloche de Noyelle's father she had no regrets whatsoever: *"Je ne regrette rien."*

In 2013, when Francis Deloche de Noyelle met with Phillip at Les Invalides, he was reassured to hear Phillip tell him he should not feel a moment's more anguish. Had Deloche de Noyelle not asked for his mother's help, neither she nor Phillip nor Sumner would have been able to hold their heads high, knowing they had played their part in defeating Hitler.

Decorated with the Légion d'Honneur and Croix de Guerre, in 2014 Phillip Jackson still treasured photograph albums telling the story of his and his parents' lives on Avenue Foch before and during the war. He kept them beside a bronze bust of his father in his room at L'Hôpital des Invalides, a stone's throw from Napoleon's tomb in central Paris. He counted himself extraordinarily fortunate to have survived at the hands of the Gestapo and a year in Neuengamme, the sinking of the *Thielbek*, a serious head injury in his seventies, and in recent years aggressive skin cancer. "My life is a story with a happy ending," he stressed.

Phillip Jackson spends his final days surrounded by other highly esteemed heroes and heroines of the French resistance, within easy walking distance of Avenue Foch. He is, however, the only one among this extraordinary cadre who can trace his roots to the north woods of Maine, who is fiercely proud of his American heritage, and is often moved to tears when he recalls his exceptionally brave and humane parents, who did the right thing at a time when so many in France opted to collaborate rather than fight.

ACKNOWLEDGMENTS

THIS BOOK COULD not have been written without the help of Phillip Jackson, who endured hours of interviews over the telephone and in person in Paris over several years. I will be forever indebted to him. He also allowed me to use many of his extraordinary photographs.

His daughter, Loraine Riemer, was extremely helpful and generous with her time and provided crucial family letters and other primary sources.

I am also indebted to Joe Manos and his family, Francis Deloche de Noyelle, the late Fritz Molden, a truly great Austrian, and his wife Hanna, Suzie Jackson, and Alain Sollier. Amy Squiers spent weeks transcribing interviews with Phillip Jackson and others. Ben Faller helped with picture research. John Snowdon took beautiful portraits yet again—an author could not hope to have a better colleague and friend.

The staffs of the following institutions helped me navigate a vast maze of archive material: the Massachussetts General Hospital, the American Hospital of Paris, the UK National Archives, US National Archives, the Bundesarchiv, the Bibliothèque Nationale de Paris, and the Château de Vincennes military archives where extraordinary assistance was provided in tracking down elusive resistance records.

It has been a pleasure to work yet again with the hugely professional team at Crown, in particular Claire Potter and my editor, Kevin Doughten. My agent, Jim Hornfischer, also showed great faith in this project from the very start.

My wife, Robin, who came up with the title and was critical in so many other ways, and my son, Felix, were both, as always, supportive beyond belief.

NOTES

PART ONE: CITY OF DARKNESS

1 **"What Nazism, epitomized by":** Jacques Delarue, *The Gestapo* (Barnsley, UK: Frontline Books, 2008), 353.

1: THE FALL

4 **repair shattered young bodies:** In 1916, before the United States entered the First World War, he had volunteered for Britain's Royal Medical Corps, arriving in France with other Americans who defied President Woodrow Wilson's 1914 call for neutrality. Sumner had survived the U-boat menace in crossing the Atlantic, and in fact the ship he crossed on was later sunk by a U-boat. When the United States entered the war, Jackson switched to the U.S. Army Medical Corps and went to work in Red Cross Hospital Number 2 on the Rue Piccini in Paris, serving under Dr. Joseph A. Blake, who was a pioneer in techniques to reconstruct badly injured faces through surgery.

4 **He was assigned to:** Many men were missing limbs and others needed amputations, which Sumner soon became an expert in. His work was extremely exhausting and dangerous, and he often labored through the night in hellish conditions while tens of thousands more men each week became casualties. For further reading on Jackson's early career see Hal Vaughan's *Doctor to the Resistance,* 1–28, and Charles Glass's *Americans in Paris,* 67–72.

4   Sumner had operated: Dr. Maurice B. Sanders, "The Mission of Dr. Sumner Jackson," *News of the Massachusetts General Hospital,* June–July 1965.

5   Sumner had seen the rise: Phillip Jackson, interview with author.

5   Sumner could not believe: Ibid.

6   "It's me or America": Ibid.

6   He was in fact: Ibid.

6   "The first time I kissed": Ibid.

7   the previous September: Ibid.

7   Sumner had thought it best: Charles Glass, *Americans in Paris,* 74.

8   Terribly afraid, the volunteer: Donald Coster, "Behind German Lines," in *Reader's Digest,* November 3, 1940.

8   It was quiet once more: Ibid.

8   The German looked as if: Ibid.

9   20mm barrels pointing skyward: Ibid.

9   "Nothing invented by man": Donald Coster, "Behind German Lines," *Reader's Digest.*

9   aimed it at his stomach: Ibid.

9   "We never see any of you": Ibid.

2: TO SAVE FRANCE

11   from Allied soldiers' skulls: Paul Richey, *Fighter Pilot,* (London: Cassell, 2004), 128.

11   with the badly wounded: According to Clemence Bock: "I can see him now at the American Hospital in a long surgical coat that reached his ankles. He invariably wore a white shirt with a tiepin joining an oxford collar—always Mr. Correct. But with a terrible temper. His patients feared and loved him. He was often intimidating, but he was mostly gentle, well read, and forever telling interesting stories about America and the Great War. . . . I do know that he treated Ernest Hemingway and his wife, all the bankers at Morgan, and Scott and Zelda Fitzgerald. . . . When he was elected to the hospital medical board, one of his fellow physicians, a sculptor, had him pose for a bust of Hippocrates. The bronze statue is still at the house on the lake." Clemence Bock, unpublished memoir.

11   Germans captured the hospital: Ibid.

11   **Then, on June 1, 1940, the:** Records of the American Hospital of Paris.

12   **might collapse without him:** Charles Glass, *Americans in Paris,* 74.

12   **"I'm glad we painted out":** Paul Richey, *Fighter Pilot,* 146.

13   **"a well-calculated psychological":** Ibid., 147. Also that day the last of 120,000 French and Belgian troops were evacuated to England.

13   **The Huns seemed to be:** Ibid.

13   **A couple of days later, a young:** Charles Glass, *Americans in Paris,* 73.

13   **Médaille Militaire onto his son's:** Ibid.

14   **"He was the eternal playboy":** Bove, *A Paris Surgeon's Story,* 221.

15   **Any other outcome was:** Phillip Jackson, interview with author.

15   **He got dressed and later:** Ibid.

16   **Finally, Toquette pulled up:** Ibid.

16   **brook eel and whitefish:** Ibid.

17   **No one wanted to be caught:** David Pryce-Jones, *Paris in the Third Reich* (New York: Holt, Rinehart, and Winston, 1981), 6.

17   **The French writer and aviator:** Ian Ousby, *Occupation* (New York: St. Martin's Press, 1998), 43.

17   **As recently as May 24:** Hanna Diamond, *Fleeing Hitler: France 1940* (Oxford, UK: Oxford University Press, 2007), 8.

17   **their windows shuttered:** Jean-Marc de Foville, *L'Entrée des Allemands à Paris, 14 Juin 1940* (Paris: Calman-Levy, 1965), 57.

18   **at the Chase Bank:** UK National Archives, KV2/2745.

18   **Sumner was far from inclined:** Charles Glass, *Americans in Paris,* 13.

19   **In a few quarters, the only:** Paul Richey, *Fighter Pilot,* 147.

3: THE FOURTEENTH

21   ***Nous vaincrons parce:*** Richard Collier, *1940: The Avalanche* (New York: Dial Press, 1979), 132.

22   **in the summer breezes:** Ibid.

23   **Meanwhile, less than a mile:** Adam Nossiter, *The Algeria Hotel* (New York: Houghton Mifflin, 2001), 3.

23   **The previous day de Martel:** Ibid.

23   **The doctor went into the reception:** Charles Bove, *A Paris Surgeon's Story,* 269.

23   **"Everything *is* dead":** Ibid., 270.

23   **and wet from the rain:** David Pryce-Jones, *Paris in the Third Reich,* 43.

24   **five feet ten inches tall:** UK National Archives, KV2/2745.

24   **made him always look:** Ibid. He was a protégé of Heydrich—the most brilliant yet also feared Nazi in the Third Reich.

24   **He himself had studied:** UK National Archives, KV2/2745.

24   **so many millions of Germans:** http://livreblanc.maurice-papon.net/interv-knochen.

24   **As SS-Obergruppenführer:** Chris McNab, *Hitler's Elite* (London: Osprey Publishing, 2013), 156.

26   **One Two Two:** The brothel would be a firm favorite with Knochen's men and his colleagues in the SS. The boîte's owner, Fabienne Jamet, loved the most fanatical Nazis' gray uniforms and their gifts of flowers and champagne for her best girls. She would later insist the German occupation was the best chapter in a long life as a Parisian hostess par excellence. The first German officers to arrive in the city looked more like excited tourists, not brutish Goths, and according to one report were "handsome boys, decent, helpful . . . above all correct." Typically, Jamet's girls would be examined three times a week for infection. Cleanliness mattered a great deal to the Germans, who were understandably strict. Sleeping with the enemy while infected was, after all, a particularly reprehensible form of sabotage.

27   **enemies of the Reich:** Jacques Delarue, *The Gestapo,* 202.

27   **dressed in an SS uniform:** National Archives UK, KV2/1668.

27   **would be running affairs:** Ibid.

27   **"demonstrations will be allowed":** Gilles Perrault and Pierre Azema, *Paris Under the Occupation* (New York: Vendome Press, 1989), 63.

27   **At some point that day:** Charles Bove, *A Paris Surgeon's Story,* 223.

27   **Among the last words he:** Adam Nossiter, *Algeria Hotel,* 3.

28   **He had made certain:** Charles Bove, *A Paris Surgeon's Story,* 223.

28   **Sumner and his colleagues:** Ibid.

4: DAY TRIPPERS

29   **"Is the last word said?":** www.guardian.co.uk/theguardian/2007/apr/29/great speeches1.

30   **Finally, de Gaulle exhorted:** www.guardian.co.uk/theguardian/2007/apr/29/greatspeeches1.

30   **Hitler's convoy circled the Arc:** Graham Robb. *Parisians: An Adventure History of Paris* (New York: Norton, 2010), 253.

31   **It was Marshal Foch:** Shrabani Basu, *Spy Princess* (New Lebanon, NY: Omega Publications, 2007), 155.

31   **"It is an armistice":** Michael Carver, *The War Lords* (London: Weidenfeld and Nicholson, 1976), 123.

31   **south, toward the Seine:** www.hitlerpages.com/pagina96a.html

32   **"why should we destroy it?":** Albert Speer, *Inside the Third Reich* (New York: Simon & Schuster, 1970), 170–73.

5: SPIES OF SUMMER

33   **"She saw them fight":** George Kennan, *Sketches from a Life* (New York: Pantheon Books, 1989), 70.

33   **"uncharitable to travelers as a desert":** Ibid.

34   **listeners at German headquarters:** Donald Coster, "Behind the German Lines," *Reader's Digest,* November 1940.

35   **If he helped Coster:** Charles Glass, *Americans in Paris,* 75.

35   **to catch eel and trout:** Phillip Jackson, interview with author.

36   **Seine for pocket money:** Ibid.

36   **Toquette's sister, Tat, kept:** Alice Barrelet, diary, August 12, 1940.

37   **"bullshit bureaucracy of old men":** Clemence Bock, unpublished memoir.

37   **"America and the Great War":** Ibid.

37   **"too much praise cannot be":** Charles Glass, *Americans in Paris,* 82.

38   **a week after his arrival:** Ibid., 136–37.

38   **Operation Torch, the Allies' successful invasion:** National Archives, US, OSS Personnel File, 1593270.

38   **diplomats like Kennan:** Donald Coster interview with Kathleen Keating: "The American Hospital in Paris During the German Occupation," May 19, 1981, 6. American Hospital of Paris Archives.

38   **"ready to sail for New York":** Donald Coster, "Behind the German Lines."

39   **due to rampant prostitution:** There was an infestation of rats because the Germans produced so much garbage and at first did not dispose of it efficiently.

6: WINGED VICTORY

41   **don their uniforms:** National Archives UK, KV2/1668.

41   **power to make arrests:** Jacques Delarue, *The Gestapo,* 202.

42   **a mile from Avenue Foch:** www.livresdeguerre.net/forum/contribution .php?index=50284.

43   **ever the nation's savior:** It was none other than Pétain, who had put an end to mutinies in 1917 during the Chemin des Dames offensive, whose many casualties Dr. Sumner Jackson had treated.

43   **"beginning to take ground":** Allan Mitchell, *Nazi Paris* (New York: Berghahn Books, 2010), 19.

44   **Hitler's mountain retreat:** Gilles Perrault and Pierre Azema, *Paris Under the Occupation,* 13.

44   **"in the occupied zone":** Thomas J. Laub, *After the Fall* (Oxford: Oxford University Press, 2010), 65.

44   **receive Wertheimer's share:** Along the Avenue Foch, the changes were notable. The Gestapo had virtually made the area its own, taking over several of the grand villas along Paris's widest avenue. The military governor had also appropriated a large mansion known as the Palais Rose on Avenue Foch. This grand home, built by the Marquis Boni de Castellane, had belonged to Mrs. Florence Jay Gould. She moved just around the corner from Knochen's base at number 72, taking up residence at 89, Rue de Malakoff.

44   **"cede their property to Aryans":** Steven Lehrer, *Wartime Sites in Paris* (New York: SF Tafel Publishers, 2013), 36.

45   **"the path of collaboration":** David Pryce-Jones, *Paris in the Third Reich,* 44.

45   **as swiftly as possible:** His immediate superior in Berlin was Adolf Eichmann, a chain-smoking thirty-four-year-old bureaucrat who would later be dubbed a "desk murderer" for his part in orchestrating the killing of more than six million Jews. That August, Eichmann had proposed that a million Jews per year for four years be moved to a special colony in Madagascar. Industrial genocide had not yet been agreed upon.

46   **"Please advise the medical staff":** Archives, American Hospital of Paris.

46   **Sumner was silent:** Diary of Alice Barrelet, October 13, 1940.

46   **singing "La Marseillaise":** Matthew Cobb, *The Resistance* (New York: Simon & Schuster, 2009), 44.

47   **Free French Forces in London:** www.cheminsdememoire.gouv.fr/en/le-11 -novembre-1940.

47   **Tomb of the Unknown Soldier:** *Les Chemins de la Memoire* 210, November 2010, 8–9.

47   **"But they are just children!":** Ibid., 46.

48   **hop on a bicycle instead:** Phillip Jackson, interview with author.

49   **the marble oyster bar:** There would eventually be so many of these roué European aristocrats sleeping with and working for the SS that they would be memorialized as *"Les Comtesses de la Gestapo."* Among the more notable were the Russian countess Mara Tchernycheff, an erstwhile model and actress, who quickly became none other than Henri Lafont's consort. One of Knochen's first sources of unofficial income came courtesy of Tchernycheff. She had tipped off her fast-living lover about thirty cases of silverware belonging to the U.S. embassy hidden in cellars on the Rue des Saints-Pères. Lafont shared the cache with Knochen and other associates in the SS. Then there was the Greek princess Mourousi, a lesbian morphine addict who would feed her habits by selling seized Jewish furniture. Last but not least was the Austrian countess Ilde von Seckendorff, code-named Mercedes, who would discover her true métier as a spy and informer for Knochen. In exchange, she would be given a majestic home of her own at 41, Avenue Foch, directly opposite Knochen's headquarters at number 72. Cyril Eder, *Les Comtesses de la Gestapo* (Paris: Grasset, 2006), 149.

49   **private patients before the war:** Phillip Jackson, interview with author.

50   **Enghien to cut wood together:** Ibid.

50   **cats and dogs and horses:** Gérard Walter, *Paris Under the Occupation* (New York: Orion Press, 1960), 79.

7: ON DOCTOR'S ORDERS

55   Pyrénées to neutral Spain: André Guillon, "Testimony of a French POW on His Time at the American Hospital of Paris," American Hospital of Paris Archives.

56   "he was in London": Ibid.

56   Sumner had to ensure: By early 1941, six months after the armistice, one floor of the hospital was still full of injured French soldiers like Guillon. They shared the floor with other Allied soldiers who had been brought from prison camps. On other floors were civilians, a third of them American. Many of the British patients had been brought to the hospital from the internment camps at Besançon, Saint-Denis, and Vittel.

56   "Portrait of an American": Clemence Bock, unpublished memoir of Sumner Jackson.

57   occupied by German forces: *New York Times,* October 30, 1914.

57   his "right-hand woman": *Time,* April 27, 1942.

58   "greediness of the Wehrmacht": René de Chambrun, *Pierre Laval, Traitor or Patriot* (New York: Charles Scribner's Sons, 1984), 70.

58   Paris before the war: David Pryce-Jones, *Paris in the Third Reich,* 235. Although Abetz was not formally accredited as ambassador—there was no peace treaty between France and Nazi Germany, merely an armistice—he nevertheless acted as if he had the full powers of an ambassador. One of his frequent guests at the German embassy, the fascist writer Louis-Ferdinand Céline, called Abetz "King Otto I"—France was referred to as "the Kingdom of Otto." King Otto genuinely loved France, especially its women. His wife, Suzanne, was indeed French, but others, younger, more malleable, with firmer thighs, were those he now most desired. Before the war, Abetz had been obsessed with a truly enchanting nineteen-year-old actress, Corinne Luchaire, and although their affair had ended, she was still among a charmed circle to be found at most functions at the German embassy. Abetz had in fact recently asked Corinne, destined to die of tuberculosis at just twenty-eight, for a definition of "collaboration" that would not offend French patriots such as the de Chambruns. "It's very simple, Your Excellency," Corinne had replied. " 'Collaboration' means basically 'give me your watch and then I'll tell you the time.' "

58   Hitler was particularly fond: Serge Jacquemard, *La Bande Bonny-Lafont* (Geneva: Scenes de Crimes), 2007, 85.

58   in a diplomatic pouch: William Stevenson, *A Man Called Intrepid* (New York: Ballantine, 1976), 337.

59   **"going to have malnutrition":** Kathleen Keating, "The American Hospital in Paris During the German Occupation," American Hospital in Paris Archives, 1981.

59   **"for the use of their army":** Ibid.

60   **he told a colleague:** Ibid.

60   **Any male who would aid:** Don Lasseter, *Their Deeds of Valor* (self-published book, 2002), 20.

61   **hired French thugs:** David Pryce-Jones, *Paris in the Third Reich*, 124.

62   **to reach his prime:** Allan Mitchell, *Nazi Paris*, 57.

63   **"permitted to remain at liberty":** *New York Times*, December 24, 1941.

63   **northeast of Paris in Compiègne:** Ibid.

63   **next Christmas France would be free:** Clara Longworth de Chambrun, *Shadows Lengthen* (New York: Scribner's, 1949), 175.

63   **an escape line to sunny Spain:** Charles Glass, *Americans in Paris*, 209.

63   **help the Allied cause:** On March 3, 1942, for the first time since France's capitulation, Paris suddenly became a target of Allied air power. In Neuilly, Sumner heard nearby antiaircraft batteries open up. He and his staff were soon standing calmly on the hospital's terrace, watching bombs explode a few miles to the south. Crowds formed on the Pont Neuf in the center of the city as if they were gazing up at a fireworks display on July 14, Bastille Day, which, like the tricolor, had been banned under occupation. It was the first great daytime raid on Paris, and its target was the Renault factory at Boulogne-Billancourt. The British and Americans badly wanted to destroy the factory: Monsieur Charles Renault was those days busy building tanks for the Germans, not cars for their autobahns. The bombing was far from accurate, however, and around five hundred Parisians were killed. The next morning a memorial to the dead was placed in the Place de la Concorde. Some 300,000 Parisians walked past. Louis Renault was of course outraged that the Allies had tried to destroy his factories. He was no collaborator. After all, he, too, was under duress, and had already been forced to hand over his home at 90, Avenue Foch, which now housed Nazi party officials. The Germans and Vichy officials exploited the bombing for all its propaganda value, using it to try to turn Parisians against the Allies. But this did not happen. Instead, like Sumner and his staff at the American Hospital, they responded with surprising nonchalance. They knew that many more losses would have to be borne if the Allies were to win and they were to be free again.

8: AVENUE BOCHE

65   **Reinhard Heydrich to France:** National Archives UK, KV2/1668.

65   **Third Reich, including France:** Ibid.

65   **"the man with the iron heart":** Mario R. Dederichs, *Heydrich: The Face of Evil* (Havertown, PA: Casemate, 2005), 92.

66   **replaced by his own cousin:** David Pryce-Jones, *Paris in the Third Reich,* 125. "The [Nazi] party wanted to take executive power away from the military," recalled Hans Speidel, a colonel on the General Staff in Paris at the time. "The crucial moment was the burning of the synagogues. . . . It served to strengthen Knochen's position. Knochen was elegant, very adroit, cultivated too, but this did not prevent him from being a party man." Source: Ibid.

66   **above the military:** Allan Mitchell, *Nazi Paris,* 57.

67   **seated at many tables:** In the Imperial Suite, Goering had examined looted art, some of it taken from Jewish homes on Avenue Foch, as he reclined within reach of a crystal bowl full of morphine tablets that sat on a side table beside another full of precious gems—rubies, black pearls. The morbidly obese *Reichsmarschall* often liked to dance with the hotel's waiters, then drift into reverie lying on a replica of Marie Antoinette's four-poster bed.

67   **rooms 266 and 268:** Steven Lehrer, *Wartime Sites in Paris*, 41.

67   **head of the French police:** National Archives UK, KV2/1668.

67   **control of the police:** There was yet another meeting with select military officials, this time at the Hôtel Majestic, a short walk from Avenue Foch. Heydrich stressed that he did not plan to use "eastern methods" in France—the scorched-earth policies of repression and extermination that had been carried out in Poland in particular. He acknowledged the growing numbers in the French resistance and the threat to security they posed. But there was no need for desperate measures. The French police under Bousquet's dynamic leadership, working closely with Knochen, would easily deal with the "terrorists"—the resistance—who were attacking German personnel with ever greater regularity. Source: Thomas J. Laub, *After the Fall,* 79.

68   **have sufficient manpower:** Ibid.

68   **"prepare the future of Europe":** http://livreblanc.maurice-papon.net/interv -Helmut.htm.

68   **Pommery champagne dynasty:** Ibid.

68   **"already on the drum":** Steven Lehrer, *Wannsee House and the Holocaust* (Jefferson, NC: McFarland, 2000), 86.

69   **"he succeeded perfectly":** Jacques Delarue, *The Gestapo*, 233.

69   **assert his new power:** National Archives UK, KV2/1668. Eventually, with the vital help of the French, 70,000 Jews in France were deported to their deaths on eighty-five convoys, among them 10,000 children. Chambrun knew Oberg on a "polite basis." Source: Ibid.

69   **Gestapo's considerable resources:** National Archives UK, KV2/2745.

70   **"fighting espionage and terrorism":** Serge Jacquemard, *La Bande Bonny-Lafont,* 50–51.

70   **vying to replace him:** Ibid., 48

71   **annihilate the Jews in France:** Cécile Desprairies, *Paris dans la Collaboration* (Paris: Seuil, 2009), 469.

71   **"this state one day":** National Archives UK, Nuremberg Trial Documents, TR.3-698, July 8, 1942.

71   **an exasperated Knochen:** Yaacov Lozowick, *Hitler's Bureaucrats* (New York: Continuum, 2002), 199.

71   **clear France of its vermin:** Carmen Callil, *Bad Faith* (London: Vintage, 2007), 287.

72   **be carrying out arrests:** Ibid. There were other dictats. While Dannecker and Eichmann conspired with the French authorities at number 31, Karl Oberg at 72, Avenue Foch, upped the ante in the war on terrorists. If French families did not turn over known resistance members within ten days of a crime—attacking the German army, for example—the SS would from then on kill all siblings and cousins over the age of 18 in retaliation.

72   **with their parents:** Theodor Dannecker, report to RSHA office IV-B-4 (Eichmann), July 6, 1942, CDJC, XLIX-35. [Centre de documentation juive contemporaine, Paris.]

72   **lists of registered Jews:** David Pryce-Jones, *Paris in The Third Reich,* 142.

72   **velodrome beside the Seine:** www.ushmm.org/wlc/en/article.php?ModuleId =10005429.

73   **"could the manhunt continue":** Jeremy Josephs, *Swastika over Paris* (London: Bloomsbury, 1989), 82.

73 **headquartered on Avenue Foch:** David Pryce-Jones, *Paris in the Third Reich*, 145.

73 **"daily or ornamental use":** Ibid., 145.

73 **they all had to go:** Mordecai Paldiel, *Churches and the Holocaust: Unholy Teaching, Good Samaritans, and Reconciliation* (Jersey City, NJ: KTAV Publishing House, 2006), 82.

74 **to the deportation centers:** Nicole Fouché, *Le Mouvement Perpétuel* (Paris: Ethiss, 1991), 66. A young Parisian called Annette Monod watched a batch of young children, who had been separated from their parents, as they were taken by French police from the City of Silence: "The gendarmes tried to have a roll call. But children and names did not correspond. Rosenthal, Biegelmann, Radetski—it all meant nothing to them. They did not understand what was wanted of them, and several even wandered away from the group. That was how a little boy approached a gendarme to play with the whistle hanging at his belt. A little girl made off to a small bank on which a few flowers were growing, and she picked some to make a bunch. The gendarmes did not know what to do. Then the order came to escort the children to the railway station nearby, without insisting on the roll call."

74 **healing and saving others:** Hal Vaughan, *Doctor to the Resistance*, 62.

9: THE SHADOW GAME

75 **They had come to arrest:** Clemence Bock, unpublished memoir.

75 **already packed a bag:** Ibid.

76 **bought a pipe cleaner:** Ibid.

76 **a rug on the floor:** Ibid.

76 **Sector C, run by the SS:** http://www.holocaustresearchproject.org/nazi occupation/frenchjews.html.

77 **abducted by the resistance:** *Time*, March 12, 1945.

77 **"interests of the American Hospital":** René de Chambrun, *Mission and Betrayal* (Stanford, CA: Hoover Institution Press, 1993), 197.

77 **German military command:** Ibid. Already attacked in America for collaborating with the Germans and for being a pathetic "mouthpiece" for his father-in-law Laval, and his godfather, Pétain, René nonetheless was vital to the survival of the hospital. He had pull in the highest circles, both in Paris and in Vichy. He got things done. Crucially, he kept the Nazis out of the hospital that Sumner had been run-

ning so well until his arrest. "It would be too long to relate all the difficulties we met with," he recalled, "time and time again, to prevent the requisition of the buildings, beds, sheets, bandages, medical supplies, etc."

77   **"released in France":** *New York Times,* October 3, 1942.

78   **by the press coverage:** Clemence Bock, unpublished memoir of Dr. Sumner Jackson.

78   **"We need the money":** Ibid.

78   **his wife Clara's name:** Ibid.

78   **private war against the Nazis:** Ibid.

78   **Dirty Anglo-American Attack:** *Le Matin,* November 9, 1942.

79   **"the end of the beginning":** Churchill, Lord Mayor's luncheon speech, November 10, 1942.

79   **"occasion he made no comment":** David Pryce-Jones, *Paris in the Third Reich,* 255.

79   **"the end of an epoch":** Yves Pourcher, *Pierre Laval Vu par Sa Fille* (Paris: La Cherche Midi, 2002), 270.

79   **a price to pay:** Pierre Abramovici, *Un Rocher Bien Occupe,* 72–82. René was in fact a wanted man. British intelligence had gathered information on him, no doubt in anticipation of a postwar trial. It was alleged that he had edited a secret news service for Pierre Laval in which he had justified Vichy's role in the Holocaust. He had also acted, it was claimed, as a representative for American companies wanting to do business with Nazi Germany, even though the United States was at war. "René de Chambrun is organizing a series of Holding Companies in the Argentine in order to conceal transactions carried out on behalf of the Germans," read one intelligence report, "the object of which is to place looted property in security. Pierre Laval, himself, is behind the scheme." And he had that summer and fall attended several luncheons at the Ritz hotel, not just to protect the American Hospital, but also to bring together collaborators and Nazis who were interested, intelligence sources maintained, in "political, economic, and financial cooperation as part of Hitler's European New Order."

79   **name of René de Chambrun:** Carmen Callil, *Bad Faith,* 305.

79   **going to be "assassinated":** "The Black List,"*Life,* August 24, 1942.

79   **"general rejection of all things German":** Allan Mitchell, *Nazi Paris,* 94.

80   **sign of "insufficient volition":** Helmut Knochen to RSHA, August 2, 1943, Bundesarchiv, Berlin, R 58/7742.

80 **Minister Joachim von Ribbentrop:** www.oocities.org/resistancehistory/caluire.html.

80 **the French resistance:** Ibid.

10: NUMBER 11

82 **they sipped chilled champagne:** Cyril Eder, *Les Comtesses de la Gestapo,* 243.

82 **not happy about it:** Clemence Bock, *Memories of Dr. Jackson,* unpublished memoir.

83 **in a 1914 yearbook:** Yearbook, Jefferson Medical College, 1914.

83 **it came to punishment:** Ibid.

83 **"'Men are good'?":** Ibid. Clemence Bock, unpublished memoir.

83 **made his nose bleed:** Phillip Jackson, interview with author.

84 **the side of some building:** Ibid.

84 **an act of resistance:** Raymond Aubrac, *The French Resistance* (Paris: Hazan, 1997), 13.

85 **also admonished Phillip:** Phillip Jackson, interview with author.

85 **used by Knochen's men:** Cécile Desprairies, *Paris dans la Collaboration* (Paris: Seuil, 2009), 480.

85 **organization under Knochen's watchful eye:** David Pryce-Jones, *Paris in the Third Reich,* 43.

85 **Knochen's counterintelligence efforts:** National Archives UK, WO 235/560.

85 **given only to the very best:** Shrabani Basu, *Spy Princess,* 156. Kieffer's headquarters at Number 84 was an impressive building, high ceilinged with tall windows. A marble staircase connected five floors. On the first were extensive radio operations for counterespionage. On the fourth were Kieffer and his secretary Katya's offices, decorated with Louis XV furniture. Katya was said to be Kieffer's mistress. Kieffer also lived in the building, enjoying superb views of Avenue Foch. A narrow corridor led from his quarters to a wooden staircase that connected to the fifth floor. Seven small rooms on this top floor, built as maids' quarters, housed captured enemy agents.

86 **for those who talked:** Kieffer had soon learned so much that he was able to pin up a detailed organizational chart of SOE's F Section—the French sector of the

Special Operations Executive, an outfit formed by Churchill in 1940 to "set Europe ablaze," to carry out sabotage, espionage, and reconnaissance in occupied Europe and to help local resistance movements.

86 Bickler's victims: While SOE enjoyed success elsewhere in occupied Europe, notably the assassination of Reinhard Heydrich in Prague, in France it had a decidedly mixed record. Many of its agents were rushed into the field with plenty of guts but insufficient training and were caught with almost comical ease. Some of SOE's brave public schoolboys had actually arrived in Paris wearing brogue shoes never seen in France, carrying obviously fake ration cards, and speaking such bad French that they had only to open their mouths to get arrested. As one captured SOE agent, Francis Cammaerts, recalled: "Those who tried to play games with the Germans were bound to lose. We were amateurs, they were professionals, and there was no hope of outsmarting them. They were skillful manipulators of information and made it appear they knew more than they did." Several captured SOE agents would later confirm that Kieffer was a skilled interrogator who rarely resorted to violence. His ever-obedient driver and a translator took over when prisoners proved uncooperative. "Well, the game is up," Kieffer often began his interviews with captured British public schoolboys. Then he would smile and point to the F Section organizational chart. "You seem to know more than I do," blurted one agent. "We know much more even than you think," replied Kieffer. "The documents that were sent to your country were read by our people before they were read by you." Kieffer needed no reminding of the critical importance of his work. He knew that no less than Adolf Hitler had a keen interest in his counterintelligence operations on Avenue Foch. Failure was completely out of the question.

87 orders from General de Gaulle: Château de Vincennes military archives, 17P 136, Goélette Frégate file.

87 intelligence organization in London: Francis Deloche de Noyelle, interview with author.

87 "Colonel Passy": Thirty-two-year-old Passy's real name was in fact Andre De Wavrin. A legendary and controversial figure in the history of the resistance, he had been born in Paris, the son of a businessman, and had joined General Charles de Gaulle in London in 1940, taking charge of the Free French's military intelligence unit, the BCRA, the Bureau Central de Renseignements et d'Action. On February 23 that year, he had parachuted into France to help unify the nascent resistance forces in France.

87 "Would you be willing to help?": Francis Deloche de Noyelle, interview with author.

87   **"did not hesitate for a second":** Ibid.

88   **of their only child:** Ibid.

88   **It was safer that way:** Phillip Jackson, interview with author.

89   **member of the network:** Ibid.

89   **would never allow it:** Radio France International, November 11, 2010.

89   **been born in Switzerland:** Phillip Jackson, interview with author.

90   **across the rough pasture:** National Archives UK, HS 9/421.

91   **as agent BOE/48:** Robert Marshall, *All the King's Men* (New York: Harper-Collins, 1988), 186.

91   **sent to the French resistance:** Ibid., 261.

91   **dying days of the war:** A year before, in the summer of 1942, SOE had decided to set up a network in Paris called Prosper. All went well at first. But then on January 22, 1943, Déricourt had arrived in France from London. It was his job to find suitable places for Lysanders to land by moonlight and to organize reception parties that would, eventually, pick up over fifty British agents. In early spring 1943, radio operator Jack Agazarian became increasingly suspicious of Déricourt. After being returned to London from France on June 16, he informed his superiors at SOE headquarters on Baker Street of his doubts about Déricourt's loyalty. His bosses refused to believe Déricourt was working for the Germans and he was allowed to stay on in France.

91   **titled *"Pour Prosper":*** Robert Marshall, *All The King's Men,* 181.

91   **hauled to Avenue Foch by the Gestapo:** Another remarkable Prosper agent, twenty-nine-year-old Noor Inayat Khan, alias Nora Baker, only just managed to avoid arrest and quickly reported back by radio to London, informing SOE of the disaster.

91   **"engaged in the breaking" of their network:** Robert Marshall, *All The King's Men,* 186.

91   **agents to their eventual deaths:** National Archives UK, WO/235.

92   **he was brutally tortured:** The Germans had first arrested Moulin, the elected head of the Eure-et-Loire region, in June 1940 after he had refused to sign a German document that incorrectly pinned blame on black French Army troops for civilian atrocities. A man of high principle, he had then tried to kill himself rather than cooperate with the Nazis, slashing his throat with a piece of broken glass. Fortunately for France, he had been saved. Then, in November 1940, the Vichy government had ordered him to dismiss all socialist officials in his region of France. When he had

refused, Pétain's regime removed him from office. Moulin had promptly joined the nascent French resistance and had managed to get to London in September 1941, under the false identity of Joseph Jean Mercier, where he had met General Charles de Gaulle, who had asked him to return to France to unify several resistance groups, to set up a coordinated "army of the shadows." That spring of 1943 he had finally succeeded in doing so but in the process his true identity had been revealed to the Gestapo. On May 7, as a hunted man, he had written to de Gaulle in London: "I am now being sought by Vichy and the Gestapo who, as a result of practices adopted by certain elements in the Resistance movements, are fully aware of my identity and my activities. I am resolved to hold on as long as possible, but if I disappear, I shall not have time to notify my successors."

92   **few hundred yards from the American Hospital:** www.holocaustresearch project.org/nazioccupation/barbie.html.

92   **"be lucky if he does":** www.onac-vg.fr/files/uploads/jean_moulin_lieux_de _memoire.pdf.

11: THE LAST SUMMER

93   **That morning, Phillip pulled:** Charles Glass, *Americans in Paris,* 321. See also Hal Vaughan, *Doctor to the Resistance,* 79–80.

94   **grandeur of Haussmann's boulevards:** Phillip Jackson, interview with author.

94   **raging in the skies above:** Ibid.

94   **"shrapnel falling everywhere":** Ibid.

94   **tail of a B-17 bomber:** National Archives, US, EE-234.

95   **blowing both their heads off:** Joe Manos, interview with author.

95   **felt himself falling into space:** Joe Manos, Escape and Evasion report, EE 234, National Archives, US. Report made November 30, 1943.

95   **landed on rocky ground:** Joe Manos, interview with author.

96   **some of his fellow crew members:** Ibid.

97   **"use by the troops":** National Archives, US, EE-234.

97   **amid the other passengers:** Joe Manos, interview with author.

98   **was the French Legion of Honor:** Ibid.

99   **"That's a crazy idea":** Joe Manos, Escape and Evasion report, NARA.

99   **at number 11, Avenue Foch:** Don Lasseter, *Their Deeds of Valor,* 373.

100   **"is left of my house":** Phillip Jackson, interview with author.

100   **near the docks:** Ibid.

101   **his equally brave wife:** Joe Manos, interview with author; Réseau Goélette file, 17 P 136, Château de Vincennes military archives.

103   **whom operated in Brittany:** Goélette Frégate archives, 17 P 136, Château de Vincennes, Paris.

103   **by motor torpedo boat:** Ibid.

103   **as the British were concerned:** Phillip Jackson, interview with author.

103   **Allied intelligence of the war:** http://news.bbc.co.uk/2/hi/europe/3663005.stm.

104   **including the one at 11, Avenue Foch:** Phillip Jackson, interview with author.

104   **Hitler's first concentration camp:** Fritz Molden, interview with author.

104   **was wounded in late 1941:** Blake Ehrlich, *Resistance—France 1940–1945* (Boston: Little, Brown, 1965), 235.

104   **sent back to Germany:** Fritz Molden, interview with author.

104   **"Étienne Paul Provost":** Hal Vaughan, *Doctor to the Resistance,* 103–4.

104   **"designs of the V-1 rocket":** Larry Collins and Dominique LaPierre, *Is Paris Burning?* (Edison, NJ: Castle Books, 2000), 190. According to these authors: "In Paris, the only trace that now remains of the mysterious Etienne Paul Provost is a dusty dossier in a two-room apartment on the rue Royer-Collard. There, in the fading archives of the Goélette network, in a brown folder marked "CLAYREC RJ4570," are the records of Posch-Pastor's service with the network and a copy of his citations." Source: Ibid.

104   **"might have been written off":** Dwight D. Eisenhower, *Crusade in Europe* (New York: Doubleday, 1948), 260. Von Camperfeld was a notable success story. But the broader picture for British intelligence, especially SOE's F Section, was far from inspiring. By October 1943, Hans Kieffer had been so successful that only one operative for SOE was still at large in Paris, twenty-nine-year-old Noor Inayat Khan, code-named Madeleine. A descendant of the Indian ruler Tipu Sultan, she had been born in Russia to an Indian Muslim father and American mother, raised in Britain and France, recruited by the SOE that February, and then dropped into France by Lysander as the first female SOE radio operator sent to help the French resistance.

It was remarkable that Madeleine was able to evade capture in Paris for so long given the dragnet of informers and the sophisticated radio detection headquartered at Avenue Foch. By moving constantly, using several addresses, including one near the American Hospital in Neuilly, transmitting to London in perfect code, changing her identity by dyeing her jet black hair, and trusting her instincts, she managed to stay a step ahead of Knochen's men. Several times, his radio experts, circling Paris in the back of disguised vans, detected her on the airwaves but were unable to track her down in time: it took around half an hour to zero in on a transmission. Noor was infuriatingly elusive, transmitting for just a few minutes and changing the crystals in her radio set to confuse her pursuers.

There were several close calls. At one point she tried to hang the aerial for her transmitter from a tree near her apartment in Neuilly when she heard a German voice. "May I help you?" asked a German officer in French. Yes, he could, she calmly replied, and the German promptly helped her attach the seventy-foot-long aerial to the tree, assuming Noor wanted to listen to music on the radio. On another occasion, while traveling on the metro, carrying her thirty-pound A Mark II transmitter/receiver inside a small suitcase, two German soldiers approached and demanded to see inside the case. "A cinematographic apparatus," she said without missing a beat. She opened the case slightly and to her relief saw that the Germans were clueless. "Well, you can see what it is," she said. "You can see all the little bulbs." The soldiers then left her alone.

Finally, Madeleine ran out of luck. As with so many SOE agents, she was betrayed. Early that October, Renée Garry, the sister of the head agent of the "Cinema" and "Phono" circuits, allegedly contacted Hans Kieffer at 84, Avenue Foch. Kieffer promptly dispatched his Swiss-born translator, bespectacled Ernst Vogt, code-named "Andre," to meet with Renée, who said she would reveal a British radio operator if she was paid 100,000 francs, around 500 pounds or $2,000 in 1943.

Vogt readily agreed. He was authorized to pay far more than she was asking. Noor was being offered at a bargain price. The going rate for an SOE agent was a million francs. Renée was paid and then revealed that Noor kept her wireless set at a house on the Rue de la Faisanderie, "parallel to the Avenue du General Serrail, which led off the Avenue Foch." In fact, her latest safe house could be seen from 84, Avenue Foch.

A couple of days later, on October 13, 1943, Vogt and a handsome Frenchman named Pierre Cartaud, also working for the Gestapo, waited for Noor at the specified address. Another agent spotted Noor entering a patisserie nearby. She was wearing a blue dress trimmed with white and a dark hat. She left the patisserie and two agents started to tail her. She turned around, saw them, and then disappeared around a corner. They gave chase but could not find her. For hours, they combed Avenue Foch and nearby streets.

Noor arrived at the safe house later that day. She turned the key in a lock on a door to an apartment. Behind the door stood Pierre Cartaud. As she entered, he tried to arrest her, grabbing her by the hands, but Noor bit his wrists savagely, drawing blood. He tried to push her onto a sofa to handcuff her but she struggled fiercely once again. So he drew his gun from his jacket and threatened to shoot her. Using one hand to aim at her, with the other he picked up a telephone and called Avenue Foch. Kieffer immediately sent Vogt and two other men for backup. Vogt later told British intelligence that when he arrived "Cartaud was standing covering her from the farthest possible corner of the room and Madeleine, sitting bolt upright on the couch, was clawing at the air in her frustrated desire to get at him, and looked exactly like a tigress."

"*Sales Boche!* (Dirty Germans!)," she kept crying.

Vogt had never seen such rage.

Madeleine was quickly taken to 84, Avenue Foch, less than a hundred yards away. Kieffer was delighted. He had finally caught the last British member of the SOE Prosper network. But, to Kieffer's great frustration, she refused to say a word for the first forty-eight hours, as had been instructed by her SOE trainers, and then when she then did open her mouth she proved to be a superb liar. Nevertheless, Kieffer was able to use her indirectly—his agents had meanwhile discovered her notebooks. Although it was strictly forbidden, she had copied down all the messages she had sent as an SOE operative.

Noor refused to reveal any secret codes when presented with the notebooks, but Kieffer knew enough to put her wireless into play, sending false messages from her to SOE headquarters in London.

Noor had been dubbed "Bang Away Lulu," so heavy was her touch on the wireless keys, yet no one at Baker Street's SOE headquarters noticed the changes in her style of transmission, in particular her "fist"—the tempo with which she tapped the keys when she sent her Morse code. There was no doubting the great courage of its agents in the field, but SOE's senior command was at times woefully amateurish when compared to the Gestapo operations on Avenue Foch. One French agent who hid Noor at her home in Paris, Emily Balachowsky, later held SOE in utter contempt: "I believe in a total incompetence of the service."

The Funkspiel with Madeleine's radio set resulted in yet another coup for the former policeman from Karlsruhe, Major Hans Kieffer: London fell for the fake Madeleine and sent three more of its agents, who were arrested by his men as soon as they landed by parachute. Madeleine herself remained uncooperative, despite continued torture and interrogation. On November 25, 1943, at about three in the morning, Kieffer was awakened in his room on the fourth floor of 84, Avenue Foch by a guard. "Bob [an SOE agent] and Madeleine had escaped," recalled Kieffer. "They, with the French resistance leader, Colonel Faye, had broken through the iron bars in the cells leading to the window of the ceiling and they climbed up onto the flat roof. By means of strips of blankets and sheets, knotted together, they let themselves down onto the balcony on the third storey of a neighboring house and there smashed a window and entered the apartment."

Noor managed to make it out of the apartment and onto Avenue Foch. Alerted to her flight, several began a manhunt. Noor was soon spotted and chased down a one-way street, where she was cornered and arrested at gunpoint. According to Kieffer, Noor refused to give her "word of honor" that she would not "attempt any further escapes." She was sent to Germany on November 27, 1943, "for safe custody" and placed in solitary confinement, shackled in chains. Classified as "highly dangerous," she continued to refuse to say a word that might help. On September 13, 1944, at Dachau concentration camp, she would be executed with a single shot to the back of the head. Her body would then be cremated. The SS were rigorous: there was to be no physical trace left behind. The last word she uttered before being murdered, aged thirty, on active service for her country was *"Liberté."*

105   for much of the war: Frank Griffiths, *Winged Hours* (London: William Kimber, 1981), 92.

105   get to Switzerland: www.lessorsavoyard.fr/Actualite/Annecy/2012/08/11/article_15_aout_1943_un_bombardier_anglais_s_ecr.shtml.

105   eating his *petit déjeuner:* http://www.iwm.org.uk/collections/item/object/80027123.

106   " 'tour of Europe'!": Frank Griffiths, *Winged Hours,* 120.

106   striking distance of Spain: Joe Manos, interview with author.

106   "bound to be challenged": Frank Griffiths, *Winged Hours,* 128.

106   "the lights of Spain": Ibid., 135.

106   left for Britain by plane: Joe Manos, Escape and Evasion report, NARA.

107   including Sumner and Toquette Jackson: Over seventy years later, in 2014, Manos would still be enormously grateful to them.

12: THE LAST METRO

110   if the Germans lost the war: Clara Longworth de Chambrun, *Shadows Lengthen,* 175.

111   more or less as they pleased: Matthew Cobb, *The Resistance,* 220.

111   "We'll all be hanged": Yves Pourcher, *Pierre Laval Vu par Sa Fille,* 312.

112   they slept beside him: Carmen Callil, *Bad Faith,* 309.

112   "or a wooden crate": David Schoenbrun, *Soldiers of the Night* (New York: New American Library, 1981), 323.

112   parked outside most cafés: Ibid., 321.

113   "Germans were quartered": Alice-Leone Moats, *No Passport for Paris* (New York: Putnam's Sons, 1945), 228–246.

113   low on General de Gaulle: Phillip Jackson, interview with author.

114   "listening to the BBC": Michael Neiberg, *The Blood of Free Men* (New York: Basic Books, 2012), 9.

114   just around the corner: Cécile Desprairies, *Paris dans la Collaboration,* 470.

115   mansions all along Avenue Foch: www.foia.cia.gov/sites/default/files/document_conversions/1705143/BERGER,%20FRIEDRICH_0006.pdf.

116   "you're being watched": Clemence Bock, unpublished memoirs.

117   **right-wing journalist Alfred Fabre-Luce:** David Pryce-Jones, *Paris in the Third Reich*, 174.

117   **"trees on the Champs-Élysées were a brilliant green":** Yves Pourcher, *Pierre Laval Vu par Sa Fille*, 317.

117   **"tired, with an absent air":** Clemence Bock, unpublished memoir.

118   **"people you know there":** Ibid.

118   **railway wagons had been damaged:** David Schoenbrun, *Soldiers of the Night*, 273.

118   *L'heure des combats viendra:* Terry Crowdy, *French Resistance Fighter* (Oxford: Osprey, 2007), 50.

118   **"dogs on the street corners":** *Defense de la France*, March 15, 1944.

119   **"a German name on the list":** Alice Moats, *No Passport for Paris*, 228.

119   **"coming to fetch them":** Jacques Delarue, *The Gestapo*, 301.

119   **Had she talked?:** National Archives, US, "Reports Headquarters, Paris 6801 MIS-X Detachment, US Forces European Theatre, 1946."

120   **including the "underground" couple:** Joe Manos, interview with author.

120   **to storm a building:** Goélette Frégate archives, 17 P 136. Château de Vincennes.

120   **resistance network were inside:** Ibid.

120   **SS captain Hugo Geissler:** Ibid.

PART THREE: NIGHT AND FOG

121   **"It was a world composed of masters":** Jacques Delarue, *The Gestapo*, 353.

13: GUESTS OF THE REICH

123   **knock on the front door:** National Archives UK, W0309/1592.

123   **"He's at the hospital":** Clemence Bock, unpublished memoir of Sumner Jackson.

123   **could be found:** Ibid.

124   **trick them or call for help:** Ibid.

124   **He felt terribly guilty:** Francis Deloche de Noyelle, interview with author.

125   **"don't say a thing":** Clemence Bock, unpublished memoir. The family was driven to Vichy. Phillip didn't sleep at all that night at number 11 when they were waiting. He packed his homework and notes for his school exam. "The men in the Milice who arrested the Jacksons were at any rate quite second-class in rank. They were not officers, just ordinary troopers. Most of the Milice were low class. They were people who couldn't get jobs, who couldn't get in the army or police, so they took their last chance with the Milice. They were the lowest of the low. They were thugs who had turned 'honest.'"

125   **may have been watched:** She would then look after the apartment, retiring to her small maid's room on the fifth floor of 11 Avenue Foch, until the end of the war, always wondering what had happened to the American family she so adored.

125   **get out and urinate:** Phillip Jackson, interview with author.

126   **Nemours . . . Nevers . . . Moulins:** Ibid.

126   **then split up the family:** National Archives UK, BT 271/106.

126   **"Would you like to have breakfast":** Clemence Bock, unpublished memoir.

126   **often with his parents:** Ibid.

127   **The weather continues to be:** Letter from Toquette to Tat, May 31, 1944.

127   **wanted him to excel:** Phillip Jackson, interview with author.

128   **tore up the ticket:** Ibid.

128   **wasted in this fight:** Robert Paxton, *Vichy France* (New York: Alfred A. Knopf, 1972), 326.

128   **"Jews and the communists":** www.history.com/this-day-in-history/pierre -laval-attempts-suicide.

128   **"thinking of France and only of her":** Geoffrey Warner, *Pierre Laval and the Eclipse of France* (New York: Macmillan, 1968), 396–97.

129   **American embassy in Vichy:** Phillip Jackson, interview with author.

129   **with three other men:** National Archives UK, W0309/1592.

130   **Not knowing was agony:** Phillip Jackson, interview with author.

130   **a whip in his hand:** Ibid.

132   **"How are things in Normandy?":** Ibid.

132   **part of the prison to another:** Ibid.

132   **"You can write to me two pages":** Jackson family archives.

132   **taken into a waiting bus:** Phillip Jackson, interview with author.

133   **"It's no use":** Ibid.

133   **fifty miles northwest of Paris:** National Archives UK, W0309/1592.

133   **Red Cross parcels:** Phillip Jackson, interview with author.

133   **nor did they go hungry:** Phillip Jackson, letter to friends, May 1945, courtesy of Loraine Riemer.

133   **deportations from Compiègne:** National Archives UK, KV2/2745.

133   **"France, arrogant, self assured":** Ibid.

133   **he was "at war":** http://livreblanc.maurice-papon.net/interv-knochen.htm.

133   **"against the Allied armies":** Ibid.

134   **"I am headed for Paris":** Jackson family archives.

135   **the heat was oppressive:** National Archives UK, W0309/1592.

135   **Others were wounded:** Ibid.

135   **by now desperately thirsty:** Phillip Jackson, interview with author.

136   **opened the boxcar doors:** National Archives UK, W0309/1592.

136   **that he resembled an ape:** Phillip Jackson, interview with author.

136   **tried to shave around it:** Ibid.

136   **His father's was 36462:** Ibid.

136   **"Since the 14th, I am at Romainville":** Private correspondence, Jackson family archives.

14: THE COUP: JULY 20, 1944

140   **uniform's belt buckles:** http://rarehistoricalphotos.com/annual-midnight-swearing-nazi-ss-troops-feldherrnhalle-munich-1938/.

140   **when his adjutant burst in:** Randall Hansen, *Disobeying Hitler* (Oxford: Oxford University Press, 2014), 42.

140   **demanding to see Oberg:** National Archives UK, KV2/1668.

140   **Knochen at number 72:** Ibid.

140   **to 72, Avenue Foch:** Ibid.

140   **"too energetically to Brehmer":** Otto Abetz, *Histoire d'une Politique Franco-Allemande, 1930–1950* (Paris: Stock, 1953), 320.

141   **"Then we'll soon have peace":** Thomas J. Laub, *After the Fall,* 284.

141   **Castiglione, close to the Opéra:** National Archives UK, KV2/1668.

142 **"accustomed to settling them"**: Alex Kershaw, *The Longest Winter* (New York: Da Capo Press, 2004), 12.

142 **"in hushing things up"**: National Archives UK, KV2/2745.

142 **brandy, listening to the radio:** Thomas J. Laub, *After the Fall,* 285.

143 **"Germans must show a united front":** Heinz Höhne, *The Order of the Death's Head* (London: Penguin, 2000), 534.

144 **operation, a mere "exercise":** Otto Abetz, *Das Offene Probleme* (Cologne: Greven Verlag, 1951), 290.

144 **deputy a more "military attitude":** National Archives UK, KV2/1668.

144 **Loyalty to Hitler was all that counted:** Michael Neiberg, *The Blood of Free Men,* 75–78.

145 **colleagues entered the dining room:** Claude Roulet, *Ritz* (Paris: Quai Voltaire, 1998), 120.

145 **German officers in France:** National Archives UK, KV2/1668.

145 **right moment to strike:** Gerhard Heller, *Un Allemand à Paris* (Paris: Editions du Seuil, 1981), 184.

15: AVE MARIA

147 **operative all the more impish:** Leo Marks, *Between Silk and Cyanide* (New York: The Free Press, 1998), 493.

147 **forty-eight hours after D-Day:** National Archives UK, HS9/1435.

147 **emerged in a courtyard:** R. J. Minney, *Carve Her Name with Pride* (London: Aramada, 1989), 188.

148 **London on seized radio sets:** National Archives UK, WO/235.

148 **in a room nearby:** Ibid.

149 **would soon be in Paris:** R. J. Minney, *Carve Her Name with Pride,* 191.

149 **the wrath of the vengeful:** Michael Neiberg, *The Blood of Free Men,* xxxi.

149 **Toquette had become close:** National Archives UK, HS9/1435.

150 **that could incriminate anyone:** www.francaislibres.net/liste/fiche.php?index=65475.

151 **"the French high society":** Raoul Nordling, *Sauver Paris* (Paris: Petite Bibliotheque Payot, 2012), 124.

151 "**wear on ceremonial occasions**": Fritz Molden, *Exploding Star* (New York: William Morrow, 1979), 125.

151 **These days the pair was arranging:** Larry Collins and Dominique Lapierre, *Is Paris Burning?,* 70.

151 **Toquette told her to stop:** Clemence Bock, unpublished memoir.

151 "**full of courage**" **as they parted:** Ibid.

152 "**No Mass tomorrow morning**": Maisie Renault, *Great Misery* (Lincoln, NE: Zea Books, 2013), 4–6.

153 **filled with intense emotion:** http://faculty.wwu.edu/jeannea/miseretrans. pdf.

155 **Then the door was closed:** Maisie Renault, *Great Misery,* 4–6.

156 "**shipped to the slaughterhouse**": Collins and Lapierre, *Is Paris Burning?,* 70.

156 **would agree to it:** Ibid.

157 **that concealed their detectors:** The resistance had even taken to issuing warnings to its "pianists"—radio operators—to be on the lookout for "fat men" in trench coats. In Paris, so effective had the tracking system become, Kieffer's men had been able to locate radio operators within half an hour of the first code being tapped out on a set's keys. But these Gestapo technicians were too busy packing up their equipment for shipment and destroying files. They had been informed that all personnel, other than combat troops, were to leave Paris in the next few days. That order had come from the very top, from Hitler himself. Traffic jams were already forming for the first time since June 1940 as trucks and cars headed north, out of Paris, bound for the Reich. Source: www.craigsimpsonbooks.com/pdfs/SOE-Educational-Aid-Leaflets-1-to-5.pdf.

157 *Germans organized evacuation detainees*: Collins and Lapierre, *Is Paris Burning?,* 70.

158 "**kill them all,**" **Abetz said:** Michael Neiberg, *The Blood of Free Men,* 127.

159 "**for your forces, Ambassador**": Raoul Nordling, *Sauver Paris,* 144–48.

159 **heroes of France's resistance:** Less than three hundred of these 2,500-odd deportees would return.

16: DAYS OF GLORY

161 **vital documents:** National Archives UK, KV2/2745.

161 **that total would return:** Allan Mitchell, *Nazi Paris,* 145.

162 **near a beautiful waterfall:** Matthew Cobb, *The French Resistance,* 258.

162 **in a convoy of fast cars:** www.memoiresdeguerre.com/article-Helmut-39991995.html.

162 **the concierge in person:** National Archives UK, KV2/1668.

164 **"Will we be able to keep our own clothes":** Virginia d'Albert Lake, *An American Heroine in the French Resistance* (New York: Fordham University Press, 2006), 152–53.

164 **"the camp at Ravensbruck":** Ibid., 155.

164 **to the Ravensbruck regime:** R. J. Minney, *Carve Her Name with Pride,* 200.

165 **acutely embarrassed by their nakedness:** Virginia d'Albert Lake, *An American Heroine in the French Resistance*, 159.

166 **"if necessary, under ruins":** Dietrich von Choltitz, *De Sébastopol à Paris* (Paris: Aubanel, 1964), 207.

166 **"Ah! General, how fortunate":** Ibid., 247.

168 **whom Himmler had wanted to be spared:** National Archives UK, KV2/2745.

169 **No one was ashamed to weep:** www.historynet.com/from-d-day-to-paris-the-story-of-a-lifetime.htm.

170 **1,750 steps of the Eiffel Tower***: Liverpool Daily Post,* August 26, 2004.

171 **"German 88 nicked one of its sides":** www.historynet.com/from-d-day-to-paris-the-story-of-a-lifetime.htm.

171 **"Everybody, one by one, hands up":** Collins and Lapierre, *Is Paris Burning?*, 297.

172 **"France, of the eternal France!":** Michael Neiberg, *The Blood of Free Men,* 237.

172 **remembered one war correspondent:** www.historynet.com/from-d-day-to-paris-the-story-of-a-lifetime.htm.

172 **"war should have ended":** Collins and Lapierre, *Is Paris Burning?*, 265.

173 **to Nazi Germany:** Charles Glass, *Americans in Paris,* 403.

173 **"had harbored American fliers":** Ibid.

174 **"Our first impression of freedom":** Clara Longworth de Chambrun, *Shadows Lengthen,* 236–47.

174 **rich friends in the country:** René de Chambrun, *Mission and Betrayal,* 165.

174 **height of the Great Terror:** Clara Longworth de Chambrun, *Shadows Lengthen,* 231.

17: NIGHT AND FOG

177 **to a train at Fürstenberg:** Virginia d'Albert Lake, *An American Heroine in the French Resistance,* 162.

178 **"France who need us":** Ibid., 165.

178 **"from 'Toquette.' Many thanks":** Jackson family archives.

178 **"to us in a confidential manner":** Ibid. Meanwhile, Toquette's family in Switzerland was furiously trying to locate Sumner and Phillip. Toquette's sister-in-law on November 1 sent a letter to Mrs. Eleanor Roosevelt at the White House asking for help in finding the Jacksons. The letter was forwarded to the State Department, which replied that it had no information on the family.

178 **daughter Tania back in London:** Virginia d'Albert-Lake, *An American Heroine in the French Resistance,* 170.

179 **"chance, it never came":** Ibid., 165.

179 **toll on women working outside:** Ibid.

179 **"until then was our only aim":** Ibid., 176.

179 **reality and nightmare had blurred:** Geneviève de Gaulle, *The Dawn of Hope* (New York: Arcade Publishing, 1998), 43.

180 **first day of a fresh year:** Virginia d'Albert-Lake, *An American Heroine in the French Resistance,* 192.

181 **"half alive, half dead":** Ibid., 193.

181 **"will power and vitality":** Ibid.

181 **"leading to her arrest":** Hal Vaughan, *Doctor to the Resistance,* 128.

181 **living on starvation rations:** Virginia d'Albert-Lake, *An American Heroine in the French Resistance,* 171.

181 **had resorted to cannibalism:** Jack G. Morrison, *Ravensbrück* (Princeton, NJ: Markus Wiener Publishers, 2000), 285.

181 a final spasm of barbarism: Like Suhren, he would be executed for war crimes.

182 SS Major Fritz Suhren: According to General de Gaulle's niece, Geneviève, who had been apprehended by Henri Lafont and handed over to Helmut Knochen on Avenue Foch, Suhren "had a crafty air about him: he reminded me of a fox, which is not exactly flattering to that poor animal." Source: Geneviève de Gaulle, *The Dawn of Hope*, 51. Suhren would be hanged in 1950.

182 burned along with their clothes: Violette Szabo, one of so many victims of the Gestapo on the Avenue Foch, would be posthumously awarded the George Cross, becoming the first woman to ever receive it. Her daughter, Tania, dressed in an outfit her mother had bought for her on a secret mission to France, was four years old when she visited Buckingham Palace with her grandparents to receive her mother's award. For several days, she had practiced her curtsy—what she called her "skirty."

> The King knew all about her mother and he proudly handed the medal to Tania.
>
> "It is for your mother," he said. "Take great care of it."
>
> Tania and her grandparents left the Palace to face a pack of press photographers who wanted Tania to show them the medal.
>
> She did so.
>
> "What an honor!" said one of the photographers.
>
> "It's for Mummy," said Tania. "I'll keep it for her till she comes home."

Source: R. J. Minney, *Carve Her Name with Pride,* 223.

183 "Army Group Rendulic in Hungary": National Archives UK, KV2/2745.

183 Henri Lafont was executed: Dominique Lormier, *La Gestapo et les Français* (Paris: Pygmalion, 2013), 77.

18: NEUENGAMME

185 and stood below the gallows: Phillip Jackson, interview with author.

185 far, just two feet: National Archives UK, W0309/1592.

186 drained of color and humanity: Phillip Jackson, interview with author.

186 Max Pauly, the camp's commandant: National Archives UK, W0309/1592.

186 "Give him a couple clouts": Ibid.

186 morning lineup at 5:00 a.m.: A prisoner who worked for the authorities who had spent eighteen years in the United States befriended Jackson and helped make his stay less hard.

186 **arms caused by malnutrition:** Clemence Bock, unpublished memoir.

187 **Hamburg into a vast inferno:** The Battle of Hamburg, code-named Operation Gomorrah, was a campaign of air raids beginning July 24, 1943, for eight days and seven nights. It was at the time the heaviest assault in the history of aerial warfare and was later called the Hiroshima of Germany by British officials.

187 **"We need a thousand pieces":** Phillip Jackson, interview with author.

187 **Phillip was among them:** Ibid.

188 **"Can you do something?":** Ibid.

189 **quite a skilled surgeon:** Ibid.

189 **"The quicker you are, the quicker":** Ibid.

190 **"energy and forcible character":** George Martelli, *Agent Extraordinary* (London: Collins, 1960), 231.

190 **his family had been deported:** Ibid.

190 **learn of his and Phillip's fates:** Ibid.

19: DELIVERANCE

191 **began with the formal roll call:** Maisie Renault, *La Grand Misère,* 170.

191 **she had a high temperature:** National Archives UK, FO 371/N363.

191 **barred them from treatment:** Jack G. Morrison, *Ravensbrück,* 240.

192 **suffering badly from dysentery:** National Archives UK, FO 371/N363.

192 **her condition grew steadily worse:** "City of Darkness," *WWII Magazine,* November 2013.

192 **giant incubator of disease:** National Archives UK, FO371/N 363.

192 **"fall into the hands of the enemy alive":** Gunther Schwarberg, "There Shall Be No Survivors, Part II," *Der Stern* magazine series, 1983.

193 **soup to mark the occasion:** Jack G. Morrison, *Ravensbrück,* 297.

193 **"This is our victory":** Count Folke Bernadotte, *Last Days of the Reich* (London: Frontline Books, 2009), 109–112.

193 **millions of enemies of the Reich:** Shown a photograph of the chief architect of the Holocaust, Reinhard Heydrich had astutely observed: "The top half is the teacher but the lower half is the sadist." Source: John Toland, *Adolf Hitler: The Definitive Biography* (London: Book Club Associates, 1977), 812.

193   **he was feeling extremely stressed:** Count Folke Bernadotte, *Last Days of the Reich,* 109–112.

193   **"humanitarian measures," recalled Bernadotte:** Ibid.

194   **Baltic port of Lübeck:** Ibid.

195   **were also to be freed:** Peter Padfield, *Himmler* (New York: MJF Books, 1990), 592.

195   **to a small barrel to defecate:** Phillip Jackson's testimony at the trial of Max Pauly, Hamburg, March 20, 1946, 63–72; National Archives UK.

196   **"French speakers up!":** "City of Darkness," *WWII Magazine,* November 2013.

196   **"I've got my patients and son":** Phillip Jackson, interview with author.

197   **where he was, beside his father:** Ibid.

197   **"bodies of his dying patients":** "City of Darkness," *WWII Magazine,* November 2013.

197   **Sumner, the "devoted American":** Ibid.

198   **untouched by by war, utterly surreal:** Maisie Renault, *La Grand Misère,* 160.

199   **"four potatoes from Ravensbruck":** Ibid.

199   **victory over Nazi bestiality:** www.fondationresistance.org/documents/dossier_them/Doc00144.pdf.

199   **"Malmo, 29 April 45":** Jackson family archives.

200   **"little more than a skeleton":** Glenn Whistler Red Cross report, Ravensbruck Trial Files, National Archives.

200   **"nervous" condition and severely malnourished:** Ibid.

PART FOUR: AFTER THE FALL

201   **"It was a world where people exterminated for pleasure":** Jacques Delarue, *The Gestapo,* 353.

20: ONE DAY IN MAY

203   **In the *Thielbek*'s hold:** The *Thielbek* was a 2,815-ton freighter.

203   **the deck and thrown overboard:** Max Arthur, "RAF Pilots Tricked," *The Independent,* London, October 16, 2000.

203   **kill them all, but how and when:** Kurt Rickert, May 17, 1946, at No. 1 C.I.C. Neumunster, National Archives UK.

204   **"assembled in the Baltic Sea":** National Archives UK, W0309/1592.

204   **"enemy naval formations":** Ibid.

204   **as if he were in a slaughterhouse:** George Martelli, *Agent Extraordinary,* 245.

204   **"breathe some clean air":** Phillip Jackson, interview with author.

204   **given orders to sink any German boat afloat:** A British army investigator, Noel Till, reported in June 1945: "The Intelligence Officer with 83 Group RAF has admitted on two occasions; first to Lt H. F. Ansell of this Team (when it was confirmed by a Wing Commander present), and on a second occasion to the Investigating Officer when he was accompanied by Lt. H. F. Ansell, that a message was received on 2 May 1945 that these ships were loaded with KZ prisoners but that, although there was ample time to warn the pilots of the planes who attacked these ships on the following day, by some oversight the message was never passed on. . . . From the facts and from the statement volunteered by the RAF Intelligence Officer, it appears that the primary responsibility for this great loss of life must fall on the British RAF personnel who failed to pass to the pilots the message they received concerning the presence of KZ prisoners on board these ships." National Archives UK, WO 309/1592.

205   **"cannon round at one ship":** www.independent.co.uk/news/uk/home-news/raf-pilots-tricked-into-killing-10000-camp-survivors-at-end-of-war-634445.html.

206   **to the edge of the deck:** Phillip Jackson, interview with author. Then he lowered himself into the cold water. He started to swim for his life. He was lucky because he was not in the target path. After a while, he realized the *Thielbek* had been severely damaged, because it started listing.

206   **dropped down into the water:** National Archives UK, W0309/1592.

206   **small town called Neustadt:** Phillip Jackson, interview with author.

207   **from the port of Lübeck:** Ibid.

207   **began to return to the shore:** Ibid.

207   **begged and screamed for their help:** Ibid.

21: HIS MAJESTY'S SERVICE

209 **green tank, its treads clanking:** National Archives UK, WO 309/1592.

209 **a plank but "in difficulties":** Phillip Jackson, letter to family, May 8, 1945.

209 **beaches strewn with bodies:** Benjamin Jacobs and Eugene Pool, *The 100-Year Secret* (Guilford, CT: The Lyons Press, 2004), 143.

209 **Neustadt to get some rest:** Ibid.

210 **"I've escaped and I'm alone now":** Radio France International, November 11, 2010.

210 **"Then come with us":** Phillip Jackson, interview with author.

210 **he needed to contact relatives:** Ibid.

210 **"How can that be?" asked Gicheny:** National Archives UK, W0309/1592.

210 **of vital use to the Allies:** George Martelli, *Agent Extraordinary,* 247.

211 **washed-up victim to another:** Phillip Jackson, interview with author.

211 **Some were around Phillip's age:** National Archives UK, W0309/1592.

211 **clearly run out of ammunition:** *Daily Telegraph,* March 18, 1982.

211 **with a severed finger:** Phillip Jackson, interview with author.

211 **"Your husband and son in Germany":** Loraine Riemer, private papers.

211 **deportees from France had not:** Stéphane Simonnet, *Atlas de la Libération de la France, Des Débarquements aux Villes Libérées* (Paris: Autrement, 2004), 68.

212 **"and it is tragic":** Phillip Jackson, interview with author.

212 **"whole family had died":** Maisie Renault, *La Grand Misère,* 170.

212 **among them for war criminals:** Phillip Jackson, interview with author.

214 **"got to killing a German":** Ibid.

214 **"when they arrived in a camp":** Ibid.

214 **"the camp to normal life":** Ibid.

215 **"going from zero to infinity":** Ibid.

215 **Hitler to Paris in June 1940:** Ibid. It was difficult to express great emotion. He had used the time in the British army as a "cooling off period."

215 **then the metro to the Place de l'Étoile:** Ibid.

216 **waiting for him at Number 11:** Ibid.

216 **happier to see her son:** Ibid. Phillip too was overjoyed. Being back at 11 Avenue Foch was scarcely believable. He had been so very lucky to get home. "I had seen people beaten, killed, and many dead bodies," he would later recall. "For the last four days at Neuengamme, I had carried corpses in wheelbarrows from one place to another. Death was all around. I had lived with it every day, slept beside it. It had become normal."

22: JUSTICE

217 **"camel hair coat with leather pockets":** National Archives UK, KV2/2745.

217 **"cell was below that of Göring":** http://livreblanc.maurice-papon.net/interv-Helmut.htm.

218 **"with dogs and guns":** Phillip Jackson, interview with author.

218 **was tagged as number one:** National Archives UK, W0309/1592.

218 **to testify in English:** Phillip Jackson, interview with author.

218 **people stood at attention at Neuengamme:** Ibid.

219 **"number nine, and number ten":** Ibid.

219 **"placing of the prisoners on the ship":** National Archives UK, W0309/1592.

219 **"the love of all that is human":** Gunther Schwarberg, *The Murders at Bullenhuser Damm* (Bloomington, IN: Indiana University Press, 1984), 102.

220 **a rope around Pauly's neck:** National Archives UK, WO 235/162.

220 **"know not what they do":** Gunther Schwarberg, *The Murders at Bullenhuser Damm*, 104–106.

220 **the Special Air Service, the SAS:** National Archives UK, KV2/1131.

220 **"condemned to death immediately":** Ibid., WO/235.

221 **"without a brutal disposition":** Ibid.

221 **worked at 84, Avenue Foch:** Ibid.

221 **"You will stop this comedy":** Sarah Helm, *A Life in Secrets* (New York: Doubleday, 2005), 355. On April 28, 1947, Kieffer wrote a final letter asking for clemency: "I beg you to mitigate the death sentence in view of my three minor children who, after the death of my wife 18 months ago, are without a mother. I also beg you to consider that my 71 years old mother lost a son in Czechoslovakia in Febuary this year and has not had any news from another son of hers from Russia for a whole year now."

221 **"Moggele, I bless you in my last hour":** Ibid., 366.

221 personally accounted for after the war: Conveniently for those who had run SOE's F section, namely Vera Atkins and Maurice Buckmaster, Kieffer took to his unmarked grave many secrets, namely the identity of "BOE 48," arguably WWII's greatest double agent: Henri Déricourt, whose treachery had destroyed the Prosper network and resulted in the deaths of many brave British agents. When the French tried Déricourt in 1948 for treason, neither Atkins nor Buckmaster testified in person for fear perhaps that the full extent of their bungling might be revealed publicly for the first time. For lack of reliable evidence, the prosecution case collapsed and Déricourt walked free. In 1962, having made a fortune smuggling opium, he was killed in a plane crash over Laos.

222 "my counterpart in the war": http://livreblanc.maurice-papon.net/interv -Helmut.htm.

222 hands of the French: Carmen Callil, *Bad Faith*, 389.

223 "deported to the East, were murdered": David Pryce-Jones, *Paris in the Third Reich*, 271.

EPILOGUE: LES INVALIDES

226 "to still have each other": Phillip Jackson, interview with author.

226 "skipped from child to adult": Ibid.

226 full-time in Enghien instead: Ibid.

226 faithful maid for over a decade: Ibid.

227 a boy at 11, Avenue Foch: Ibid.

228 *Je ne regrette rien*: Francis Deloche de Noyelle, interview with author.

228 "happy ending," he stressed: Phillip Jackson, interview with author.

BIBLIOGRAPHY

Abramovici, Pierre. *Un Rocher Bien Occupe.* Paris: Editions Du Seuil, 2001.

Americans in France: A Directory, 1939–1940. Paris: American Chamber of Commerce in France, 1940.

Aubrac, Lucie. *Outwitting the Gestapo,* translated by Konrad Bieber. Lincoln, NE: University of Nebraska Press, 1985.

Beach, Sylvia. *Shakespeare and Company.* London: Faber and Faber, 1960.

Blumenson, Martin. *The Vildé Affair.* London: Robert Hale, 1977.

Bonnet, Marie-Josèphe. *Tortionnaires, Truands et Collabos.* Rennes: Editions Ouest-France, 2013.

Bove, Dr. Charles, with Dana Lee Thomas. *A Paris Surgeon's Story.* New York: Little, Brown and Company, 1956.

Brome, Vincent. *The Way Back.* New York: W. W. Norton, 1957.

Buisson, Patrick. *1940–1945: Annees Erotiques.* Paris: Albin Michel, 2008.

Callil, Carmen. *Bad Faith.* London: Vintage, 2007.

Campbell, Christy. *Target London.* London: Abacus, 2013.

Chavelet, Elisabeth. *Avenue Foch.* Paris: France Loisirs, 1984.

Cobb, Matthew. *The Resistance.* New York: Simon & Schuster, 2009.

Cointet, Michèle. *La Milice Française.* Paris: Fayard, 2013.

Cole, Hubert. *Laval: A Biography.* London: Heinemann, 1963.

Collier, Richard. *1940: The World in Flames.* London: Hamish Hamilton, 1979.

Collins, Larry, and Dominique Lapierre. *Is Paris Burning?* New York: Simon & Schuster, 1965.

Cowles, Virginia. *Looking for Trouble.* London: Hamish Hamilton, 1941.

d'Albert-Lake, Virginia. *An American Heroine in the French Resistance: The Diary and Memoir of Virginia d'Albert-Lake,* ed. Judy Barrett Litoff. New York: Fordham University Press, 2006.

de Brinon, Fernand. *Mémoires.* Paris: La P. Internationale, 1949.

de Chambrun, Adolphe. *Impressions of Lincoln and the Civil War: A Foreigner's Account,* trans. General Adelbert de Chambrun. New York: Random House, 1952.

de Chambrun, René. *I Saw France Fall: Will She Rise Again?* New York: William Morrow and Company, 1940.

———. *Mission and Betrayal, 1940–1945: Working with Franklin Roosevelt to Help Save Britain and Europe.* Stanford, CA: Hoover Institution Press, 1992.

———. *Pierre Laval: Traitor or Patriot?* New York: Charles Scribner's Sons, 1984.

———. *Sorti du Rang.* Paris: Atelier Marcel Jullian, 1980.

de Saint-Exupéry, Antoine. *Wartime Writings, 1939–1944.* New York: Harcourt, Brace, Jovanovich, 1986.

Delarue, Jacques. *The Gestapo.* Barnsley, UK: Frontline Books, 2008.

Desprairies, Cécile. *Paris dans La Collaboration.* Paris: Seuil, 2009.

Eder, Cyril. *Les Comtesses de la Gestapo.* Paris: Grasset, 2006.

Ehrlich, Blake. *Resistance.* Boston: Little, Brown, 1965.

Friedman, David M. *The Immortalists.* New York: Harper Perennial, 2008.

Foot, M. R. D. *MI9.* London: Biteback Publishing, 2011.

———. *SOE.* London: BBC Books, 1984.

Fourcade, Marie-Madeleine. *Noah's Ark.* New York: Dutton, 1974.

Fuller, Jean Overton. *Déricourt.* Salisbury: Michael Russell, 1989.

Gildea, Robert. *Marianne in Chains: In Search of the German Occupation of France, 1940–1945.* New York: Macmillan, 2002.

Glass, Charles. *Americans in Paris.* New York: Penguin, 2010.

Griffiths, Frank. *Winged Hours.* London: William Kimber, 1981.

Heller, Gerhard. *Un Allemand à Paris.* Paris: Edition de Seuil, 1981.

Hollard, Florian. *Michel Hollard.* Paris: Le Cherche Midi, 2005.

Horne, Alistair. *Seven Ages of Paris.* New York: Alfred A. Knopf, 2003.

Humbert, Agnes. *Resistance.* New York: Bloomsbury, 2004.

Jackson, Julian. *France: The Dark Years 1940–1944.* Oxford: Oxford University Press, 2001.

Jacobs, Benjamin, and Eugene Pool. *The 100-Year Secret.* Guilford, CT: The Lyons Press, 2004.

Jacquemard, Serge. *La Bande Bonny-Lafont.* Geneva: Editions Scenes de Crimes, 2007.

Josephs, Jeremy. *Swastika over Paris.* London: Bloomsbury, 1989.

Jucker, Ninetta. *Curfew in Paris: A Record of the German Occupation.* London: The Hogarth Press, 1960.

Kennan, George. *Sketches from a Life.* New York: Pantheon Books, 1989.

Kladstrup, Don and Petie. *Wine and War.* New York: Broadway Books, 2001.

Koestler, Arthur. *Scum of the Earth.* London: Cape, 1941. Reprinted Eland Books, 1991.

Kramer, Rita. *Flames in the Field.* London: Penguin, 1996.

Lagard, Dorothy. *American Hospital of Paris: A Century of Adventure, 1906–2006.* Paris: Le Cherche-Midi, 2006.

Laub, Thomas J. *After the Fall.* Oxford: Oxford University Press, 2010.

Litoff, Judy Barrett. *An American Heroine in the French Resistance.* New York: Fordham University Press, 2006.

Longworth de Chambrun, Clara. *Shadows Lengthen: The Story of My Life.* New York: Charles Scribner's Sons, 1949.

———. *Shadows Like Myself.* New York: Charles Scribner's Sons, 1936.

Lottman, Herbert. *The Fall of Paris: June 1940.* London: Sinclair-Stevenson, 1992.

———. *Pétain: Hero or Traitor: The Untold Story.* New York: William Morrow and Company, 1985.

Lozowick, Yaacov. *Hitler's Bureaucrats.* New York: Continuum, 2002.

Marks, Leo. *Between Silk and Cyanide.* New York: The Free Press, 1998.

Marrus, Michael R., and Robert O. Paxton. *Vichy France and the Jews*. New York: Basic Books, 1981.

Marshall, Bruce. *The White Rabbit*. London: Pan Books, 1980.

Martelli, George, with Michel Hollard. *The Man Who Saved London: The Story of Michel Hollard, D.S.O., Croix de Guerre*. London: Companion Book Club, 1960.

Maurois, André. *Why France Fell*, trans. from French by Denver Lindley. London: The Bodley Head, 1941.

Mazzeo, Tilar. *The Hotel on Place Vendôme*. New York: Harper Collins, 2014.

Michel, Henri. *Paris Allemand*. Paris: Albin Michel, 1981.

Minney, R. J. *Carve Her Name with Pride*. London: Aramada, 1989.

Mitchell, Allan. *The Devil's Captain*. New York: Beghahn Books, 2011.

———. *Nazi Paris*. New York: Berghahn Books, 2008.

Moats, Alice-Leone. *No Passport for Paris*. New York: G. P. Putnam's Sons, 1945.

Moorehead, Caroline. *A Train in Winter*. New York: Harper Collins, 2011.

Moss, Norman. *Nineteen Weeks: Britain, America, and the Fateful Summer of 1940*. London: Aurum Press, 2004.

Neiberg, Michael. *The Blood of Free Men*. New York: Basic Books, 2012.

Némirovsky, Irène. *Suite Française*. New York: Alfred A. Knopf, 2006.

Nordling, Raoul. *Sauver Paris*. Paris: Petite Bibliotheque Payot, 2012.

Nossiter, Adam. *The Algeria Hotel*. New York: Houghton Mifflin, 2001.

Ousby, Ian. *Occupation: The Ordeal of France, 1940–1944*. London: Pimlico, 1999.

Paxton, Robert O. *Vichy France: Old Guard and New Order, 1940–1944*. New York: W. W. Norton and Company (also, London: Barrie & Jenkins), 1972.

Peabody, Polly. *Occupied Territory*. London: The Cresset Press, 1941.

Perrault, Gilles, and Pierre Azema. *Paris Under the Occupation*. New York: The Vendome Press, 1989.

Pourcher, Yves. *Pierre Laval Vu par Sa Fille d'après Ses Carnets Intimes*. Paris: Le Cherche-Midi, 2002.

Pryce-Jones, David. *Paris in the Third Reich: A History of the German Occupation, 1940–1944*. London: Collins, 1981.

Rankin, Nicholas. *Ian Fleming's Commandos*. London: Faber and Faber, 2011.

Renault, Maisie. *La Grande Misère*. Paris: Chavane, 1948.

Reynolds, Quentin. *The Wounded Don't Cry*. London: Cassell and Company, 1941.

Riding, Alan. *And the Show Went On*. New York: Vintage, 2011.

Rock, George. *History of the American Field Service, 1920–1955*. New York: American Field Service Publication, undated.

Rosbottom, Ronald C. *When Paris Went Dark*. New York: Little, Brown, 2014.

Roulet, Claude. *Ritz*. Paris: Quai Voltaire, 1998.

Schellenberg, Walter. *The Labyrinth*. New York: Da Capo, 2000.

Schoenbrun, David. *Soldiers of the Night*. New York: New American Library, 1981.

Schwarberg, Gunther. *The Murders at Bullenhuser Damm*. Bloomington, IN: Indiana University Press, 1984.

Sevareid, Eric. *Not So Wild a Dream*. New York: Alfred A. Knopf, 1946.

Shirer, William L. *The Collapse of the Third Republic: An Inquiry into the Fall of France in 1940*. New York: Simon & Schuster, 1969.

———. *20th Century Journey: Memoir of a Life and the Times, vol. I: The Start, 1904–1930*. Boston: Little, Brown and Company, 1984.

Smith, Richard Harris. *OSS*. Guildford, CT: The Lyons Press, 2005.

Spotts, Frederic. *The Shameful Peace*. New Haven, CT: Yale University Press, 2008.

Tartière, Drue, with M. R. Werner. *The House near Paris: An American Woman's Story of Traffic in Patriots*. New York: Simon and Schuster, 1946.

Tillion, Germaine. *Ravensbruck*. Rome: Fazi Editore, 2012.

Toland, John. *Adolf Hitler*. New York: Doubleday and Company, 1976.

Vaughan, Hal. *Doctor to the Resistance: The Heroic True Story of an American Surgeon and His Family in Occupied France*. Washington, DC: Brassey's, 2004.

Vinen, Richard. *The Unfree French*. New Haven: Yale University Press, 2006.

Walter, Gérard. *Paris Under the Occupation*. New York: Orion Press, 1960.

Weitz, Margaret Collins. *Sisters in the Resistance*. New York, John Wiley & Sons, 1995.

INDEX

ABOUT THE AUTHOR

ALEX KERSHAW is the *New York Times* bestselling author of several books on World War II, including *The Bedford Boys, The Longest Winter,* and *The Liberator*. He lives in Williamstown, Massachusetts.

www.alexkershaw.com